TM

 W9-CAF-766

TM

References for the Rest of Us! ®

BESTSELLING BOOK SERIES FROM IDG

Are you intimidated and confused by computers? Do you find that traditional manuals are overloaded with technical details you'll never use? Do your friends and family always call you to fix simple problems on their PCs? Then the *...For Dummies®* computer book series from IDG Books Worldwide is for you.

...For Dummies books are written for those frustrated computer users who know they aren't really dumb but find that PC hardware, software, and indeed the unique vocabulary of computing make them feel helpless. *...For Dummies* books use a lighthearted approach, a down-to-earth style, and even cartoons and humorous icons to diffuse computer novices' fears and build their confidence. Lighthearted but not lightweight, these books are a perfect survival guide for anyone forced to use a computer.

> *"I like my copy so much I told friends; now they bought copies."*
>
> **— Irene C., Orwell, Ohio**

> *"Quick, concise, nontechnical, and humorous."*
>
> **— Jay A., Elburn, Illinois**

> *"Thanks, I needed this book. Now I can sleep at night."*
>
> **— Robin F., British Columbia, Canada**

Already, millions of satisfied readers agree. They have made *...For Dummies* books the #1 introductory level computer book series and have written asking for more. So, if you're looking for the most fun and easy way to learn about computers, look to *...For Dummies* books to give you a helping hand.

TM

IDG BOOKS
WORLDWIDE

EXCEL 97 PROGRAMMING FOR WINDOWS® FOR DUMMIES®

by John Walkenbach

IDG Books Worldwide, Inc.
An International Data Group Company

Foster City, CA ♦ Chicago, IL ♦ Indianapolis, IN ♦ New York, NY

Excel 97 Programming For Windows® For Dummies®

Published by
IDG Books Worldwide, Inc.
An International Data Group Company
919 E. Hillsdale Blvd.
Suite 400
Foster City, CA 94404
www.idgbooks.com (IDG Books Worldwide Web site)
www.dummies.com (Dummies Press Web site)

Library of Congress Catalog Card No.: 97-72409

ISBN: 0-7645-0132-1

Printed in the United States of America

10 9 8 7 6 5 4 3 2

1O/RV/RQ/ZY/IN

Distributed in the United States by IDG Books Worldwide, Inc.

Distributed by Macmillan Canada for Canada; by Transworld Publishers Limited in the United Kingdom; by IDG Norge Books for Norway; by IDG Sweden Books for Sweden; by Woodslane Pty. Ltd. for Australia; by Woodslane (NZ) Ltd. for New Zealand; by Addison Wesley Longman Singapore Pte Ltd. for Singapore, Malaysia, Thailand, Indonesia and Korea; by Norma Comunicaciones S.A. for Colombia; by Intersoft for South Africa; by International Thomson Publishing for Germany, Austria and Switzerland; by Toppan Company Ltd. for Japan; by Distribuidora Cuspide for Argentina; by Livraria Cultura for Brazil; by Ediciencia S.A. for Ecuador; by Ediciones ZETA S.C.R. Ltda. for Peru; by WS Computer Publishing Corporation, Inc., for the Philippines; by Unalis Corporation for Taiwan; by Contemporanea de Ediciones for Venezuela; by Computer Book & Magazine Store for Puerto Rico; by Express Computer Distributors for the Caribbean and West Indies. Authorized Sales Agent: Anthony Rudkin Associates for the Middle East and North Africa.

For general information on IDG Books Worldwide's books in the U.S., please call our Consumer Customer Service department at 800-762-2974. For reseller information, including discounts and premium sales, please call our Reseller Customer Service department at 800-434-3422.

For information on where to purchase IDG Books Worldwide's books outside the U.S., please contact our International Sales department at 650-655-3200 or fax 650-655-3297.

For information on foreign language translations, please contact our Foreign & Subsidiary Rights department at 650-655-3021 or fax 650-655-3281.

For sales inquiries and special prices for bulk quantities, please contact our Sales department at 650-655-3200 or write to the address above.

For information on using IDG Books Worldwide's books in the classroom or for ordering examination copies, please contact our Educational Sales department at 800-434-2086 or fax 317-596-5499.

For press review copies, author interviews, or other publicity information, please contact our Public Relations department at 650-655-3000 or fax 650-655-3299.

For authorization to photocopy items for corporate, personal, or educational use, please contact Copyright Clearance Center, 222 Rosewood Drive, Danvers, MA 01923, or fax 978-750-4470.

is a trademark under exclusive license to IDG Books Worldwide, Inc., from International Data Group, Inc.

About the Author

John Walkenbach is one of the country's leading authorities on spreadsheet software. He's principal of JWalk and Associates Inc., a Southern California-based consulting firm that specializes in spreadsheet application development. John is also a shareware developer, and his most popular product is the Power Utility Pak add-in for Excel. John has written more than 250 articles and reviews for publications such as *PC World, InfoWorld, Windows,* and *PC/Computing.* In addition, he's authored about 20 other spreadsheet books, including *Excel For Windows 97 Bible, Excel 97 For Windows For Dummies Quick Reference,* and *Excel 97 For Windows Power Programming with VBA.* He also maintains The Spreadsheet Page on the World Wide Web (http://www.jwalk.com). When he's not banging away on his computer keyboard, he's probably banging away on one of his guitars, trying to cop a few blues licks from Freddie King.

Dedication

This book is dedicated to my wonderful daughter, Kate.

Acknowledgments

This book is in your hands right now because of the talented people at IDG Books Worldwide, Inc. I've been fortunate to have been associated with IDG Books since their early days, and I've watched the company evolve into the publishing powerhouse it is today. Many thanks to the two SP's who edited this book: Susan Pink and Suzanne Packer Thomas. They helped make this a Special Project. Special thanks to Colin Banfield, an e-mail buddy who served as technical reviewer for this project. He caught quite a few of my errors and made some great suggestions.

The ideas for many of the topics in this book came from two sources: The Excel Forum on CompuServe, and the comp.apps.spreadsheets Usenet group on the Internet. Thanks to all who frequent these services. Your problems were the inspiration for more than a few of the examples I present in this book.

Thanks also to the following people, who unknowingly helped me out by providing daily background entertainment: Tori Amos, Keola Beamer, Beavis and Butt-Head, David Bromberg, J.J. Cale, Eric Clapton, Chick Corea, Jimmy Dawkins, Enya, Emmylou Harris, Bugs Henderson, Lightnin' Hopkins, Caroline Lavelle, John Lennon, Sarah McLachlan, Natalie Merchant, Joni Mitchell, Alanis Morissette, Willie Nelson, Liz Phair, Leon Russell, Howard Stern, Liz Story, Randy Travis, Muddy Waters, Doc Watson, and many, many more.

ABOUT IDG BOOKS WORLDWIDE

Welcome to the world of IDG Books Worldwide.

IDG Books Worldwide, Inc., is a subsidiary of International Data Group, the world's largest publisher of computer-related information and the leading global provider of information services on information technology. IDG was founded more than 25 years ago and now employs more than 8,500 people worldwide. IDG publishes more than 275 computer publications in over 75 countries (see listing below). More than 90 million people read one or more IDG publications each month.

Launched in 1990, IDG Books Worldwide is today the #1 publisher of best-selling computer books in the United States. We are proud to have received eight awards from the Computer Press Association in recognition of editorial excellence and three from *Computer Currents'* First Annual Readers' Choice Awards. Our best-selling *...For Dummies*® series has more than 50 million copies in print with translations in 38 languages. IDG Books Worldwide, through a joint venture with IDG's Hi-Tech Beijing, became the first U.S. publisher to publish a computer book in the People's Republic of China. In record time, IDG Books Worldwide has become the first choice for millions of readers around the world who want to learn how to better manage their businesses.

Our mission is simple: Every one of our books is designed to bring extra value and skill-building instructions to the reader. Our books are written by experts who understand and care about our readers. The knowledge base of our editorial staff comes from years of experience in publishing, education, and journalism — experience we use to produce books for the '90s. In short, we care about books, so we attract the best people. We devote special attention to details such as audience, interior design, use of icons, and illustrations. And because we use an efficient process of authoring, editing, and desktop publishing our books electronically, we can spend more time ensuring superior content and spend less time on the technicalities of making books.

You can count on our commitment to deliver high-quality books at competitive prices on topics you want to read about. At IDG Books Worldwide, we continue in the IDG tradition of delivering quality for more than 25 years. You'll find no better book on a subject than one from IDG Books Worldwide.

John Kilcullen
CEO
IDG Books Worldwide, Inc.

Steven Berkowitz
President and Publisher
IDG Books Worldwide, Inc.

*Eighth Annual
Computer Press
Awards ≥1992*

*Ninth Annual
Computer Press
Awards ≥1993*

*Tenth Annual
Computer Press
Awards ≥1994*

*Eleventh Annual
Computer Press
Awards ≥1995*

IDG Books Worldwide, Inc., is a subsidiary of International Data Group, the world's largest publisher of computer-related information and the leading global provider of information services on information technology. International Data Group publishes over 275 computer publications in over 75 countries. More than 90 million people read one or more International Data Group's publications each month. International Data Group's publications include: **ARGENTINA:** Buyer's Guide, Computerworld Argentina, PC World Argentina; **AUSTRALIA:** Australian Macworld, Australian PC World, Australian Reseller News, Computerworld, IT Casebook, Network World, Publish, Webmaster; **AUSTRIA:** Computerwelt Österreich, Networks Austria, PC Tip Austria; **BANGLADESH:** PC World Bangladesh; **BELARUS:** PC World Belarus; **BELGIUM:** Data News; **BRAZIL:** Annuário de Informática, Computerworld, Connections, Macworld, PC Player, PC World, Publish, Reseller News, Supergamepower; **BULGARIA:** Computerworld Bulgaria, Network World Bulgaria, PC & MacWorld Bulgaria; **CANADA:** CIO Canada, Client/Server World, ComputerWorld Canada, InfoWorld Canada, NetworkWorld Canada, WebWorld; **CHILE:** Computerworld Chile, PC World Chile; **COLOMBIA:** Computerworld Colombia, PC World Colombia; **COSTA RICA:** PC World Centro America; **THE CZECH AND SLOVAK REPUBLICS:** Computerworld Czechoslovakia, Macworld Czech Republic, PC World Czechoslovakia; **DENMARK:** Communications World Danmark, Computerworld Danmark, Macworld Danmark, PC World Danmark, Techworld Denmark; **DOMINICAN REPUBLIC:** PC World Republica Dominicana; **ECUADOR:** PC World Ecuador; **EGYPT:** Computerworld Middle East, PC World Middle East; **EL SALVADOR:** PC World Centro America; **FINLAND:** MikroPC, Tietoverkko, Tietoviikko; **FRANCE:** Distributique, Hebdo, Info PC, Le Monde Informatique, Macworld, Reseaux & Telecoms, WebMaster France; **GERMANY:** Computer Partner, Computerwoche, Computerwoche Extra, Computerwoche FOCUS, Global Online, Macwelt, PC Welt; **GREECE:** Amiga Computing, GamePro Greece, Multimedia World; **GUATEMALA:** PC World Centro America; **HONDURAS:** PC World Centro America; **HONG KONG:** Computerworld Hong Kong, PC World Hong Kong, Publish in Asia; **HUNGARY:** ABCD CD-ROM, Computerworld Szamitastechnika, Internetto online Magazine, PC World Hungary, PC-X Magazin Hungary; **ICELAND:** Tolvuheimur PC World Island; **INDIA:** Information Communications World, Information Systems Computerworld, PC World India, Publish in Asia; **INDONESIA:** InfoKomputer PC World, Komputek Computerworld, Publish in Asia; **IRELAND:** ComputerScope, PC Live!; **ISRAEL:** Macworld Israel, People & Computers/Computerworld; **ITALY:** Computerworld Italia, Macworld Italia, Networking Italia, PC World Italia; **JAPAN:** DTP World, Macworld Japan, Nikkei Personal Computing, OS/2 World Japan, SunWorld Japan, Windows NT World, Windows World Japan; **KENYA:** PC World East African; **KOREA:** Hi-Tech Information, Macworld Korea, PC World Korea; **MACEDONIA:** PC World Macedonia; **MALAYSIA:** Computerworld Malaysia, PC World Malaysia, Publish in Asia; **MALTA:** PC World Malta; **MEXICO:** Computerworld Mexico, PC World Mexico; **MYANMAR:** PC World Myanmar; **NETHERLANDS:** Computer! Totaal, LAN Internetworking Magazine, LAN World Buyers Guide, Macworld Netherlands, Net, WebWereld; **NEW ZEALAND:** Absolute Beginners Guide and Plain & Simple Series, Computer Buyer, Computer Industry Directory, Computerworld New Zealand, MTB, Network World, PC World New Zealand; **NICARAGUA:** PC World Centro America; **NORWAY:** Computerworld Norge, CW Rapport, Datamagasinet, Financial Rapport, Kursguide Norge, Macworld Norge, Multimediaworld Norge, PC World Ekspress Norge, PC World Nettverk, PC World Norge, PC World ProduktGuide Norge; **PAKISTAN:** Computerworld Pakistan; **PANAMA:** PC World Panama; **PEOPLE'S REPUBLIC OF CHINA:** China Computer Users, China Computerworld, China InfoWorld, China Telecom World Weekly, Computer & Communication, Electronic Design China, Electronics Today, Electronics Weekly, Game Software, PC World China, Popular Computer Week, Software Weekly, Software World, Telecom World; **PERU:** Computerworld Peru, PC World Profesional Peru, PC World SoHo Peru; **PHILIPPINES:** Click!, Computerworld Philippines, PC World Philippines, Publish in Asia; **POLAND:** Computerworld Poland, Computerworld Special Report Poland, Cyber, Macworld Poland, Networld Poland, PC World Komputer; **PORTUGAL:** Cerebro/PC World, Computerworld/Correio Informático, Dealer World Portugal, Mac*In/PC*In Portugal, Multimedia World; **PUERTO RICO:** PC World Puerto Rico; **ROMANIA:** Computerworld Romania, PC World Romania, Telecom Romania; **RUSSIA:** Computerworld Russia, Mir PK, Publish, Seti; **SINGAPORE:** Computerworld Singapore, PC World Singapore, Publish in Asia; **SLOVENIA:** Monitor; **SOUTH AFRICA:** Computing SA, Network World SA, Software World SA; **SPAIN:** Communicaciones World España, Computerworld España, Dealer World España, Macworld España, PC World España; **SRI LANKA:** Infolink PC World; **SWEDEN:** CAP&Design, Computer Sweden, Corporate Computing Sweden, Internetworld Sweden, it branschen, Macworld Sweden, MaxiData Sweden, MikroDatorn, Nätverk & Kommunikation, PC World Sweden, PCaktiv, Windows World Sweden; **SWITZERLAND:** Computerworld Schweiz, Macworld Schweiz, PCtip; **TAIWAN:** Computerworld Taiwan, Macworld Taiwan, NEW ViSiON/Publish, PC World Taiwan, Windows World Taiwan; **THAILAND:** Publish in Asia, Thai Computerworld; **TURKEY:** Computerworld Turkiye, Macworld Turkiye, Network World Turkiye, PC World Turkiye; **UKRAINE:** Computerworld Kiev, Multimedia World Ukraine, PC World Ukraine; **UNITED KINGDOM:** Acorn User UK, Amiga Action UK, Amiga Computing UK, Apple Talk UK, Computing, Macworld, Parents and Computers UK, PC Advisor, PC Home, PSX Pro, The WEB; **UNITED STATES:** Cable in the Classroom, CIO Magazine, Computerworld, DOS World, Federal Computer Week, GamePro Magazine, InfoWorld, I-Way, Macworld, Network World, PC Games, PC World, Publish, Video Event, THE WEB Magazine, and WebMaster; online webzines: JavaWorld, NetscapeWorld, and SunWorld Online; **URUGUAY:** InfoWorld Uruguay; **VENEZUELA:** Computerworld Venezuela, PC World Venezuela, and **VIETNAM:** PC World Vietnam.   5/7/98

Publisher's Acknowledgments

We're proud of this book; please register your comments through our IDG Books Worldwide Online Registration Form located at http://my2cents.dummies.com.

Some of the people who helped bring this book to market include the following:

Acquisitions, Editorial, and Media Development

Project Editor: Susan Pink

Acquisitions Editor: Michael Kelly

Technical Editor: Colin Banfield

Editorial Manager: Mary C. Corder

Editorial Assistants: Chris H. Collins, Michael D. Sullivan

Special Help

Suzanne Thomas, Associate Editor
Stephanie Koutek, Proof Editor

Production

Project Coordinator: Valery Bourke

Layout and Graphics: Elizabeth Cárdenas-Nelson, J. Tyler Connor, Dominique DeFelice, Pamela Emanoil, Maridee V. Ennis, Todd Klemme, Jane E. Martin, Tom Missler, Mark C. Owens, Heather Pearson, Anna Rohrer, Brent Savage, M. Anne Sipahimalani, Michael A. Sullivan

Proofreaders: Henry Lazarek, Christine Berman, Kelli Botta, Joel K. Draper, Rachel Garvey, Nancy Price, Robert Springer

Indexer: Infodex Indexing Services Inc.

General and Administrative

IDG Books Worldwide, Inc.: John Kilcullen, CEO; Steven Berkowitz, President and Publisher

IDG Books Technology Publishing: Brenda McLaughlin, Senior Vice President and Group Publisher

Dummies Technology Press and Dummies Editorial: Diane Graves Steele, Vice President and Associate Publisher; Mary Bednarek, Director of Acquisitions and Product Development; Kristin A. Cocks, Editorial Director

Dummies Trade Press: Kathleen A. Welton, Vice President and Publisher; Kevin Thornton, Acquisitions Manager

IDG Books Production for Dummies Press: Michael R. Britton, Vice President of Production and Creative Services; Cindy L. Phipps, Manager of Project Coordination, Production Proofreading, and Indexing; Kathie S. Schutte, Supervisor of Page Layout; Shelley Lea, Supervisor of Graphics and Design; Debbie J. Gates, Production Systems Specialist; Robert Springer, Supervisor of Proofreading; Debbie Stailey, Special Projects Coordinator; Tony Augsburger, Supervisor of Reprints and Bluelines

Dummies Packaging and Book Design: Robin Seaman, Creative Director; Kavish + Kavish, Cover Design

◆

The publisher would like to give special thanks to Patrick J. McGovern, without whom this book would not have been possible.

◆

Contents at a Glance

Cartoons at a Glance

By Rich Tennant

Real Programmers think an eight-hour day is for sissies.

page 9

"C'MON BRICKMAN, YOU KNOW AS WELL AS I DO THAT 'NOSE-SCANNING' IS OUR BEST DEFENSE AGAINST UNAUTHORIZED ACCESS TO PERSONAL FILES."

page 363

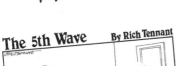

"...AND FOR THE HI-TECH MAN IN YOUR LIFE, WE HAVE THIS LOVELY PC-ON-A-ROPE."

page 325

Real Programmers have trouble supressing homicidal tendencies when asked "Are you sure?"

page 31

"WELL, RIGHT OFF, THE RESPONSE TIME SEEMS A BIT SLOW."

page 91

Real Programmers either smoke two packs of cigarettes a day, or they don't smoke at all.

page 217

AFTER SPENDING 9 DAYS WITH 12 DIFFERENT VENDORS AND READING 26 BROCHURES, DAVE HAD AN ACUTE ATTACK OF TOXIC OPTION SYNDROME.

page 287

Fax: 978-546-7747 • E-mail: the5wave@tiac.net

Table of Contents

Introduction

∙ ∙

*G*reetings, prospective Excel programmer!

Thanks for buying my book. I think you'll find that it offers a fast, enjoyable way to discover the ins and outs of Microsoft Excel programming. Even if you don't have the foggiest idea of what programming is all about, this book can help you make Excel jump through hoops in no time (well, it will take *some* time).

Unlike most programming books, this one is written in plain English, and even normal people can understand it. Even better, it's filled with information of the "just the facts, ma'am" variety — and not the drivel you might need once every third lifetime.

What This Book Covers

Go to any large bookstore and you'll find many Excel books (far too many, as far as I'm concerned). This quick overview can help you decide whether this book is really right for you. *Excel 97 Programming For Windows For Dummies*

- ✔ Is designed for intermediate to advanced Excel users who want to learn Visual Basic for Applications (VBA) programming
- ✔ Requires no previous programming experience
- ✔ Covers the most commonly used commands
- ✔ Is appropriate for Excel 97 (also known as Excel 8)
- ✔ Just might make you crack a smile occasionally — it even has cartoons

If you are using Excel 95 or Excel 5, you need to know right now that this is not the correct book for you. Although Excel 97 seems very similar to the previous versions of Excel, *programming* Excel 97 is quite different — so different, in fact, that you're likely to become very confused. If you're still using a pre-97 version of Excel, locate a copy of my *Excel Programming For Windows 95 For Dummies*.

This is *not* an introductory Excel book. If you're looking for a general-purpose Excel book, check out any of the following books, which are all published by IDG Books Worldwide, Inc:

✔ *Excel 97 For Windows For Dummies*, by Greg Harvey

✔ *Excel 97 Bible*, by John Walkenbach (yep, that's me)

✔ *Excel 97 For Windows For Dummies Quick Reference,* by John Walkenbach (me again)

Notice that the title of this book isn't *The Complete Guide to Excel 97 Programming For Dummies*. I don't cover all aspects of Excel programming — but then again, you probably don't want to know *everything* about this topic. In the unlikely event you want a more comprehensive Excel programming book, you might try *Excel 97 For Windows Power Programming with VBA*, by John Walkenbach (is this guy prolific, or what?).

So You Want to Be a Programmer . . .

Besides earning money to pay my bills, my main goal in writing this book is to teach Excel users how to use the VBA language — a tool that helps you significantly enhance the power of the world's most popular spreadsheet. Using VBA, however, involves programming. (Yikes! The *p* word.)

If you're like most computer users, the word *programmer* conjures up an image of someone who looks and behaves nothing like you. Perhaps words such as *nerd*, *geek*, and *dweeb* come to mind.

Fact is, times have changed. Computer programming has become much easier, and even so-called normal people now engage in this activity. *Programming* simply means developing instructions that the computer automatically carries out. *Excel programming* refers to the fact that you can instruct Excel to automatically do things that you normally do manually — saving you lots of time and (you hope) reducing errors. I could go on, but I need to save some good stuff for Chapter 1.

If you've read this far, it's a safe bet that you need to become an Excel programmer. This could be something you came up with yourself or (more likely) something your boss decided. In this book, I tell you enough about Excel programming so that you won't feel like an idiot the next time you're trapped in a conference room with a group of Excel aficionados. And by the time you finish this book, you can honestly say, "Yeah, I do some Excel programming."

Why Bother?

Most Excel users never bother to learn VBA programming. Your interest in this topic definitely places you among an elite group. Welcome to the fold! If you're still not convinced that this programming stuff is a good idea, I've come up with a few good reasons why you should take the time to learn VBA programming:

- ✔ **It will make you more marketable.** Like it or not, Microsoft's applications are extremely popular. You may already know that all applications in MS Office 97 support VBA — and you can expect to see even more apps using VBA in the future. The more you know about VBA, the better your chances for advancement in your job.

- ✔ **It lets you get the most out of your software investment** (or, more likely, your *employer's* software investment). Using Excel without knowing VBA is sort of like buying a TV set and watching only the odd-numbered channels.

- ✔ **It will improve your productivity (eventually).** Learning VBA definitely takes some time, but you'll more than make up for this in the amount of time you ultimately save because you're more productive. Sort of like what they told you about going to college.

- ✔ **It's fun (well, sometimes).** Some people really enjoy making Excel do things that are otherwise impossible. By the time you finish this book, you just might be one of those people.

Now are you convinced?

What I Assume about You

People who write books usually have a target reader in mind. For this book, my target reader is a conglomerate of dozens of Excel users I've met over the years (either in person or — more frequently — out in cyberspace). The following points more or less describe my hypothetical target reader:

- ✔ You have access to a PC at work — and probably at home.

- ✔ You're running Windows 95 (or Windows NT) and Excel 97.

- ✔ You've been using computers for several years.

- ✔ You use Excel frequently in your work, and you consider yourself to be more knowledgeable than the average Excel user.

✔ You need to make Excel do some things that you currently can't make it do.

✔ You have little or no programming experience.

✔ You need to accomplish some work, and you have a low tolerance for thick, boring computer books.

Obligatory Typographical Conventions Section

All computer books have a section like this. (I think some federal law requires it.) Read it or skip it.

Sometimes, I refer to key combinations — which means you hold down one key while you press another. For example, Ctrl+Z means you hold down the Ctrl key while you press Z.

For menu commands, I use a distinctive character to separate menu items. For example, you use the following command to open a workbook file:

```
File⇨Open
```

Notice the underlined *hot keys*. You press these keys to invoke the command from the keyboard (as opposed to using a mouse). In this case, you press Alt+F and then O.

Any text you need to enter appears in **bold**. For example, I might say, enter **=SUM(B:B)** in cell A1.

Excel programming involves developing *code* — that is, the instructions Excel follows. All code in this book appears in a monospace font, like this:

```
Range("AnnualTotal").Select
```

Some long lines of code don't fit between the margins in this book. In such cases, I use the standard VBA line continuation character sequence: a space followed by an underscore character. Here's an example:

```
Selection.PasteSpecial Paste:=xlValues, Operation:=xlNone, _
    SkipBlanks:=False, Transpose:=False
```

When you enter this code, you can type it as written or place it on a single line (omitting the space and the underscore character).

How This Book Is Organized

I divided this book into seven major parts, each of which contains several chapters. Although I arranged the chapters in a fairly logical sequence, you can read them in any order you choose. Here's a quick preview of what's in store for you.

Part I: Introducing VBA

Part I has but two chapters. I introduce the VBA language in the first chapter. In Chapter 2, I let you get your feet wet right away by taking you on a hands-on guided tour.

Part II: How VBA Works with Excel

In writing this book, I assumed that you already know how to use Excel. The four chapters in Part II give you a better grasp on how VBA is implemented in Excel. These chapters are all important, so don't skip past them, okay?

Part III: Programming Concepts

The eight chapters in Part III get you into the nitty-gritty of what programming is all about. You may not need to know all this stuff, but you'll be glad it's there if you ever do need it.

Part IV: Developing Custom Dialog Boxes

One of the coolest parts of programming in Excel is designing custom dialog boxes (well, at least *I* like it). The four chapters in Part IV show you how to create dialog boxes that look like they came straight from the software lab at Microsoft.

Part V: Creating Custom Toolbars and Menus

Part V has two chapters, both of which address *user interface* topics. One chapter deals with creating custom menus; the other describes how to customize toolbars.

Part VI: Putting It All Together

The three chapters in Part VI pull together information from the previous chapters. You find out how to develop custom worksheet functions, create add-ins, and design user-oriented applications.

Part VII: The Part of Tens

Traditionally, books in the *...For Dummies* series contain a final part that consists of short *top 10*-type chapters. Because I'm a sucker for tradition, this book has several such chapters that you can peruse at your convenience. (If you're like most readers, you'll turn to this part first.)

Marginal Icons

Somewhere along the line, a market research company must have shown that publishers can sell more copies of their computer books if they stick icons in the margins of those books. *Icons* are those little pictures that supposedly draw your attention to various features, or help you decide whether something is worth reading.

I don't know if this research is valid, but I'm not taking any chances. So here are the icons you'll encounter in your travels from front cover to back cover:

This icon flags material you might consider technical. You might find it interesting, but you can safely skip it if you're in a hurry.

Don't skip information marked with this icon. It identifies a shortcut that can save you lots of time (and maybe even allow you to leave the office at a reasonable hour).

This icon tells you when you need to store information in the deep recesses of your brain for later use.

Read anything marked with this icon. Otherwise, you may lose your data, blow up your computer, cause a nuclear meltdown — or maybe even ruin your whole day.

This icon signals a feature that's new to Excel 97. If you're upgrading from Excel 95, this information will help you with the transition.

A Blatant Plug

You might be interested in a shareware product I developed: the Power Utility Pak for Excel 97. It contains 31 useful Excel utilities, 40 new worksheet functions, and enhanced shortcut menus. The best part is that I developed it using VBA exclusively.

Thousands of people throughout the planet use the product, which normally sells for $39.95. But because you bought my book, you can get your very own copy absolutely free — well, there *is* a small shipping and handling charge. And if you're curious, you can even get the VBA source files so you can see what goes on behind the scenes (and maybe even snag a useful programming trick or two along the way). Check out the coupon in the back of the book for details.

Wanna Reach Out?

I enjoy hearing from readers, so please don't hesitate to send me your questions, comments, or suggestions. The best way to contact me is by e-mail:

```
john@j-walk.com
```

And if you're really ambitious, I urge you to point your World Wide Web browser to my very own Web site — which is packed to the gills with even more Excel goodies. The URL is

```
http://www.j-walk.com/ss/
```

If you haven't reached the on-ramp to the information superhighway, you can contact me through traditional mail in care of the publisher.

Now What?

Reading this introduction was your first step. Now, it's time to move on and become a programmer (there's that *p* word again!).

If you're a programming virgin, I strongly suggest that you start with Chapter 1 and progress in chapter order until you've discovered enough. Chapter 2 gives you some immediate hands-on experience, so you'll have the illusion that you're making quick progress.

But it's a free country (at least it was when I wrote these words); I won't sic the Computer Book Police on you if you opt to thumb through randomly and read whatever strikes your fancy.

I hope you have as much fun reading this book as I did writing it.

Part I
Introducing VBA

The 5th Wave   By Rich Tennant

Re·al Pro·gram·mers

Real Programmers think an eight-hour day is for sissies.

In this part . . .

Every book must start somewhere. This one starts by introducing you to VBA (and I'm sure you two will become very good friends over the course of a few dozen chapters). After the introductions are made, Chapter 2 walks you through a real-live Excel programming session.

Chapter 1

What Is VBA?

*T*his chapter is completely devoid of hands-on training stuff. It does, however, contain some essential background information that will assist you on your way to becoming an Excel programmer. In other words, this chapter paves the way for everything else that follows and gives you a feel for how Excel programming fits into the overall scheme of the universe.

Okay, So What Is VBA?

VBA, which stands for *Visual Basic for Applications*, is a programming language developed by Microsoft — you know, the company run by the richest man in the United States. Excel — along with the other members of Microsoft Office 97 — includes the VBA language.

Don't confuse VBA with VB (which stands for Visual Basic). VB is a programming language that lets you create standalone executable programs (you know, those EXE files). Although VBA and VB have a lot in common, they are different animals. And to confuse things even more, there's also something called VBScript (Visual Basic Script) — which is a programming language that's used for Web pages and other applications, including Outlook 97. Again, VBScript has a lot in common with VBA, but it's definitely not the same.

In a nutshell, VBA is the tool you use to develop macros (or programs) that control Excel.

A few words about terminology

With the introduction of VBA in Excel 5, the terminology used to describe the Excel programmable features got a bit muddy. For example, VBA is a programming language, but it also serves as a macro language. So what do you call something written in VBA and executed in Excel? Is it a *macro*, or is it a *program?* Excel's online help often refers to VBA procedures as macros, so I use that terminology. But I also call this stuff a program.

By the way, *macro* does *not* stand for Messy And Confusing Repeated Operation. Rather, it comes from the Greek *makros*, which means large — which also describes your paycheck after you become an expert macro programmer.

What Can You Do with VBA?

You're undoubtedly aware that people use Excel for thousands of different tasks. Here are just a few examples:

- Keeping lists of things, such as customers, students' grades, or Christmas gift ideas
- Budgeting and forecasting
- Analyzing scientific data
- Creating invoices and other forms
- Developing charts and maps from data
- Blah, blah, blah

This list could go on and on, but I think you get the idea. My point is simply that Excel is used for a wide variety of applications, and everyone reading this book has different needs and expectations regarding Excel. But one thing virtually every reader has in common is the *need to automate some aspects of Excel*. That, dear reader, is what VBA is all about.

For example, you might create a VBA macro to format and print your month-end sales report. After developing and debugging the macro, you can execute the macro with a single command, causing Excel to perform many time-consuming procedures automatically. Rather than struggle through a tedious sequence of commands, you can grab a cup of joe and let your computer do the work — which is how it's supposed to be, right?

Kodak had an advertising slogan: "You press the button, we do the rest." That statement pretty much sums up the appeal of macros. You execute a macro with a single action (perhaps a button click), and the macro automatically does lots of cool things for you.

In the following sections, I briefly describe some common uses for VBA macros. One or two of these may push your button.

Insert a text string automatically

If you often need to enter your company name into worksheets, you can create a macro to do the typing for you. You can also extend this concept as far as you like. For example, you might develop a macro that automatically types a list of all salespeople who work for your company. This is a very simple — but quite handy — use for VBA.

Automate a task you perform frequently

Assume you're a sales manager and you need to prepare a month-end sales report to keep your boss happy. If the task is straightforward, you can develop a VBA macro to do it for you. Your boss will be impressed by the consistently high quality of your reports, and you'll be promoted to a new job for which you are highly unqualified.

Automate repetitive operations

If you need to perform the same action on, say, 12 different Excel work-books, you can record a macro while you perform the task on the first workbook and then let the macro repeat your action on the other work-books. The nice thing about this is that Excel never complains about being bored.

Create a custom command

Do you find that you often issue the same sequence of Excel menu com-mands? If so, you can save yourself a few seconds by developing a macro that combines these commands into a single custom command, which you can execute with a single keystroke.

Create a custom toolbar button

You can customize the Excel toolbars with your own buttons that execute macros you write. Quite impressive.

Create a custom menu command

You can also customize Excel's menus with your own commands that execute macros you write. Even more impressive.

Create a simplified front end for users who don't know much about Excel

In almost any office, you can find lots of people who don't really understand how to use computers (sound familiar?). Using VBA, you can make it easy for these inexperienced users to perform useful work. For example, you can set up a foolproof data entry template so that you don't have to waste *your* time doing mundane work.

Develop new worksheet functions

Although Excel includes numerous built-in functions, you can create custom worksheet functions that can greatly simplify your formulas. I guarantee you'll be surprised by how easy this is. (I show you how to do this in Chapter 21.) Even better, the Paste Function dialog box displays your custom functions, making them appear to be built-in Excel functions.

Create complete, turnkey, macro-driven applications

If you're willing to spend some time, you can use VBA to create large-scale applications complete with custom dialog boxes, online help, and lots of other accoutrements.

Create custom add-ins for Excel

You're probably familiar with some of the add-ins that ship with Excel (for example, the Analysis ToolPak is a popular add-in). Most of these were created with Excel macros. I developed my Power Utility Pak add-in using only VBA. With some help from this book, you can create your own add-ins.

Advantages and Disadvantages of VBA

In this section, I briefly describe the good things about VBA — and I also explore its darker side.

VBA advantages

You can automate almost anything you do in Excel. To do so, you write instructions that Excel carries out. Automating a task by using VBA offers several advantages:

- Excel always executes the task in exactly the same way (in most cases, consistency is a good thing).
- Excel performs the task much faster than you could do it manually (unless, of course, you're Clark Kent).
- Excel always performs the task without errors (which probably can't be said about you or me).
- The task can be performed by someone who doesn't know anything about Excel.
- You can do things in Excel that are otherwise impossible — which can make you a very popular person around the office.

A personal anecdote

Excel programming has its own challenges and frustrations. One of my books, *Excel 5 For Windows Power Programming Techniques*, included a disk containing the examples I discuss in the book. I compressed these files so that they would fit on a single disk. Trying to be clever, I wrote a VBA program to expand the files and copy them to the appropriate directories. I spent a lot of time writing and debugging the code, and I tested it thoroughly on three different computers.

Imagine my surprise when I started receiving e-mail from readers who could not install the files. With a bit of sleuthing, I eventually discovered that the readers who were having the problem had all upgraded to Excel 5.0c (I developed my installation program using Excel 5.0a). It turns out that the Excel 5.0c upgrade featured a very subtle change that caused my macro to bomb. Because I'm not privy to Microsoft's plans, I couldn't anticipate this problem. Needless to say, this author suffered lots of embarrassment and had to e-mail corrections to hundreds of frustrated readers.

VBA disadvantages

It's only fair that I give equal time to listing the disadvantages (or *potential* disadvantages) of VBA:

- ✔ You have to learn how to write programs in VBA (but that's why you bought this book, right?). Fortunately, it's not as difficult as you might expect.

- ✔ Other people who need to use the VBA programs you develop must have their own copies of Excel. It would be nice if you could press a button that transforms your Excel/VBA application into a standalone program, but that isn't possible (and probably never will be).

- ✔ Sometimes, things go wrong. In other words, you can't blindly assume that your VBA program will always work correctly under all circumstances. Welcome to the world of debugging.

- ✔ VBA is a moving target. As you know, Microsoft is continually upgrading Excel. You may discover that VBA code you've written doesn't work properly with a future version of Excel. Take it from me, I discovered this the hard way, as detailed in the "A personal anecdote" sidebar.

VBA in a Nutshell

Following is a quick and dirty summary of what VBA is all about. Of course, I describe all this stuff in excruciating detail later in the book.

- ✔ **You perform actions in VBA by writing (or recording) code in a VBA module.** You view and edit VBA modules using the Visual Basic Editor (VBE).

- ✔ **A VBA module consists of subroutine procedures.** A subroutine procedure is basically computer code that performs some action on or with objects. The following example shows a simple subroutine called Test:

```
Sub SimpleProcedure()
    Sum = 1 + 1
    MsgBox "The answer is " & Sum
End Sub
```

- ✔ **A VBA module can also have function procedures.** A function procedure returns a single value, and you can call it from another VBA procedure or even use it as a function in a worksheet formula. Here's an example of a function named AddTwo:

```
Function AddTwo(arg1, arg2)
    AddTwo = arg1 + arg2
End Function
```

✔ **VBA manipulates objects.** Excel provides more than 100 objects that you can manipulate. Examples of objects include a workbook, a worksheet, a range on a worksheet, a chart, and a rectangle. You have many, many more objects at your disposal, and you can manipulate them using VBA code.

✔ **Objects are arranged in a hierarchy.** Objects can act as *containers* for other objects. For example, Excel itself is an object called Application, and it contains other objects such as Workbook objects and CommandBar objects. The Workbook object can contain other objects, such as Worksheet objects and Chart objects. A Worksheet object can contain objects such as Range objects and PivotTable objects. The term *object model* refers to the arrangement of these objects (see Chapter 4 for details).

✔ **Objects of the same type form a collection.** For example, the Worksheets collection consists of all the worksheets in a particular workbook. The Charts collection consists of all Chart objects in a workbook. Collections are themselves objects.

✔ **You refer to an object by specifying its position in the object hierarchy, using a dot as a separator.** For example, you can refer to the workbook BOOK1.XLS as

```
Application.Workbooks("Book1.xls")
```

This refers to the workbook BOOK1.XLS in the Workbooks collection. The Workbooks collection is contained in the Application object (that is, Excel). Extending this to another level, you can refer to Sheet1 in Book1 as

```
Application.Workbooks("Book1.xls").Worksheets("Sheet1")
```

As shown in the following example, you can take this to still another level and refer to a specific cell:

```
Application.Workbooks("Book1.xls").Worksheets("Sheet1").Range("A1")
```

✔ **If you omit specific references, Excel uses the *active* objects.** If Book1 is the active workbook, you can simplify the preceding reference as follows:

```
Worksheets("Sheet1").Range("A1")
```

If you know that Sheet1 is the active sheet, you can simplify the reference even more:

```
Range("A1")
```

✔ **Objects have properties.** You can think of a property as a *setting* for an object. For example, a Range object has such properties as Value and Name. A Chart object has such properties as HasTitle and Type. You can use VBA to determine object properties and to change properties.

✔ **You refer to a property of an object by combining the object's name with the property's name, separated by a period.** For example, you can refer to the value in cell A1 on Sheet1 as follows:

```
Worksheets("Sheet1").Range("A1").Value
```

✔ **You can assign values to variables.** To assign the value in cell A1 on Sheet1 to a variable called *Interest*, use the following VBA statement:

```
Interest = Worksheets("Sheet1").Range("A1").Value
```

✔ **Objects have methods.** A *method* is an action Excel performs with an object. For example, one of the methods for a Range object is ClearContents. This method clears the contents of the range.

✔ **You specify a method by combining the object with the method, separated by a period.** For example, the following statement clears the contents of cell A1:

```
Worksheets("Sheet1").Range("A1").ClearContents
```

✔ **VBA includes all the constructs of modern programming languages, including arrays and looping.**

Believe it or not, the preceding list pretty much describes VBA in a nutshell. Now you just have to find out the details. That's the purpose of the rest of this book.

An Excursion into Versions

If you plan to develop VBA macros, you should have some understanding of Excel's history. I know you weren't expecting a history lesson, but this is important stuff.

Here's a list of all the major Excel for Windows versions that have seen the light of day, along with a few words about how they handle macros:

✔ **Excel 2:** The original version of Excel for Windows was called version 2 (rather than 1) so that it would correspond to the Macintosh version. Excel 2 first appeared in 1987, and nobody uses it anymore, so you can pretty much forget that it ever existed.

✔ **Excel 3:** Released in late 1990, this version features the XLM macro language. A few people live in a time warp and still use this version.

✔ **Excel 4:** This version hit the streets in early 1992. It also uses the XLM macro language. A fair number of people still use this version. (They subscribe to the philosophy *if it ain't broke, don't fix it.*)

✔ **Excel 5:** This one came out in early 1994. It was the first version to use VBA (but it also supported XLM). Many people continue to use this version because they are reluctant to move up to Windows 95.

✔ **Excel 95:** Technically known as Excel 7 (there is no Excel 6), this version began shipping in the summer of 1995. It's a 32-bit version and requires Windows 95 or Windows NT. It has a few enhancements to VBA, and it supports the XLM language. Excel 95 uses the same file format as Excel 5.

✔ **Excel 97:** This version (a.k.a. Excel 8) was born in January 1997. It requires Windows 95 or Windows NT. It has *many* enhancements, and features an entirely new interface for programming VBA macros. Excel 97 also uses a new file format (which cannot be opened by previous versions).

So what's the point of this mini history lesson? If you plan to distribute your Excel/VBA files to other users, it's vitally important that you understand which version of Excel they use. For example, if you develop a macro and save it in the Excel 97 file format, users running previous versions of Excel will not even be able to open the file.

Excel's other macro language

VBA made its debut with Excel 5, which was released in 1994. Previous versions of Excel incorporate a completely different macro language called XLM (which stands for Excel Macro). Most people who know about such things consider VBA to be a giant step forward. Microsoft, however, didn't want to abandon its loyal users by making them switch to VBA cold turkey. Therefore, Excel 5, Excel 95, and Excel 97 still support XLM macros.

Microsoft keeps XLM around mainly for compatibility purposes. People who wrote macros in earlier versions of Excel can still execute those macros when they run Excel 5 or Excel 95.

For the most part, you can just ignore the fact that another macro language lurks behind the scenes. This book covers VBA exclusively.

Chapter 2
Jumping Right In

● ●

In This Chapter

▶ A hands-on, step-by-step example of developing a useful macro

▶ Recording your actions using the Excel macro recorder

▶ Examining and testing the recorded code

▶ Changing the recorded macro

● ●

I'm not much of a swimmer, but I have learned that the best way to get into a cold body of water is to jump right in — no sense prolonging the agony. By wading through this chapter, you can get your feet wet immediately, yet not get in over your head. By the time you reach the end of this chapter you just might start feeling better about this whole programming business. This chapter provides a step-by-step demonstration of how to develop a simple, but useful, VBA macro.

What You'll Be Doing

In this example, you create a useful macro that converts selected formulas to their current values. Sure, you can do this without a macro, but it's a multistep procedure.

To convert a range of formulas to values, you normally complete the following steps:

1. **Select the range that contains the formulas to be converted.**

2. **Copy the range to the Clipboard.**

3. **Choose Edit⇨Paste Special.**

4. **Click the Values option button in the Paste Special dialog box, which is shown in Figure 2-1.**

5. **Click OK.**

Figure 2-1:
Use the
Values
option in
the Paste
Special
dialog box
to copy
formulas as
values.

6. Press Esc.

This clears the cut-copy mode indicator (the moving border) in the worksheet.

The macro you create in this chapter accomplishes all these steps in a single action. As detailed in the following sections, you start by recording your actions as you go through these steps. Then, you test the macro to see whether it works. Finally, you edit the macro to add some finishing touches. Ready?

First Steps

To prepare for what is to come, start Excel and open a new workbook. Next, enter some values and formulas into the worksheet. It doesn't matter what you enter. This step simply provides something to work with. Figure 2-2 shows how my workbook looks at this point. The bottom row and the rightmost column contain formulas.

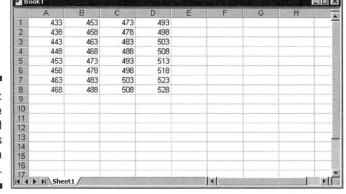

Figure 2-2:
Sample
values and
formulas
in a
worksheet.

Recording the Macro

Okay, here comes the hands-on part. Follow these instructions carefully:

1. **Select the range of cells that contains your formulas.**

   The selection can include both values and formulas. In my case, I chose the range A1:D8.

2. **Choose Tools⇨Macro⇨Record New Macro.**

   The Record Macro dialog box appears, shown in Figure 2-3.

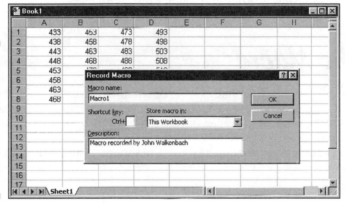

Figure 2-3:
The Record
Macro
dialog box
appears
when you
are about to
record a
macro.

3. **Enter a name for the macro.**

   Excel provides a default name, but it's better to use a more descriptive name for your macro. ConvertFormulas is a good name.

4. **Enter Shift+C (for an uppercase C) as the shortcut keys.**

   Specifying a shortcut key lets you execute the macro by pressing a key combination — in this case, Ctrl+Shift+C.

5. **Click OK.**

   The dialog box closes, and Excel's macro recorder is turned on. From this point, Excel monitors everything you do and converts it to VBA code. Notice that a two-button toolbar appears and the status bar displays *Recording.*

6. **Choose Edit⇨Copy (or press Ctrl+C).**

   This copies the selected range of cells to the Clipboard.

7. **Choose Edit⇨Paste Special.**

   Excel displays the Paste Special dialog box.

8. **Click the Values option.**

9. **Click OK to close the dialog box.**

10. **Press Esc to cancel the Excel cut-copy mode indicator.**

    The moving border is removed from the selection — which is Excel's way of telling you that data is ready to be copied.

11. **Choose Tools⊏>Macro⊏>Stop Recording. Or click the Stop Recording button on the mini-toolbar that's floating on your screen.**

    The macro recorder is turned off.

Congratulations! You just created your first Excel VBA macro. You might want to phone your mother and tell her the good news.

Testing the Macro

Now you can try out this macro and see whether it works properly. To test your macro, you need to add some more formulas to the worksheet. (You wiped out the original formulas during the process of recording the macro.)

1. **Enter some new formulas in the worksheet — again, any formulas will do.**

2. **Select the range that contains the formulas.**

3. **Press Ctrl+Shift+C.**

In a flash, Excel executes the macro. The macro converts all the formulas in the selected range to their current values.

Another way to execute the macro is to choose the Tools⊏>Macro⊏>Macros command (or press Alt+F8) to display the Macros dialog box. Select the macro from the list (in this case, ConvertFormulas) and click OK. Make sure you select the range to be converted before you execute the macro.

Examining the Macro

So far, you've recorded a macro and tested it. And if you're a curious type, you're probably wondering what this macro looks like.

Excel stores the recorded macro in the workbook, but you can't actually view the macro in Excel. To view (or modify) a macro, you must activate the Visual Basic Editor (VBE, for short).

In previous versions of Excel, VBA macros were stored in Module sheets, which were visible from Excel. Excel 97 provides a new way of working with VBA code.

To see the macro:

1. **Choose Tools⇨Macro⇨Visual Basic Editor. (Better yet, press Alt+F11 — a shortcut key that will become very familiar to you.)**

   The Visual Basic Editor window appears, as shown in Figure 2-4. The VBE window contains several other windows and is probably very intimidating. Don't fret; you'll get used to it.

2. **In the VBE window, locate the window called Project.**

   The Project window (also known as the Project Explorer window) contains a list of all workbooks that are currently open. Each project is arranged as a "tree" and can be expanded (to show more information) or contracted (to show less information).

3. **Select the project that corresponds to the workbook in which you recorded the macro.**

   If you haven't saved the workbook, the project is probably called VBAProject (Book1).

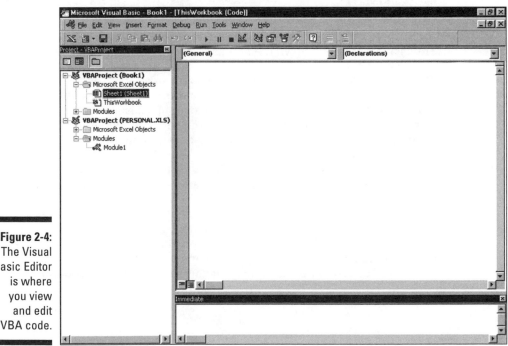

Figure 2-4:
The Visual Basic Editor is where you view and edit VBA code.

4. **Double-click the line labeled Modules.**

The tree will expand to show Module1, which is the only module in the project.

5. **Double-click Module1.**

The VBA code in that module is displayed in another window. Figure 2-5 shows how it looks on my screen. Because the VBE window is highly customizable, your screen may not look exactly the same.

The code in Module1 should look like this:

```
Sub ConvertFormulas()
'
' ConvertFormulas Macro
' Macro recorded by John Walkenbach
'
' Keyboard Shortcut: Ctrl+Shift+C
'
    Selection.Copy
    Selection.PasteSpecial Paste:=xlValues,
Operation:=xlNone, _
    SkipBlanks:= False, Transpose:=False
    Application.CutCopyMode = False
End Sub
```

At this point, the macro probably looks like Greek to you. Don't worry. Travel a few chapters down the road, and all will be as clear as Evian.

The ConvertFormulas macro (also known as a *subroutine*, or *sub*) consists of several statements. Excel executes the statements one by one, from top to bottom. A statement preceded by an apostrophe (') is a comment. Comments are included only for information purposes and are essentially ignored. In other words, Excel doesn't execute comments.

The first actual VBA statement (which begins with the word *Sub*) identifies the macro as a subroutine and gives its name — you provided this name before you started recording the macro. The next statement tells Excel to copy the cells in the selection. The next statement corresponds to the options you selected in the Paste Special dialog box (this statement occupies two lines, using VBA's line continuation character — a space followed by an underscore). The next statement cancels the Excel cut-copy mode indicator. The last statement simply signals the end of the subroutine.

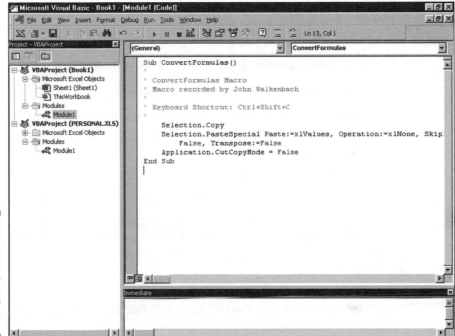

Figure 2-5:
The VBE,
displaying
the VBA
code in
Module1 of
Book1

Modifying the Macro

This macro is fairly useful, saving you a few seconds every time you need to convert formulas to values, but it's also dangerous. As you may have noticed, after executing this macro, you can't choose the Edit⇨Undo command. In other words, if you execute this macro accidentally, you have no way to convert the values back to the original formulas.

In this section, you make a minor addition to the macro to prompt users to verify their intentions before the formula-to-value conversion takes place. Issuing such a warning isn't completely foolproof, but it's better than nothing.

Actually, you can develop macros that can be undone with the Edit⇨Undo command. That, however, is a bit beyond the scope of this book.

You need to provide a pop-up message asking the user to confirm the macro by clicking Yes or No. Fortunately, a VBA statement lets you do this quite easily.

Working in a VBA module is much like working in a word processing document (except there's no word wrap). You can press Enter to start a new line, and the familiar editing keys work as expected.

Here's how you modify the macro to include the warning:

1. **In the VBE, activate the Module1 module.**

2. **Move the cursor directly above the Selection.Copy statement.**

3. **Press Enter to start a new line, and then type the following VBA statements:**

```
Answer = MsgBox("Convert formulas to values?", vbYesNo)
If Answer <> vbYes Then Exit Sub
```

To make the new statements line up with the existing statements, press Tab before typing the new statements. Indenting text is optional, but it makes your macros easier to read. Your macro should now look like the example in Figure 2-6.

Figure 2-6:
The Convert-Formulas subroutine after you add two statements.

```
Book1 - Module1 (Code)
(General)                                    ConvertFormulas

Sub ConvertFormulas()
'
' ConvertFormulas Macro
' Macro recorded by John Walkenbach
'
' Keyboard Shortcut: Ctrl+Shift+C
'
    Answer = MsgBox("Convert formulas to values?", vbYesNo)
    If Answer <> vbYes Then Exit Sub
    Selection.Copy
    Selection.PasteSpecial Paste:=xlValues, Operation:=xlNone, SkipBlanks:= _
        False, Transpose:=False
    Application.CutCopyMode = False
End Sub
```

These new statements cause Excel to display a message box with two buttons: Yes and No. The user's button click is stored in a variable named Answer. If the Answer is not equal to Yes, Excel exits the subroutine with no further action (<> represents *not equal to*). Figure 2-7 shows this message box in action.

Activate a worksheet and try out the revised macro to see how it works. To test your macro, you may need to add some more formulas to your worksheet. Press Alt+F11 to return to Excel.

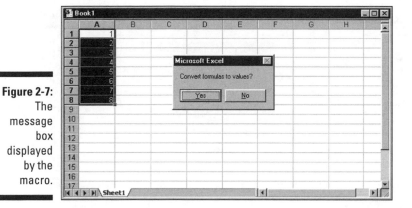

You'll find that clicking the No button cancels the macro, and the formulas in the selection remain intact. When you click the No button, Excel executes the *Exit Sub* part of the macro. If you click Yes, the macro continues its normal course of action.

If you find this macro useful, you should save the workbook file.

More about This Macro

By the time you finish this book, you'll completely understand how the ConvertFormulas macro works — and you'll be able to develop more-sophisticated macros. For now, I'll wrap up the example with a few additional points about the macro:

- ✔ For this macro to work, its workbook must be open. If you close the workbook, the macro doesn't work (and the Ctrl+Shift+C shortcut key has no effect).

- ✔ As long as the workbook containing the macro is open, you can run the macro while any workbook is active. In other words, the macro's own workbook doesn't have to be active.

- ✔ The macro isn't perfect. One of its flaws is that it generates an error if the selection isn't a range. If you select a chart and then press Ctrl+Shift+C, the macro will grind to a halt and you'll see the error message in Figure 2-8. In Chapter 14, I show you how to correct this problem.

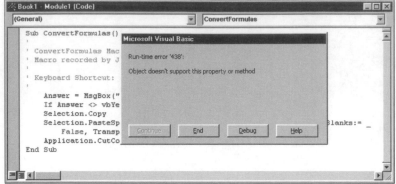

Figure 2-8:
VBA's way
of telling
you
something's
wrong.

- ✔ Before you started recording the macro, you assigned it to a new shortcut key. This is just one of several ways to execute the macro.

- ✔ You could enter this macro manually rather than record it. To do so, you need a good understanding of VBA (be patient, you'll get there).

- ✔ The two statements you added after the fact are examples of VBA statements that you *cannot* record.

- ✔ You could store this macro in your Personal Macro Workbook. If you were to do so, the macro would be available automatically whenever you start Excel. See Chapter 6 for details about your Personal Macro Workbook.

- ✔ You could also convert the workbook to an add-in file (more about this in Chapter 22).

You've now been initiated into the world of Excel programming. (Sorry, there's no secret handshake.) I hope this chapter helps you realize that Excel programming is something you can actually do — and even live to tell about it. Keep reading. Subsequent chapters almost certainly answer any questions you have, and you'll soon understand exactly what you did in this hands-on session.

Part II
How VBA Works with Excel

Re·al Pro'gram·mers

Real Programmers have trouble supressing homicidal tendencies when asked "Are you sure?"

In this part . . .

The next four chapters provide the necessary foundation for discovering the ins and outs of VBA. You find out about modules (the sheets that store your VBA code) and are introduced to the Excel object model (something you won't want to miss). You also discover the difference between subroutines and functions, and you get a crash course in the Excel macro recorder.

Chapter 3

Introducing the Visual Basic Editor

- -

In This Chapter

▶ What is the Visual Basic Editor?

▶ Visual Basic Editor parts

▶ What goes into a VBA module

▶ Three ways to get VBA code into a module

▶ Customizing the VBA environment

- -

As an experienced Excel user, you know a good deal about workbooks, formulas, charts, and other Excel goodies. Now it's time to expand your horizons and explore an entirely new aspect of Excel: the Visual Basic Editor (VBE).

The VBE is new to Excel 97. In previous versions of Excel, you edit VBA code in a VBA module — which is a sheet in a workbook. VBE is a vastly improved development environment.

What Is the VBE?

The Visual Basic Editor is a separate application that works seamlessly with Excel 97. By "seamlessly," I mean that Excel takes care of the details of opening VBE when you need it. And you can't run VBE separately; Excel 97 must be running in order for the VBE to run.

Activating the VBE

The quickest way to activate the VBE window is to press Alt+F11 when Excel is active. To return to Excel, press Alt+F11 again.

Tool Bar   Menu Bar

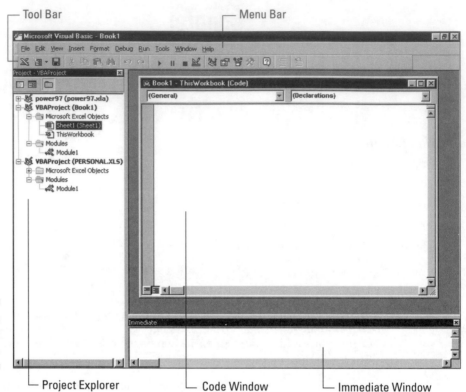

Figure 3-1:
The VBE
window.

Project Explorer   Code Window   Immediate Window

VBE parts

Figure 3-1 shows the VBE window, maximized to fill the entire screen. Because there's a lot going on in the VBE, it's a good idea to maximize the window so that you can see as much as possible without scrolling and dragging windows around.

Chances are, your VBE window won't look exactly like the window shown in Figure 3-1. This window is highly customizable — you can hide windows, change their sizes, "dock" them, rearrange them, and so on.

The VBE actually has even more parts than are shown in the figure. I discuss these additional components in Chapter 13 (which deals with debugging) and in Part IV (in which I discuss custom dialog boxes).

Menu bar

The VBE menu bar, of course, works like every other menu bar you've encountered. It contains commands that you use to do things with the various components in the VBE. Also, you'll find that many of the menu commands have shortcut keys associated with them.

The VBE also features shortcut menus. As you'll discover, you can right-click virtually anything in a VBE window and you'll get a shortcut menu of common commands.

Toolbar

The Standard toolbar, which is directly under the menu bar by default, is one of four VBE toolbars available. VBE toolbars work just like those in Excel 97: You can customize toolbars, move them around, display other toolbars, and so on. Use the View⇨Toolbars command to work with VBE toolbars.

Project Explorer window

The Project Explorer window displays a tree diagram that consists of every workbook that is currently open in Excel (including add-ins and hidden workbooks). I discuss this window in more detail in the next section ("Working with the Project Explorer").

If the Project Explorer window is not visible, press Ctrl+R. To hide the Project Explorer window, click the Close button in its title bar (or right click anywhere in the Project Explorer window and select Hide from the shortcut menu).

Code window

A Code window (sometimes known as a Module window) contains VBA code. Every item in a project has an associated Code window. To view a Code window for an object, double-click the object in the Project Explorer window. For example, to view the Code window for the Sheet1 object, double-click Sheet1 in the Project Explorer window. Unless you've added some VBA code, the Code window will be empty.

You'll learn more about Code windows later in this chapter (see "Working with a Code Window").

Immediate window

The Immediate window may or may not be visible. If the Immediate window isn't visible, press Ctrl+G. To close the Immediate window, click the Close button in its title bar (or right-click anywhere in the Immediate window and select Hide from the shortcut menu).

The Immediate window is most useful for executing VBA statements directly and for debugging your code. If you're just starting out with VBA, this window won't be all that useful, so feel free to hide it to get it out of the way. By the time you finish Chapter 13, you'll be able to appreciate this window.

Working with the Project Explorer

When you're working in the VBE, each Excel workbook and add-in that's open is a project. You can think of a project as a collection of objects arranged as an outline. You can "expand" a project by clicking the plus sign (+) at the left of the project's name in the Project Explorer window. You "contract" a project by clicking the minus sign (-) to the left of a project's name. Figure 3-2 shows a Project Explorer window with three projects listed (one add-in and two workbooks).

Figure 3-2:
A Project
Explorer
window
with three
projects
listed.

Every project expands to show at least one "node" called Microsoft Excel Objects. This node expands to show an item for each sheet in the workbook (each sheet is considered an object), and another object called ThisWorkbook (which represents the Workbook object). If the project has any VBA modules, the project listing also shows a Modules node. And, as you'll see in Part IV, a project may also contain a node called Forms — which contains UserForm objects (also known as custom dialog boxes).

The concept of objects may be a bit fuzzy. However, I guarantee that things will become much clearer in subsequent chapters, so don't be too concerned if you don't really understand what's going on at this point.

Adding a new VBA module

To add a new VBA module to a project, select the project's name in the Project Explorer window and choose Insert⇨Module. Or you can right-click the project's name and choose Insert⇨Module from the shortcut menu.

When you record a macro, Excel automatically inserts a VBA module to hold the recorded code.

Removing a VBA module

If you need to remove a VBA module form a project, select the module's name in the Project Explorer window and choose File⇨Remove *xxx,* where *xxx* is the name of the module. Or you can right-click the module's name and choose Remove *xxx* from the shortcut menu.

Exporting and importing objects

Every object in a project can be saved to a separate file. Saving an individual object in a project is known as exporting. And, it stands to reason, that you can also import objects into a project. Exporting and importing objects might be useful if you want to use a particular object (such as a VBA module or a UserForm) in a different project.

To export an object, select it in the Project Explorer window and choose File⇨Export File (or press Ctrl+E). You'll get a dialog box that asks for a filename. Note that the object remains in the project (only a copy of it is exported).

To import a file into a project, select the project's name in the Explorer window and choose File⇨Import File. You'll get a dialog box that asks for a file. You can import a file only if it has been exported using the File⇨Export File command.

Working with a Code Window

As you become proficient with VBA, you'll be spending *lots* of time working in Code windows. Macros that you record are stored in a module, and you can type VBA code directly into a VBA module. Just to make sure you're straight with the concept, remember that a VBA module holds your VBA code, and a VBA module is displayed in a Code window.

Minimizing and maximizing windows

At any given time, VBE may have lots of Code windows. Figure 3-3 shows an example of what I mean.

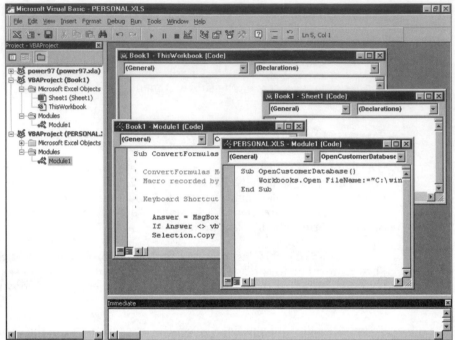

Figure 3-3:
Code
window
overload.

Code windows are much like worksheet windows in Excel. You can minimize them, maximize them, hide them, rearrange them, and so on. Most people find it much easier to maximize the Code window that they're working on. Doing so lets you see more code and keeps you from getting distracted. To maximize a Code window, click the maximize button in its title bar (or just double-click its title bar). To restore a Code window (make it non-maximized), click the Restore button in its title bar.

Sometimes, you may want to have two or more Code windows visible. For example, you might want to compare the code in two modules — or copy code from one module to another.

Minimizing a Code window gets it out of the way. You can also click the Close button in a Code window's title bar to close the window completely. To open it again, just double-click the appropriate object in the Project Explorer window.

Pause for a terminology break

I need to digress for a moment to discuss terminology. Throughout this book, I use the terms *subroutine*, *routine*, *procedure*, and *macro*. You may be a bit confused by these terms (I don't blame you). Programming folks usually use the word *procedure* to describe an automated task. Technically, a procedure can be a subroutine or a function — both of which are sometimes called *routines*. I use all these terms pretty much interchangeably. As detailed in the following chapters, however, there is an important difference between subroutines and functions. For now, don't worry about the terminology. Just try to understand the concepts.

What goes in a module?

In general, a VBA module can hold three types of code:

- ✔ **Subroutine procedures:** A *subroutine* is a set of instructions that performs some action.

- ✔ **Function procedures:** A *function* is a set of instructions that returns a single value (similar in concept to a worksheet function such as SUM).

- ✔ **Declarations:** A *declaration* is a statement of information that you provide to VBA. For example, you can declare the data type for variables you plan to use.

A single VBA module can store any number of subroutines, functions, and declarations. How you organize a VBA module is completely up to you. Some people prefer to keep all their VBA code for an application in a single VBA module; others like to split up the code into several different modules. It's a personal choice.

Getting VBA code into a module

An empty VBA module is like the fake food you see in the windows of some Chinese restaurants; it looks good, but it doesn't really do much for you. Before you can do anything meaningful, you must have some VBA code in the VBA module. You can get VBA code into a VBA module in three ways:

- ✔ By entering the code directly

- ✔ By using the Excel macro recorder to record your actions and convert them to VBA code

- ✔ By copying the code from a module and pasting it to a different module

Entering code directly

Sometimes, the best route is the most direct one. Entering code directly involves . . . well, entering the code directly. In other words, you type the code by using your keyboard. Entering and editing text in a VBA module works pretty much as you might expect. You can select text and copy it or cut it, paste it to another location, and so on.

You can use the Tab key to indent some of the lines. This isn't really necessary, but it's a good habit to acquire, because it makes your code easier to read. As you study the code I present in this book, you'll understand why this is helpful.

A single line of VBA code can be as long as you like. However, you may want to use the line continuation character to break up lengthy lines of code. To continue a single line of code (also known as a *statement*) from one line to the next, end the first line with a space followed by an underscore (_). Then, continue the statement on the next line. Here's an example of a single line of code split into three lines.

```
Selection.Sort Key1:=Range("A1"), _
    Order1:=xlAscending, Header:=xlGuess, _
    Orientation:=xlTopToBottom
```

This statement would perform exactly the same way if it were entered in a single line (with no line continuation characters). Notice that I indented the second and third lines of this statement. Indenting makes it clear that these lines are not separate statements.

Excel limits you to using no more than nine line continuation characters in a single statement. If you try to use more, you'll be rudely interrupted with a message from the big guy. This is no big deal; just combine a few lines by removing the line continuation characters and everything will be fine.

A VBA module has multiple levels of undo and redo. Therefore, if you delete a statement that you shouldn't have, you can press Ctrl+Z repeatedly (or use the Undo button on the toolbar) until the statement comes back. After undoing, you can press F4 (or use the Redo button on the toolbar) to redo the changes you've undone. This undo/redo business is more complicated to describe than it is to use. I recommend that you play around with this feature until you understand how it works.

Ready to enter some real live code? Try this:

1. **In Excel, start a new workbook.**

2. **Press Alt+F11 to activate the VBE.**

3. Click on the new workbook's name in the Project Explorer window.

4. Choose Insert⇨Module to insert a VBA module into the project.

5. Type the following code into the module:

```
Sub GuessName()
    Msg = "Is your name " & Application.UserName & "?"
    Ans = MsgBox(Msg, vbYesNo)
    If Ans = vbNo Then MsgBox "Oh, never mind."
    If Ans = vbYes Then MsgBox "I must be clairvoyant!"
End Sub
```

6. To execute this subroutine, make sure the cursor is located anywhere within the text you typed, and press F5 (which is a shortcut for the Run⇨Run Sub/UserForm command).

If you entered the code correctly, Excel executes the subroutine, and you can respond to the simple dialog box shown in Figure 3-4.

Figure 3-4:
The message box displayed by the GuessName subroutine.

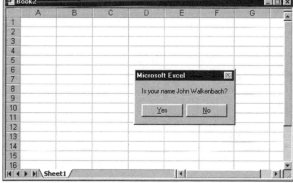

When you enter the code listed above, you might notice that the VBE makes some adjustments to the text you enter. For example, VBE automatically inserts the End Sub statement. And if you omit the space before or after an equal sign, VBE inserts the space for you. Also, VBE changes the color of some text and capitalizes some words. This is all perfectly normal, so don't be alarmed. It's just VBE's way of keeping things neat and readable.

At this point, it's not important that you understand how this code works; that will become clear as you progress through this book.

If you followed the steps listed above, you've just written a VBA subroutine, also known as a macro. When you press F5, Excel quickly compiles the code and executes it. In other words, Excel evaluates each statement and does what you told it to do (don't let this newfound power go to your head). You can execute this macro any number of times — although it tends to lose its appeal after a few dozen times.

For the record, this simple subroutine uses the following concepts (all of which are covered later in this book):

✔ Defining a subroutine procedure (the first line)

✔ Assigning a value to a variable (Msg and Ans)

✔ Concatenating (joining) a string (using the & operator)

✔ Using a built-in VBA function (MsgBox)

✔ Using built-in VBA constants (vbYesNo, vbNo, and vbYes)

✔ Using an If-Then construct (twice)

✔ Ending a subroutine procedure (the last line)

Not bad for a beginner, eh?

Using the macro recorder

Another way you can get code into a VBA module is by recording your actions using the Excel macro recorder. If you worked through the hands-on exercise in Chapter 2, you already have some experience with this technique.

There is absolutely no way you can record the GuessName subroutine shown in the preceding section. You can only record things that you can do directly in Excel. Displaying a message box is not in Excel's normal repertoire (it's a VBA thing). The macro recorder is useful, but for most macros you'll probably have to enter at least *some* code manually.

Here's a step-by-step example that shows you how to record a macro that simply turns off the cell gridlines in a worksheet. If you want to try this example, start with a new, blank workbook and follow these steps:

1. **Activate a worksheet in the workbook (any worksheet will do).**

2. **Choose Tools➪Macro➪Record New Macro.**

   Excel displays its Record Macro dialog box.

3. Just click OK to accept the defaults.

Excel automatically inserts a new VBA module named Module1. From this point on, Excel converts your actions into VBA code. While recording, Excel displays the word *Recording* in the status bar. Excel also displays a miniature floating toolbar that contains two toolbar buttons: Stop Recording and Relative Reference.

4. Choose Tools⇨Options.

Excel displays its Options dialog box.

5. Click the View tab, remove the check mark from the Gridlines option, and click OK to close the dialog box.

If the worksheet you're using has no gridlines, put a check mark next to the Gridlines option to turn on gridlines.

6. Click the Stop Recording button on the miniature toolbar.

Excel stops recording your actions.

To view this newly recorded macro, press Alt+F11 to activate the VBE. Locate the workbook's name in the Project Explorer window. You'll see that the project has a Modules node with one module listed: Module1. Double-click Module1 to view the Code window for the module.

Here's the code generated by your actions:

```
Sub Macro1()
    ActiveWindow.DisplayGridlines = False
End Sub
```

To try out this macro, activate a worksheet that has gridlines displayed. Then, choose Tools⇨Macro⇨Macros (or press Alt+F8). Excel displays a dialog box that lists all the available macros. Select Macro1 and click the Run button. Excel executes the macro, and the gridlines magically disappear. Are you beginning to see how this macro business can be fun?

Of course, you can execute any number of commands and perform any number of actions while the macro recorder is running. Excel dutifully translates your mouse movements and keystrokes to VBA code. It works similarly to a tape recorder, but Excel never runs out of tape.

The preceding macro isn't really all that useful. To make it useful, activate the module and change the statement to

```
ActiveWindow.DisplayGridlines = _
    Not ActiveWindow.DisplayGridlines
```

This modification makes the macro serve as a toggle. If gridlines are displayed, the macro turns them off. If gridlines are not displayed, the macro turns them on. Oops, I'm getting ahead of myself — sorry, but I couldn't resist that simple enhancement.

Copying VBA code

The final method for getting code into a VBA module is to copy it from another module. For example, a subroutine or function you write for one project might also be useful in another project. Rather than waste time reentering the code, you can simply activate the module and use the normal Clipboard copy and paste procedures to copy it into a different VBA module. After pasting the code into a VBA module, you can modify the code if necessary.

Customizing the VBA Environment

If you're serious about becoming an Excel programmer, you'll be spending a lot of time with VBA modules on your screen. To help you make things as comfortable as possible (no, please keep your shoes on), the VBE provides quite a few customization options.

When VBE is active, choose Tools⇨Options. You'll see a dialog box with four tabs: Editor, Editor Format, General, and Docking. I discuss some of the most useful options in the sections that follow.

Using the Editor tab

Figure 3-5 shows the options you access by clicking the Editor tab of the Options dialog box.

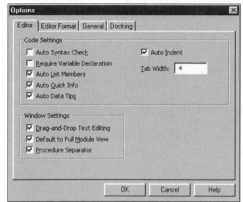

Figure 3-5:
The Editor
tab of the
Options
dialog box.

Auto Syntax Check option

The Auto Syntax Check setting determines whether the VBE pops up a dialog box if it discovers a syntax error while you're entering your VBA code. The dialog box tells roughly what the problem is. If you don't choose this setting, VBE flags syntax errors by displaying them in a different color from the rest of the code, and you don't have to deal with any dialog boxes popping up on your screen. I usually keep this setting turned off because I find the dialog boxes annoying, and I can usually figure out what's wrong with a statement. But when I was a VBA newbie, I found this assistance quite helpful.

Require Variable Declaration option

If the Require Variable Declaration option is set, VBE inserts the following statement at the beginning of each new VBA module you insert:

```
Option Explicit
```

Changing this setting affects only new modules, not existing modules. If this statement appears in your module, you must explicitly define each variable you use. In Chapter 7, I explain why you should develop this habit.

Auto List Members option

If the Auto List Members option is set, VBE provides some help when you're entering your VBA code by displays a list that contains information that would logically complete the statement you're typing. I like this option and always keep it turned on. Figure 3-6 shows an example of this (which will make lots more sense when you actually start writing VBA code).

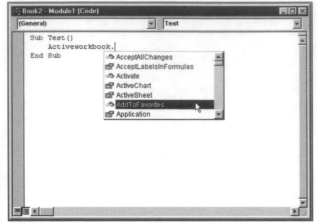

Figure 3-6:
An example
of Auto List
Members.

Auto Quick Info option

If the Auto Quick Info option is set, VBE displays information about functions and their arguments as you type. This can be very helpful. Figure 3-7 shows this feature in action.

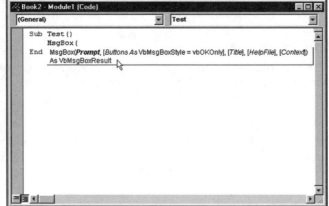

Figure 3-7:
An example
of Auto
Quick Info
offering
help about
the MsgBox
function.

Auto Data Tips option

If the Auto Data Tips option is set, VBE displays the value of the variable over which your cursor is placed when you're debugging code. When you enter the wonderful world of debugging (as described in Chapter 13), you'll appreciate this option.

Auto Indent setting

The Auto Indent setting determines whether VBE automatically indents each new line of code by the same amount as the previous line. I'm big on using indentations in my code, so I keep this option on.

Use the Tab key to indent your code, not the spacebar. Also, you can use Shift+Tab to "unindent" a line of code.

VBE's Edit toolbar (which is hidden by default) contains two useful buttons: Indent and Outdent. These buttons let you quickly indent or "unindent" a block of code. Select the code and then click one of these buttons to change the indenting of the block.

Drag-and-Drop Text Editing option

The Drag-and-Drop Text Editing option, when enabled, lets you copy and move text by dragging and dropping. I keep this option on, but I hardly ever remember to use it.

Default to Full Module View option

The Default to Full Module View option sets the default state for new modules (it doesn't affect existing modules). If set, procedures in the Code window appear as a single scrollable list. If this option is turned off, you can see only one procedure at a time.

Procedure Separator option

When the Procedure Separator option is turned on, separator bars are displayed at the end of each procedure in a Code window. I like the idea of separator bars, so I keep this option turned on.

Using the Editor Format tab

Figure 3-8 shows the Editor Format tab of the Options dialog box.

Code Colors option

The Code Colors option lets you set the text color (foreground and background) and indicator color displayed for various elements of VBA code. This is largely a matter of personal preference. Personally, I find the default colors to be just fine. But for a change of scenery, I occasionally play around with these settings.

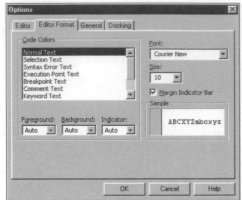

Font option

The Font option lets you select the font that's used in your VBA modules. For best results, stick with a fixed-width font such as Courier New. In a fixed-width font, all characters are exactly the same width. This makes your code more readable because the characters are nicely aligned vertically and you can easily distinguish multiple spaces.

Size setting

The Size setting specifies the size of the font in the VBA modules. This setting is a matter of personal preference determined by your video display resolution and your eyesight.

Margin Indicator Bar option

This option controls the display of the vertical margin indicator bar in your modules. You should keep this turned on; otherwise you won't be able to see the helpful graphical indicators when you're debugging your code.

Using the General tab

Figure 3-9 shows the options available under the General tab in the Options dialog box. In almost every case, the default settings are just fine.

Using the Docking tab

Figure 3-10 shows the Docking tab of the Options dialog box. These options determine how the various windows in the VBE behave. When a window is docked, it is fixed in place along one of the edges of the VBE window. This

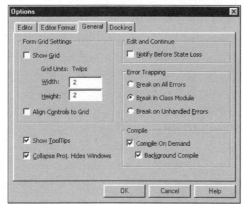

Figure 3-9:
The General
tab of the
Options
dialog box.

makes it much easier to identify and locate a particular window. If you turn off all docking, you'll have a big mess of windows that will be very confusing. Generally, you'll find that the default settings work fine.

This chapter presented everything you need to know to get started using the VBE. All of the windows might be a bit overwhelming at first, but you'll soon get used to them. You can find more about the VBE in Part IV, which discusses UserForms (custom dialog boxes).

Figure 3-10:
The
Docking tab
of the
Options
dialog box.

Chapter 4

Introducing the Excel Object Model

*E*veryone is familiar with the word *object*. The *American Heritage Dictionary* defines it as follows:

> **ob·ject** (òb'jĭkt, -jèkt´) *noun.* Something perceptible by one or more of the senses, especially by vision or touch; a material thing.

Well folks, forget this definition. In the world of programming, the word *object* has a different meaning. You often see it used as part of the expression *object-oriented programming,* or OOP for short. OOP is based on the idea that software consists of distinct objects, which have attributes (or properties) and can be manipulated. These objects are not material things. Rather, they exist in the form of bits and bytes.

In this chapter, I introduce you to the Excel object model. By the time you finish this chapter, you'll have a reasonably good understanding of what OOP is all about — and why you need to understand this concept to become a VBA programmer. After all, Excel programming really boils down to manipulating Excel's objects. It's as simple as that.

The material in this chapter may be a bit overwhelming. But please take my advice and plow through it, even if you don't fully grasp it. This important concept will make lots more sense as you progress through the book.

Excel Is an Object?

You've used Excel for quite a while, but you probably never really thought of it as being an object. The more you work with VBA, the more you'll view Excel in those terms. You'll soon understand that Excel is an object, and that it contains other objects. Those objects, in turn, contain still more objects. In other words, VBA programming involves working with an object hierarchy.

At the top of this hierarchy is the Application object — in this case, Excel itself (the mother of all objects).

The Object Hierarchy

An Application object contains other objects. Following is a list of the 15 objects contained in the Excel Application:

- Addin
- Assistant
- AutoCorrect
- CommandBar
- Debug
- Dialog
- FileFind
- FileSearch
- Name
- ODBCError
- RecentFiles
- VBE
- Window
- Workbook
- WorksheetFunction

Excel 97 includes quite a few new objects, so many of the objects listed here are not available in previous versions of Excel.

Each object contained in the Application object can contain other objects. For example, a Workbook object can contain the following objects:

- ✔ Chart
- ✔ CommandBar
- ✔ CustomView
- ✔ DocumentProperty
- ✔ Mailer
- ✔ Name
- ✔ PivotCache
- ✔ RoutingSlip
- ✔ Style
- ✔ VBProject
- ✔ Window
- ✔ Worksheet

In turn, each of these objects can contain still *other* objects. Consider a Worksheet object (which is contained in a Workbook object — which is contained in the Application object). A Worksheet object can contain the following objects:

- ✔ ChartObject
- ✔ Comment
- ✔ HPageBreak
- ✔ Hyperlink
- ✔ Name
- ✔ OLEObject
- ✔ Outline
- ✔ PageSetup
- ✔ PivotTable
- ✔ QueryTable
- ✔ Range
- ✔ Scenario
- ✔ Shape
- ✔ VPageBreak

Visualizing objects

The online help system for Excel 97 displays the complete Excel object model graphically. To find this diagram, follow these steps:

1. **Activate the VBE.**

2. **Choose Help⇨Contents and Index.**

   The Visual Basic For Applications Help Topics window appears.

3. **In the Help Topics window, double-click Microsoft Excel Visual Basic Reference.**

4. **Double-click Shortcut to Microsoft Excel Visual Basic Reference.**

   A new Help Topics window (Microsoft Excel Visual Basic) appears.

5. **Select the Contents tab, and then double-click Microsoft Excel Visual Basic Reference.**

6. **Double-click Microsoft Excel Objects.**

You'll see the help window shown in the accompanying figure.

If the preceding steps don't work for you, the most likely cause is that the VBA help files are not installed. You'll need to rerun the Setup program for Excel (or Office) and choose the Custom option to specify that you want the VBA help files installed. Unlike the initial installation, this will take only a few minutes.

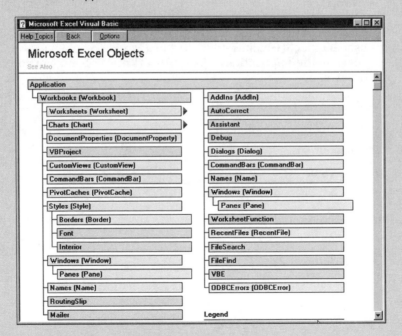

At this point in your introduction to Excel programming, this diagram may add to your confusion. But one day in the not-too-distant future, something will click, and you'll actually find this diagram enlightening.

Put another way, if you want to do something with a range on a particular worksheet, you may find it helpful to visualize that range in the following manner:

Range ⇨ contained in Worksheet ⇨ contained in Workbook ⇨ contained in Excel

Is this beginning to make sense?

Before you come down with a bad case of "object overload," it's important to understand that you will never have a need to use most of the objects available to you. In fact, most of your VBA work will involve only a few objects.

Understanding Collections

Another key concept in VBA programming is *collection*. A collection is a group of objects of the same type. And to add to the confusion, a collection is itself an object.

Here are a few examples of commonly used collections:

- ✔ **Workbooks**: A collection of all currently open Workbook objects
- ✔ **Worksheets**: A collection of all Worksheet objects contained in a particular Workbook object
- ✔ **Charts**: A collection of all Chart objects (chart sheets) contained in a particular Workbook object
- ✔ **Sheets**: A collection of all sheets (regardless of their type) contained in a particular Workbook object
- ✔ **Shapes**: A collection of all Shape objects contained in a particular Worksheet object

You may notice that the names of collections are all plural — which makes sense (at least to me).

Referring to Objects

I presented the information in the previous sections to prepare you for the next concept: how to refer to objects in your VBA code. Referring to an object is important because you must identify the object that you want to work with. After all, VBA can't read your mind — at least the current version can't.

You can work with an entire collection of objects in one fell swoop. More often, however, you need to work with a specific object in a collection (such as a particular worksheet in a workbook). To reference a single object from a collection, you put the object's name or index number in parentheses after the name of the collection, like this:

```
Worksheets("Sheet1")
```

Notice that the sheet's name is in quotation marks. If you omit the quotation marks, Excel won't be able to identify the object.

If Sheet1 is the first (or only) worksheet in the collection, you can also use the following reference:

```
Worksheets(1)
```

In this case, the number is *not* in quotation marks. Bottom line? If you refer to an object by using its name, use quotation marks. If you refer to an object by using its index number, use a plain number without quotation marks.

Another collection, called Sheets, contains all the sheets (regardless of their type) in a workbook. If Sheet1 is the first sheet in the workbook, you can reference it as

```
Sheets(1)
```

Avoiding ambiguity

When you refer to an object that's contained in another object, you often must qualify the reference to the object by connecting object names with the dot (.) operator. Consider this example: What if you have two workbooks open and they both contain a worksheet named Sheet1? To eliminate this potential ambiguity, you need to qualify the reference by adding the object's *container*, like this:

```
Workbooks("Book1").Worksheets("Sheet1")
```

To refer to a specific range (such as cell A1) on a worksheet named Sheet1 in a workbook named Book1, you can use the following expression:

```
Workbooks("Book1").Worksheets("Sheet1").Range("A1")
```

Simplifying object references

Technically, the fully qualified reference for the preceding example also includes the Application object, as follows:

```
Application.Workbooks("Book1").Worksheets("Sheet1").Range("A1")
```

You can, however, omit the Application object in your references (it is assumed). If the Book1 object is the active workbook, you can even omit that object and use the following reference:

```
Worksheets("Sheet1").Range("A1")
```

And (I think you know where I'm going with this), if Sheet1 is the active worksheet, you can use an even simpler expression:

```
Range("A1")
```

Contrary to what some people may think, Excel does not have a Cell object. A *cell* is simply a Range object that consists of just one element.

Object Properties and Methods

Although knowing how to refer to objects is important, you can't do anything useful by simply referring to an object (as in the examples in the previous sections). To accomplish anything meaningful, you must do one of two things:

- ✔ Read or modify an object's *properties*
- ✔ Specify a *method* of action to be used with an object

With literally thousands of properties and methods available, you can easily be overwhelmed. I've been working with this stuff for years and I'm *still* overwhelmed. But as I've said before and I'll say again: You'll find that you'll never use most of the available properties and methods.

Another slant on McObjects, McProperties, and McMethods

Here's an analogy that may help you understand the relationships between objects, properties, and methods in VBA. In this analogy, I compare Excel with a fast-food restaurant chain.

The basic unit in Excel is a workbook object. In a fast-food chain, the basic unit is an individual restaurant. In Excel, you can add workbooks and close workbooks, and all the open workbooks are part of Workbooks, the collection of workbook objects. Similarly, the management of a fast-food chain can add restaurants and close restaurants; you can view all the restaurants in the chain as a collection of Restaurant objects.

An Excel workbook is an object, but it also contains other objects such as Worksheets and Charts. Furthermore, each object in a workbook can contain its own objects. For example, a worksheet can contain Range objects, PivotTable objects, Shape objects, and so on.

Continuing with the analogy, a fast-food restaurant contains objects such as Kitchen, DiningArea, and ParkingLot. Furthermore, management can add or remove objects from the Restaurant object. For example, a particular Restaurant object may get a new DriveupWindow object. Each of these objects can contain other objects. For example, the Kitchen object has a Stove object, a VentilationFan object, a Chef object, a Sink object, and so on.

Excel's object's have properties. For example, a Range object has properties such as Value and Name, and a Shape object has properties such as Width and Height. Not surprisingly, objects in a fast-food restaurant also have properties. For example, the Stove object has properties such as Temperature and NumberofBurners. The VentilationFan has its own set of properties (TurnedOn, RPM, and so on).

In addition to properties, Excel's objects have methods, each of which performs an operation on an object. For example, the ClearContents method erases the contents of a Range object. An object in a fast-food restaurant also has methods. You can easily envision a ChangeThermostat method for a Stove object, or a SwitchOn method for a VentilationFan object.

In Excel, methods sometimes change an object's properties. A Range object's ClearContents method changes the Range's Value property. Similarly, the ChangeThermostat method affects a Stove object's Temperature property.

With VBA, you can write or record subroutine procedures to manipulate Excel's objects. In a fast-food restaurant, the management can give orders to manipulate the objects in the restaurants ("Turn on the stove and switch the ventilation fan to high").

The next time you visit your favorite fast-food joint, just say, "I'll have a Burger object with the Onion property set to False."

Object properties

Every object has properties. You can think of properties as attributes that describe the object. An object's properties determine how it looks, how it behaves, and whether it is visible. Using VBA, you can do two things with an object's properties:

 ✔ Examine the current setting for a property

 ✔ Change the property's setting

For example, a single-cell Range object has a property called Value. The Value property stores the value contained in the cell. You can write VBA code to display the Value property, or you may write VBA code to set the Value property to a specific value. The following subroutine uses the VBA built-in MsgBox function to pop up a box that displays the value in cell A1 on Sheet1 (see Figure 4-1):

```
Sub ShowValue()
    Contents - Worksheets("Sheet1").Range("A1").Value
    MsgBox Contents
End Sub
```

MsgBox is a useful function; you'll often use it to display results while Excel executes your VBA code. I tell you more about this function in Chapter 15.

Figure 4-1:
This
message
box
displays the
Value
property of
a Range
object.

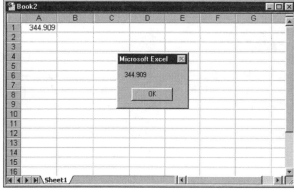

The code in the preceding example displays the current setting of a cell's Value property. What if you want to change the setting for that property? The following subroutine changes the value displayed in cell A1 by changing the cell's Value property:

```
Sub ChangeValue()
    Worksheets("Sheet1").Range("A1").Value = 934
End Sub
```

After Excel executes this subroutine, cell A1 on Sheet1 contains the value 934.

Each object has its own set of properties, although some properties are common to many objects. For example, many (but not all) objects have a Visible property. Most objects also have a Name property.

Some object properties are read-only, which means that you can find out the property's value, but you can't change it.

As I mention earlier in this chapter, a collection is also an object. This means that a collection also has properties. For example, you can determine how many workbooks are open by accessing the Count property of the Worksheets collection. The following VBA subroutine displays a message box that tells you how many workbooks are open:

```
Sub CountBooks()
    MsgBox Workbooks.Count
End Sub
```

Object methods

In addition to properties, objects have methods. A *method* is an action you perform with an object. A method can change an object's properties, or make the object do something.

This simple example uses the Calculate method on a Range object to calculate the formula in cell A1 on Sheet1:

```
Sub CalcCell()
    Worksheets("Sheet1").Range("A1").Calculate
End Sub
```

Most methods also take one or more *arguments*. An argument is a value that further specifies the action to perform. You place the arguments for a method after the method, separated by a space.

The following example activates Sheet1, and then copies the contents of cell A1 to cell B1 using the Copy method of the Range object. In this example, the Copy method has one argument — the destination range for the copy operation:

```
Sub CopyOne()
    Worksheets("Sheet1").Activate
    Range("A1").Copy Range("B1")
End Sub
```

Notice that I omit the worksheet reference when I refer to the Range objects. I could do this safely because I used a statement to activate Sheet1 (using the Activate method).

Because a collection is also an object, collections have methods. The following subroutine uses the Add method for the Workbooks collection:

```
Sub AddAWorkbook()
    Workbooks.Add
End Sub
```

As you may expect, this statement creates a new workbook. In other words, it adds a new workbook to the Workbooks collection.

Object Events

In this section, I briefly touch on one more topic that you'll need to know about: Events. Objects respond to various events that occur. For example, when you're working in Excel and you activate a different workbook, an Activate event occurs. You could, for example, have a VBA macro that is designed to execute whenever an Activate event occurs.

Excel supports many events, but not all objects can respond to all events. And some objects don't respond to any events. The concept of an event becomes clear in Chapter 11 (which is devoted to that topic), and also in Part IV (which discusses custom dialog boxes).

Finding Out More

You find out more about objects, properties, and methods in the following chapters. You may also be interested in three other excellent tools:

✔ VBA's online help

✔ The Object Browser

✔ Auto List Members

Using online help

The VBA online help system describes every object, property, and method that is available to you. This is an excellent resource for finding out about VBA and is more comprehensive than any book on the market.

If you're working in a VBA module and you want information about a particular object, method, or procedure, just move the cursor to the word you're interested in and press F1. In a few seconds, you'll see the appropriate help topic, complete with cross-references and perhaps even an example or two.

Figure 4-2 shows a screen from the online help system — in this case, for a Worksheet object. You can click Properties to get a complete list of this object's properties; click Methods to get a listing of its methods, or click Events to get a listing of the events it responds to.

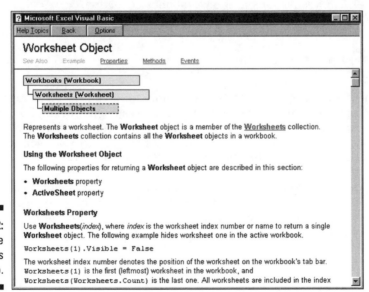

Figure 4-2: An example of VBA's online help.

Using the Object Browser

The VBE includes another tool, known as the Object Browser. As the name implies, this tool lets you browse through the objects available to you. The Object Browser may not be of much value now, but you'll probably find it more useful as you gain experience with VBA.

To access the Object Browser, press F2 when the VBE is active (or choose View⇨Object Browser). You'll see a window like the one shown in Figure 4-3.

The drop-down list at the top contains a list of all object libraries that are currently available. If you want to browse through Excel's objects, select Excel from the drop-down list.

The second drop-down list is where you enter a search string. For example, if you want to look at all Excel objects that deal with links, type **link** into the second field and click the Binoculars icon. The Search Results window will display everything in the object library that contains the text *link*. If you see something that looks like it may be of interest, press F1 for more information.

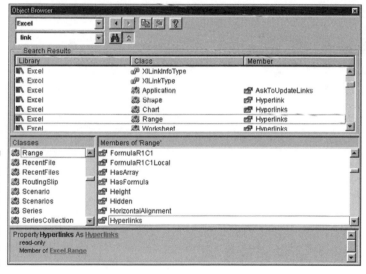

Figure 4-3: Browsing for objects with the Object Browser.

Chapter 5

VBA Subroutines and Functions

• •

In This Chapter

▶ Understanding the difference between subroutines and functions

▶ Executing subroutines (many ways)

▶ Executing functions (two ways)

• •

*S*everal times in previous chapters, I mention the term *subroutine*, and I allude to that fact that *functions* also play a role in VBA. In this chapter, I clear up any confusion you may have about the use of subroutines and functions in VBA.

Subroutines versus Functions

The VBA code that you write in the Visual Basic Editor is known as a *procedure*. You can actually write two types of procedures:

▸ **A subroutine procedure:** A group of VBA statements that perform an action (or actions) with Excel.

▸ **A function procedure:** A group of VBA statements that perform a calculation and return a single value.

Most macros you write in VBA are subroutine procedures. You can think of a subroutine as being like a command: Execute the subroutine and something happens (of course, exactly *what* happens depends on the subroutine's code).

A function is also a procedure, but it's quite different from a subroutine. You're already familiar with the concept of a function. Excel includes many *worksheet* functions that you use every day (well, at least every weekday). Examples include SUM, PMT, and VLOOKUP. You use these worksheet functions in formulas. Each function takes one or more arguments (although a few functions don't use any arguments). The function does some behind-the-scenes calculations, and returns a single value. The same goes for functions that you develop with VBA.

Looking at subroutines

Every subroutine procedure starts with the keyword Sub, and ends with an End Sub statement. Here's an example:

```
Sub UpdateSalesSummary()
    [VBA code goes here]
End Sub
```

This example shows a subroutine named UpdateSalesSummary. A set of parentheses follows the subroutine name. In most cases, these parentheses are empty. However, you may pass arguments to subroutines from other subroutines or functions. If your subroutine uses arguments, you list these between the parentheses.

When you record a macro with the Excel macro recorder, the result is always a subroutine procedure.

As you see later in this chapter, Excel provides quite a few ways to execute a VBA subroutine.

Looking at functions

Every function procedure starts with the keyword Function and ends with an End Function statement. Here's an example:

```
Function CubeRoot(number)
    [VBA code goes here]
End Function
```

This function, named CubeRoot, takes one argument (named *number*), which is enclosed in parentheses. Functions can have no arguments, one argument, or multiple arguments. When you execute the function, it returns a single value.

You can execute a function in only two ways. You can execute it from another procedure (a subroutine or another function) or use it in a worksheet formula.

You can't use the Excel macro recorder to record a function. You must manually enter every function that you create.

A few words about arguments

You're probably well aware of the normal definition of *argument* — but this term has a different meaning in the world of programming. An argument is a value that is passed to a subroutine or a function procedure. The procedure then uses that argument to do its thing.

To better understand the concept, think of the worksheet functions you use regularly. Most of them take one or more arguments.

For example, Excel's SQRT function takes one argument — that is then used in the calculation. The function returns the square root of the argument. Some of the Excel worksheet functions don't take any arguments. (RAND and NOW are two examples.) Arguments passed to VBA subroutines and functions work the same way. Some procedures require arguments, and others do not.

Naming subroutines and functions

Like humans and pets, every subroutine and function procedure must have a name. When naming subroutines and functions, you must follow a few rules:

✔ You can use letters, numbers, and some punctuation characters, but the first character must be a letter.

✔ The name can't look like a cell reference. For example, if you try to name a subroutine AC45, Excel complains because that name resembles a cell address.

✔ You can't use any spaces or periods in the name.

✔ VBA does not distinguish between uppercase and lowercase letters.

✔ You can't embed any of the following characters in a name: #, $, %, &, or !

✔ Names can be no longer than 254 characters. (Of course, you would never make a procedure name this long.)

Ideally, a procedure's name should describe the routine's purpose. A good rule of thumb is to create a name by combining a verb and a noun — for example, ProcessData, PrintReport, Sort_Array, or CheckFilename.

Some programmers prefer using sentence-like names that provide a complete description of the subroutine. Some examples include WriteReportToTextFile and Get_Print_Options_and_Print_Report. The use of such lengthy names has its pros and cons. On the one hand, such names are descriptive and unambiguous. On the other hand, they are difficult to type.

Everyone develops a naming style, but the main objectives should be to make the names descriptive and to avoid meaningless names such as DoIt, Update, and Fix.

Executing Subroutines

Although you may not know much about *developing* subroutines at this point, I'm going to jump ahead a bit and discuss how to *execute* subroutines. This is important, because a subroutine is worthless unless you know how to execute it.

By the way, *executing* a subroutine means the same thing as *running* a subroutine, or *calling* a subroutine. You can use whatever terminology you like.

You can execute a VBA subroutine in many ways — that's one reason why you can do so many useful things with subroutines. Here's an exhaustive list of the ways in which you can execute a subroutine (well, at least all the ways I could think of):

- With the Run⇨Run Sub/UserForm command (in the VBE). Or you can press the F5 shortcut key. Excel executes the subroutine at the cursor position. This method doesn't work if the subroutine requires one or more arguments.

- From the Macro dialog box (which you open by choosing Tools⇨ Macro⇨Macros). Or you can press the Alt+F8 shortcut key. When the Macro dialog box appears, just select the subroutine you want and click Run. This dialog box lists only the subroutines that don't require an argument.

- Using the Ctrl+key shortcut assigned to the subroutine (assuming you assigned one).

- By clicking a button or a shape on a worksheet. The button or shape must have a subroutine assigned to it.

- From another subroutine you write.

- From a Toolbar button (see Chapter 20).

- From a custom menu you develop (see Chapter 19).

- Automatically, when you open or close a workbook (see Chapter 11).

- When an event occurs. As I detail in Chapter 11, these events include saving the workbook, making a change to a cell, activating a sheet, and other things.

- From the Immediate window in the VBE. Just type the name of the subroutine and press Enter.

Excel 5 and Excel 95 made it very easy to assign a macro to a new menu item on the Tools menu. For some unknown reason, this feature is not available in Excel 97.

I demonstrate some of these techniques in the following sections. Before I can do that, you need to enter a subroutine into a VBA module. Start with a new workbook and press Alt+F11 to activate the VBE. Select the workbook in the Project window and choose Insert⟹Module to insert a new module. Then enter the following into the module:

```
Sub SampleSub()
    Num = InputBox("Enter a positive number")
    MsgBox Num ^ 0.5 & " is the square root."
End Sub
```

This simple subroutine asks the user for a number, and then displays the square root of that number in a message box. Figures 5-1 and 5-2 show what happens when you execute this subroutine.

Figure 5-1:
Using the
VBA built-in
InputBox
function to
get a
number.

Figure 5-2:
Displaying
the square
root of a
number by
using the
MsgBox
function.

By the way, SampleSub is not an example of a *good* macro. It doesn't check for errors, so you can easily make it fail (try clicking the Cancel button to see what I mean).

Executing the subroutine directly

The quickest way you can execute this subroutine is to do so directly from the VBA module in which you defined it. Activate the VBE and select the VBA module that contains the subroutine. Move the cursor anywhere in the subroutine, and press F5 (or choose Run⊃Run Sub/UserForm). Respond to the subroutine's request, and click OK. The subroutine displays the square root of the number you entered.

You can't use the Run⊃Run Sub/UserForm command to execute a subroutine that uses any arguments because you have no way to pass the arguments to the subroutine. If the subroutine contains one or more arguments, the only way to execute the subroutine is to call it from another procedure — which must supply the argument(s).

Executing the subroutine from the Macro dialog box

Next, activate Excel (Atl+F11 is the express route) and choose Tools⊃ Macro⊃Macros. Excel displays the dialog box shown in Figure 5-3. Select the macro, and click Run (or just double-click the macro's name in the list box).

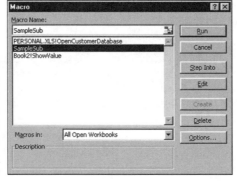

Figure 5-3: The Macro dialog box lists all available subroutines.

Assigning a shortcut key

Before you can execute a macro by pressing a key combination, you have to set things up. Specifically, you must assign a shortcut key to the macro.

When you begin recording a macro, you have the opportunity to assign a shortcut key in the Record Macro dialog box. If you create the subroutine without using the macro recorder, you can assign a shortcut key (or change an existing shortcut key) using the following procedure:

1. **Choose Tools⇨Macro⇨Macros.**

2. **Select the subroutine name in the list box.**

   In this example, the subroutine is named SampleSub.

3. **Click the Options button.**

   Excel displays the dialog box shown in Figure 5-4.

Figure 5-4:
The Macro
Options
dialog box
lets you
choose
options for
your
macros.

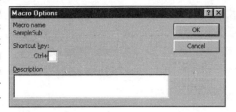

4. **Click the Shortcut Key option, and enter a letter in the box labeled Ctrl.**

   The letter you enter corresponds to the key combination you want to use for executing the macro. For example, if you enter the letter *s*, you can then execute the macro by pressing Ctrl+S. If you enter an uppercase letter, you need to add the Shift key to the key combination. For example, if you enter *S* (uppercase), you can execute the macro by pressing Ctrl+Shift+S.

5. **Click OK and then click Close to close the Macro dialog box.**

The shortcut keys you assign to macros override Excel's built-in shortcut keys. For example, if you assign Ctrl+S to a macro, you can't use this shortcut key to save your workbook. This is usually not a big deal because Excel always provides other ways to execute commands.

Excel does *not* use the following keys in its Ctrl+key combinations: E, J, L, M, Q, and T. Excel doesn't use too many Ctrl+Shift+key combinations. In fact, you can safely use any of them *except* F, O, and P.

Executing the macro from a button or shape

You can create still another means for executing the macro by assigning the macro to a button (or any other shape) on a worksheet. To try this, activate a worksheet, and then add a button from the Forms toolbar. To display the Forms toolbar, right-click any toolbar and choose Forms from the shortcut menu. Next, click the Button tool on the Forms toolbar. Then drag in the worksheet to create the button.

After you add the button to your worksheet, Excel jumps right in and displays the Assign Macro dialog box shown in Figure 5-5. Select the macro you want to assign to the button, and click OK.

Figure 5-5:
When you add a button to a worksheet, Excel automatically displays the Assign Macro dialog box.

You can assign a macro also to any other shape or object. For example, if you'd like to execute a macro when the user clicks a Rectangle object, add the Rectangle to the worksheet (use the Rectangle button on the Drawing toolbar). Then right-click the rectangle and choose Assign Macro from its shortcut menu. Select the macro from the Assign Macro dialog box and click OK.

Executing the macro from another subroutine

As I mention earlier in this chapter, you can execute a subroutine also from another subroutine. If you want to give this a try, activate the VBA module that holds the SampleSub routine, and then enter this new subroutine (either above or below SampleSub — it makes no difference):

```
Sub NewSub()
    Call SampleSub
End Sub
```

Now, execute the NewSub macro. The easiest way to do this is to move the cursor anywhere within the NewSub code and press F5. Notice that this NewSub subroutine simply executes the SampleSub subroutine.

By the way, the keyword Call is optional. The statement could consist of only the subroutine's name. I find, however, that using the Call keyword makes it perfectly clear that a subroutine is being called.

Executing Functions

Functions, unlike subroutines, can be executed in only two ways:

- ✔ By calling the function from another subroutine or function
- ✔ By using the function in a worksheet formula

Here's a simple function you can try. Enter this function into a VBA module:

```
Function Squared(number)
    Squared = number * number
End Function
```

This function is pretty wimpy — it merely squares the number passed to it as its argument.

Calling the function from a subroutine

Because you can't execute this function directly, you must call it from another procedure. Enter the following simple procedure in the same VBA module that contains the Squared function:

```
Sub CallerSub()
    MsgBox Squared(25)
End Sub
```

When you execute the CallerSub procedure (using any of the methods I describe earlier in this chapter), Excel displays a message box like the one shown in Figure 5-6.

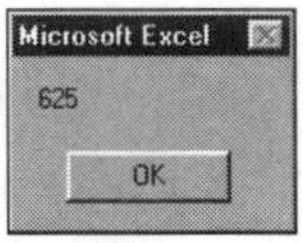

Figure 5-6:
This
message
box
displays the
result
obtained by
calling a
custom
function.

It's pretty easy to see what's going on. The MsgBox statement refers to a custom function (Squared) and passes an argument (the number in parentheses) to this function. The Squared function computes the answer and returns it to the MsgBox statement. The MsgBox statement then displays the result. Try changing the argument that's passed, and run the CallerSub macro again. You'll see that it works just like it should.

Calling a function from a worksheet formula

Now it's time to call this custom VBA function from a worksheet formula. Activate a worksheet in the same workbook that holds the Squared function definition. Then enter the following formula into any cell:

```
=Squared(45)
```

The cell displays 2025, which is indeed 45 squared.

As you might expect, you can use a cell reference as the argument for the Squared function. For example, if cell A1 contains a value, you can enter **=Squared(A1)**. In this case, the function returns the number obtained by squaring the value in A1.

You can use this function any number of times in the worksheet. And this function even appears in the Paste Function dialog box. Click the Paste Function toolbar button, and scroll down to the User Defined category. As shown in Figure 5-7, the Paste Function lists your very own function.

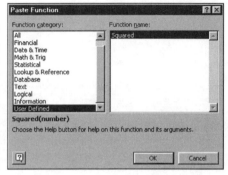

Figure 5-7:
The Squared function appears in the Paste Function dialog box.

If you want the Paste Function dialog box to display a description of the function, choose Tools⇨Macro⇨Macros. Excel displays the Macro dialog box, but Squared doesn't appear in the list. (Squared is a function, and this list shows only subroutines.) Don't fret. Simply type the word **Squared** and then click the Options button. Enter a description of the function in the box labeled Description. Close the Options dialog box and then close the Macro dialog box by clicking the Cancel button. This descriptive text now appears in the Paste Function dialog box.

By now, things may be starting to come together for you. (I wish I had this book when *I* was starting out.) You've found out lots about subroutines and functions. You still have a lot more to find out, but the finer points come later. You start creating macros in Chapter 6, which discusses the ins and outs of developing macros using the Excel macro recorder.

Chapter 6
Using the Excel Macro Recorder

In This Chapter

▶ Recording your actions using the Excel built-in macro recorder

▶ Understanding the types of macros you can record

▶ Setting the appropriate options for macro recording

*I*f you're reading this book in chapter number order, you know that you can use two methods for developing a subroutine macro:

✔ Record it, using the Excel macro recorder

✔ Write it (knowledge of VBA required)

This chapter deals with the ins and outs of using the Excel macro recorder. Recording a macro isn't always the best approach — and some macros simply can't be recorded, no matter how hard you try. You'll see, however, that the Excel macro recorder is very useful and is an excellent learning tool.

Is It Live, or Is It VBA?

Recording a macro is sort of like using a tape recorder. Turn it on, do your thing, and then turn it off after you're finished. This analogy, however, only goes so far. Table 6-1 compares tape recording with macro recording.

Table 6-1	Tape Recording versus Macro Recording	
	Tape Recorder Recorder	**Excel Macro**
What equipment is required?	A tape recorder and a microphone.	A computer and a copy of Excel.
What is recorded?	Sounds.	Actions taken in Excel.
Where is the recording stored?	On magnetic tape.	In a VBA module.
How do you play it back?	Rewind the tape, and press Play.	Choose Tools⇨Macro (or various other methods).
Can you edit the recording?	Yes, if you have the proper equipment.	Yes, if you know what you're doing.
Can you copy the recording?	Yes, if you have a second tape recorder.	Yes (no additional equipment required).
Is the recording accurate?	Depends on the situation and the quality of the equipment.	Depends on how you set things up.
What if you make a mistake?	Re-record the tape (or edit it if possible).	Re-record the macro (or edit it if possible).
Can you view the recording?	No, it's just a bunch of magnetic impulses.	Yes, by activating a VBA module.
Can you make money with the recording?	Yes, if it's good (editing usually required).	Yes, but you need to do a lot of editing first.

Recording Basics

You take the following basic steps when you record a macro (I describe these steps in more detail later in this chapter):

1. **Think about what you want the macro to do.**

2. **Get things set up properly.**

   This step determines how well your macro works.

3. **Determine whether you want the recording to be relative or absolute.**

4. **Choose Tools⇨Macro⇨Record New Macro.**

   Excel displays its Record Macro dialog box.

5. **Enter a name, shortcut key, macro location, and description.**

   This step is optional.

6. **Click OK in the Record Macro dialog box.**

   Excel automatically inserts a VBA module. From this point, Excel converts your actions into VBA code. It also displays a miniature floating toolbar, which contains two toolbar buttons: Stop Recording and Relative Reference.

7. **Perform the actions you want to record, using the mouse or the keyboard.**

8. **After you're finished, click the Stop Recording button on the miniature toolbar (or choose Tools⇨Macro⇨Stop Recording).**

   Excel stops recording your actions.

9. **Test the macro to make sure that it works correctly.**

Types of Macros Appropriate for Recording

The macro recorder is best suited for simple, straightforward macros. For example, you might want to record a macro that applies certain formatting to a selected range. Or you can record a macro that sets up row and column headings for a new worksheet.

As I mention in the preceding chapter, you can't use the macro recorder to create function procedures.

You may also find the macro recorder helpful for developing more-complex macros. Often, I record some actions and then copy the recorded code into another, more complex macro. In most cases, you need to edit the recorded code and add some new VBA statements.

The macro recorder *cannot* generate code for any of the following tasks:

✔ Performing any type of repetitive looping

✔ Performing any type of conditional actions (using an If-Then statement)

✔ Assigning values to variables

✔ Specifying data types

✔ Displaying pop-up messages

✔ Displaying custom dialog boxes

I describe these concepts later in the book. But for now, just understand that the macro recorder isn't the ultimate answer for programming Excel.

The limited capability of the macro recorder certainly doesn't diminish the importance of this tool. I make this point throughout the book: *Recording your actions is perhaps the best way to learn VBA.* When in doubt, try recording. Although the result may not be exactly what you want, viewing the recorded code might steer you in the right direction.

Preparing to Record

Before you take the big step and turn on the macro recorder, spend a minute or two thinking about what you're going to do. Remember, you record a macro so that Excel can automatically repeat the actions you record.

Ultimately, the success of a recorded macro depends on five factors:

✔ How the workbook is set up while you record the macro

✔ What is selected when you start recording

✔ Whether you use absolute or relative recording mode

✔ The accuracy of your recorded actions

✔ The context in which you play back the recorded macro

The importance of these factors becomes crystal clear in the next section when I walk you through an example.

Relative or Absolute?

When recording your actions, Excel normally records absolute references to cells (this is the default recording mode). Very often, this is the *wrong* recording mode. If you use relative recording, Excel records relative references to cells.

In the following sections, I demonstrate the difference between absolute and relative recording mode.

Recording in absolute mode

Follow these steps to record a simple macro in absolute mode. This macro simply enters three month names into a worksheet:

1. **Choose Tools➪Macro➪Record New Macro.**
2. **Type** Absolute **as the name for this macro.**
3. **Click OK to begin recording.**
4. **Activate cell B1, and type** Jan **in that cell.**
5. **Move to cell C1, and type** Feb.
6. **Move to cell D1, and type** Mar.
7. **Click cell B1 to activate it again.**
8. **Stop the macro recorder.**

Press Alt+F11 to activate the VBE, and then examine the Module1 module. Excel generates the following code:

```
Sub Absolute()
    Range("B1").Select
    ActiveCell.FormulaR1C1 = "Jan"
    Range("C1").Select
    ActiveCell.FormulaR1C1 = "Feb"
    Range("D1").Select
    ActiveCell.FormulaR1C1 = "Mar"
    Range("B1").Select
End Sub
```

When executed, this macro selects cell B1 and inserts the month names in the range B1:D1 Then the macro reactivates cell B1.

These same actions occur regardless of which cell is active when you execute the macro. A macro recorded using absolute references always produces the same results when it is executed. In this case, the macro always enters the names of the first three months into the range B1:D1.

Recording in relative mode

In some cases, however, you want your recorded macro to work with cell locations in a *relative* manner. In the preceding example, you may want the macro to start entering the month names in the active cell. In such a case, you need to use relative recording.

The Stop Recording toolbar, which consists of only two buttons, is displayed when you are recording a macro. You can change the manner in which Excel records your actions by clicking the Relative Reference button on the Stop Recording toolbar. This button is a toggle. When the button appears in a pressed state, the recording mode is relative. When the button appears normally, you are recording in absolute mode.

Figure 6-1 shows the Relative Reference button in its normal state (left) and in its pressed state (right). If you have trouble telling the difference, you're not alone.

Figure 6-1:
The two
states of
the Relative
Reference
button.

You can change the recording method at any time, even in the middle of recording.

To see how this works, erase the cells in B1:D1 and then perform the following steps:

1. **Activate cell B1.**
2. **Choose Tools⇨Macro⇨Record New Macro.**
3. **Name this macro Relative.**
4. **Click OK to begin recording.**
5. **Click the Relative Reference button to change the recording mode to relative.**

   When you click this button, it will appear pressed.
6. **Enter the first three month names in B1:D1, as in the previous example.**
7. **Select cell B1.**
8. **Stop the macro recorder.**

Notice that this procedure differs slightly from the previous example. In this example, you activate the beginning cell *before* you start recording. This is an important step when you record macros that use the active cell as a base.

Unlike the previous macro (which you recorded in absolute mode), this one always starts entering text in the active cell. Try it. Move the cell pointer to any cell and then execute the Relative macro. The month names are always entered beginning at the active cell.

With the recording mode set to relative, the code Excel generates is quite different from the previous example:

```
Sub Relative()
    ActiveCell.FormulaR1C1 = "Jan"
    ActiveCell.Offset(0, 1).Range("A1").Select
    ActiveCell.FormulaR1C1 = "Feb"
    ActiveCell.Offset(0, 1).Range("A1").Select
    ActiveCell.FormulaR1C1 = "Mar"
    ActiveCell.Offset(0, -2).Range("A1").Select
End Sub
```

Notice that the code generated by the macro recorder refers to cell A1. This may seem strange, because you never used cell A1 during the recording of the macro. This is simply a by-product of the way the macro recorder works. (I discuss this in more detail in Chapter 8 when I talk about the Offset method.) At this point, all you need to know is that the macro works like it should.

The important point here is that the macro recorder has two distinct modes, and you need to be aware of which mode you're using. Otherwise, you may not get the results you expected.

What Gets Recorded?

When you turn on the macro recorder, Excel converts your mouse and keyboard actions into valid VBA code. I could probably write several pages describing how Excel does this, but the best way to understand the process is by watching the macro recorder in action. Follow these steps:

1. **Start with a blank workbook.**

2. **Make sure that the Excel window is not maximized.**

3. **Press Alt+F11 to activate the VBE window (and make sure that *this* window is not maximized).**

4. **Arrange the Excel window and the VBE window so that both are visible. (For best results, minimize any other applications that are running.)**

5. **Activate Excel, Choose Tools⊅Macro⊅Record New Macro, and click OK to start the macro recorder.**

   Excel inserts a new module (named Module1) and starts recording on that sheet.

6. **Activate the VBE window.**

7. **In the Project Explorer window, double-click Module1 to display that module in the Code window.**

Your screen should look something like the example in Figure 6-2.

Now, play around for a while: Select various Excel commands, and watch the code being generated in the VBE window. Select cells, enter data, format cells, use the menus and toolbars, create a chart, manipulate graphics objects, and so on — go crazy! I guarantee you'll be enlightened as you watch Excel spit out the code before your very eyes.

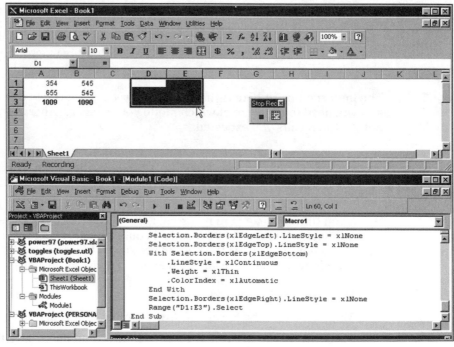

Figure 6-2: A convenient window arrangement for watching the macro recorder do its thing.

Recording Options

When recording your actions to create VBA code, you have several options. Recall that the <u>T</u>ools⇨<u>M</u>acro⇨<u>R</u>ecord New Macro command displays the Record Macro dialog box before recording begins, as shown in Figure 6-3.

Figure 6-3:
The Record
Macro
dialog box
provides
several
recording
options.

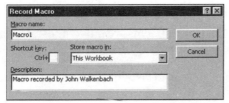

This dialog box gives you quite a bit of control over your macro. In the following sections, I describe your options.

Macro Name

You can enter a name for the subroutine that you are recording. By default, Excel uses the names Macro1, Macro2, and so on for each macro you record. I usually just accept the default name, and change the name of the subroutine later. You, however, may prefer to name the macro up front — the choice is yours.

Shortcut key

The Shortcut key option lets you execute the macro by pressing a shortcut key combination. For example, if you enter **w** (lowercase), you can execute the macro by pressing Ctrl+w. If you enter **W** (uppercase), the macro comes alive when you press Ctrl+Shift+W.

You can add or change a shortcut key at any time, so you don't need to set this option when recording a macro.

Store macro in

The Store macro in option tells Excel where to store the macro that it is recording. By default, Excel puts the recorded macro in a module in the active workbook. If you prefer, you can record it in a new workbook (Excel opens a blank workbook) or in your Personal Macro Workbook.

Description

When you record a macro, the macro begins with five lines of comments (three of them blank) that list the macro name, the user's name, and the date. You can put anything you like here, or nothing at all. As far as I'm concerned, the Description option is a waste of time because I always end up deleting these lines in the module.

Previous versions of Excel offered a choice of macro languages (VBA or the old XLM macro language). Although Excel 97 still executes XLM macros, it can no longer record such macros — which is just as well because you wouldn't want to record your macro using the outdated XLM macro langauge anyway.

Your Personal Macro Workbook

If you create some VBA macros that you find particularly useful, you may want to store these routines in your Personal Macro Workbook. Excel stores this workbook (PERSONAL.XLS) in your EXCEL\XLSTART directory (which may be named something like OFFICE\ XLSTART). Whenever you start Excel, this workbook is loaded. It's a hidden workbook, so it's out of your way. When you record a macro, one of your options is to record it to your Personal Macro Workbook.

You won't have a Personal Macro Workbook unless you record a macro and specify the Personal Macro Workbook as the location for the macro. After you do so, this workbook is created for you automatically.

To examine your Personal Macro Workbook, activate the VBE.

Is This Thing Efficient?

You might think that recording a macro would generate some award-winning VBA code — better than you could write manually. Think again. In many cases, the recorder spits out lots of extraneous garbage — and it often generates code that's less than efficient.

Don't get me wrong. I'm a staunch supporter of the macro recorder. It's a great tool for helping you learn VBA. Except for simple macros, however, I've never used a recorded macro without fixing it up a bit (usually, *quite* a bit).

To demonstrate just how inefficient the macro recorder's code can be, try this:

1. **Turn on the macro recorder.**

2. **Choose File➪Page Setup.**

   The Page Setup dialog box appears.

3. **Click the Page Tab.**

4. **Change the page orientation to Landscape, and click OK.**

5. **Turn off the macro recorder.**

To take a look at the macro, activate the Module1 sheet. This single — and very simple — command generates the following code:

```
Sub Macro1()
'
' Macro1 Macro
' Macro recorded by John Walkenbach
'
    With ActiveSheet.PageSetup
        .PrintTitleRows = ""
        .PrintTitleColumns = ""
    End With
    ActiveSheet.PageSetup.PrintArea = ""
    With ActiveSheet.PageSetup
        .LeftHeader = ""
        .CenterHeader = ""
        .RightHeader = ""
        .LeftFooter = ""
```

(continued)

(continued)

```
        .CenterFooter = ""
        .RightFooter = ""
        .LeftMargin = Application.InchesToPoints(0.75)
        .RightMargin = Application.InchesToPoints(0.75)
        .TopMargin = Application.InchesToPoints(1)
        .BottomMargin = Application.InchesToPoints(1)
        .HeaderMargin = Application.InchesToPoints(0.5)
        .FooterMargin = Application.InchesToPoints(0.5)
        .PrintHeadings = False
        .PrintGridlines = False
        .PrintComments = xlPrintNoComments
        .PrintQuality = 600
        .CenterHorizontally = False
        .CenterVertically = False
        .Orientation = xlLandscape
        .Draft = False
        .PaperSize = xlPaperLetter
        .FirstPageNumber = xlAutomatic
        .Order = xlDownThenOver
        .BlackAndWhite = False
        .Zoom = 100
    End With
End Sub
```

You may be surprised by the amount of code generated by this single command. (It was the first time I tried something like this.) Although you changed only one setting in the Page Setup dialog box, Excel generated code that reproduces *all* the settings in the dialog box.

This is a good example of macro recording overkill. If you want a macro that simply switches the page setup to landscape mode, you can simplify this macro considerably by deleting the extraneous code. This makes the macro easier to read, and the macro will also run faster because it doesn't perform any unnecessary tasks. You can simplify this macro as follows:

```
Sub Macro1()
    With ActiveSheet.PageSetup
        .Orientation = xlLandscape
    End With
End Sub
```

I deleted all the code except the line that sets the Orientation property. Actually, you can simplify this macro even more because you don't really need the With..End With construct:

```
Sub Macro1()
    ActiveSheet.PageSetup.Orientation = xlLandscape
End Sub
```

In this case, the macro changes the Orientation property of the PageSetup object on the active sheet. All other properties are unchanged. By the way, xlLandscape is a built-in constant that VBA provides to make things easier for you. I discuss built-in constants in Chapter 7.

Rather than record this macro, you could enter it directly into a VBA module. To do so, you have to know which objects, properties, and methods to use. Although the recorded macro isn't all that great, by recording it, you learned that the PageSetup object has an Orientation property. This example shows how the macro recorder can help you learn VBA.

This chapter pretty much sums it up when it comes to using the macro recorder. The only thing missing is experience. The more you work with the macro recorder, the more you'll realize that it's a great tool.

Part III

Programming Concepts

The 5th Wave   By Rich Tennant

"WELL, RIGHT OFF, THE RESPONSE TIME SEEMS A BIT SLOW."

In this part . . .

This is the part of the book that you've been waiting for. In the next eight chapters, you find out about all the essential elements of Excel programming. And in the process, you see some illuminating examples that you can adapt to your own needs.

Chapter 7

Essential VBA Language Elements

● ●

In This Chapter

▶ When, why, and how to use comments in your code

▶ Using variables and constants

▶ How to tell VBA what type of data you're using

▶ Scoping variables

▶ Assigning information to variables

▶ All about arrays

▶ Why you may need to use labels in your procedures

● ●

*B*ecause VBA is a real-live programming language, it uses many elements that are common to all programming languages. In this chapter, I cue you in to several of these elements: comments, variables, constants, data types, arrays, and a few other goodies. If you've programmed using other languages, some of this material will be familiar. If you're a programming newbie, it's time to roll up your sleeves and get busy.

Using Comments in Your Code

A *comment* is the simplest type of VBA statement. Because VBA ignores these statements, they can consist of anything you want. Comments are for your own use. You can insert a comment to remind yourself why you did something, or to clarify some particularly elegant code you wrote. Use comments liberally to describe what the code does (which isn't always obvious by reading the code itself). Often, code that makes perfect sense today mystifies you tomorrow.

You begin a comment with an apostrophe ('). VBA ignores any text that follows an apostrophe in a line of code. You can use a complete line for your comment, or insert your comment at the end of a line of code.

The following example shows a VBA subroutine with three comments (though they're not necessarily *good* comments):

```
Sub Comments()
'   This subroutine does nothing of value
    x = 0    'x represents nothingness
    'Display the result
    MsgBox x
End Sub
```

The "apostrophe indicates a comment" rule has one exception. VBA doesn't interpret an apostrophe inside a set of quotation marks as a comment indicator. For example, the following statement doesn't contain a comment, even though it has an apostrophe:

```
Msg = "Can't continue"
```

You can also use the Rem keyword to mark a line of code as a comment. Here's an example:

```
Rem — The next statement prompts the user for a name
```

The Rem keyword is a holdover from previous versions of BASIC; VBA includes it for compatibility. Rem works only for complete lines of code. The apostrophe is the preferred method for inserting comments.

Often, you want to test a procedure without a particular statement or group of statements. Rather than delete the statements, simply turn them into comments by inserting apostrophes. VBA ignores these statements when it executes the routine. Then, simply remove the apostrophes to convert the comments back to statements.

The VBE makes it easy to "comment out" a block of statements and then convert the comments back to statements. In the VBE, choose View⇨ Toolbars⇨Edit to display the Edit toolbar (see Figure 7-1). To convert a block of statements to comments, select the statements and click the Comment Block button. To remove the apostrophes, select the statements and click the Uncomment Block button.

Although comments can be helpful, not all comments are created equal. For example, the following procedure uses lots of comments, but they really add nothing of value:

Figure 7-1:
The VBE
Edit toolbar
contains
several
useful
buttons.

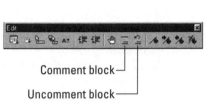

Comment block
Uncomment block

```
Sub BadComments()
'   Declare variables
    Dim x As Integer
    Dim y As Integer
    Dim z As Integer
'   Start the routine
    x = 100 ' Assign 100 to x
    y = 200 ' Assign 200 to y
'   Add x and y and store in z
    z = x + y
'   Show the result
    MsgBox z
End Sub
```

Everyone develops his or her own style of commenting. To be useful, however, comments must convey information that's not immediately obvious from reading the code. Otherwise, your comments just chew up bytes.

The following tips can help you make effective use of comments:

✔ Briefly describe the purpose of each subroutine or function you write.

✔ Use comments to keep track of changes you make to a procedure.

✔ Use a comment to indicate that you're using a function or a construct in an unusual or nonstandard manner.

✔ Use comments to describe the variables you use, especially if you don't use meaningful variable names.

✔ Use a comment to describe any workarounds you develop to overcome bugs in Excel.

✔ Get into the habit of writing comments as you develop code, rather than saving this task for a final step.

Using Variables, Constants, and Data Types

VBA's main purpose in life is to manipulate data. VBA stores the data in your computer's memory; it may or may not end up on disk. Some data resides in objects, such as worksheet ranges. Other data is stored in *variables* that you create.

Understanding variables

A variable is simply a named storage location in your computer's memory. You have lots of flexibility in naming your variables, so you should make the variable names as descriptive as possible. You assign a value to a variable using the equal sign operator (more about this later in the "Using Assignment Statements" section).

Here are some examples of statements that use variables (the variable names are on the left side of the equal signs):

```
x = 1
InterestRate = 0.075
LoanPayoffAmount = 243089
DataEntered = False
x = x + 1
MyNum = YourNum * 1.25
UserName = "Bob Johnson"
DateStarted = #3/14/96#
```

VBA enforces a few rules regarding variable names:

- ✔ You can use letters, numbers, and some punctuation characters, but the first character must be a letter.

- ✔ You cannot use any spaces or periods in a variable name.

- ✔ VBA does not distinguish between uppercase and lowercase letters.

- ✔ You cannot use the following characters in a variable name: #, $, %, &, or ! (See the "Another way of data-typing variables" sidebar later in this chapter.)

- ✔ Variable names can be no longer than 254 characters. Of course, you're only asking for trouble if you use names as long as this.

To make variable names more readable, programmers often use mixed case (for example, InterestRate) or the underscore character (interest_rate).

VBA has many reserved words that you can't use for variable names or procedure names. Reserved words are

- ✔ Built-in function names, such as Ucase and Sqr
- ✔ Lanuage words, such as Sub, With, and For

If you attempt to use one of these names as a variable, you get an error message. So, if an assignment statement produces an error message, double-check and make sure that the variable name isn't a reserved word.

Compared to previous versions, Excel 97 is more flexible when it comes to using reserved words as variable names. You can use many reserved words as variable names if you declare the variable using a Dim statement. I cover the concept of declaring variables later in this chapter (see the section "Declaring and scoping variables").

What are VBA's data types?

When I talk about *data type*, I'm referring to the manner in which a program stores data in memory — for example, as integers, real numbers, or strings. Although VBA can take care of these details automatically, it does so at a cost. (There's no free lunch.) Letting VBA handle your data typing results in slower execution and inefficient use of memory. For small applications, this usually doesn't present much of a problem. But for large or complex applications, which may be slow or need to conserve every last byte of memory, you need to be on familiar terms with data types.

Because VBA can automatically handle all the details involved in dealing with data, it makes life easy for programmers. This is not so with all programming languages. For example, some languages are *strictly typed*, which means the programmer must explicitly define the data type for every variable used.

VBA has a variety of built-in data types. Table 7-1 lists the most-common types of data that VBA can handle.

Table 7-1	VBA's Built-In Data Types	
Data Type	*Bytes Used*	*Range of Values*
Boolean	2	True or False
Integer	2	–32,768 to 32,767
Long	4	–2,147,483,648 to 2,147,483,647

(continued)

Table 7-1 (continued)

Data Type	Bytes Used	Range of Values
Single	4	−3.402823E38 to 1.401298E45
Double (negative)	8	−1.79769313486232E308 to −4.94065645841247E-324
Double (positive)	8	4.94065645841247E−324 to 1.79769313486232E308
Currency	8	−922,337,203,685,477.5808 to 922,337,203,685,477.5807
Date	8	1/1/100 to 12/31/9999
String	1 per char	Varies
Object	4	Any defined object
Variant	Varies	Any data type
User defined	Varies	Varies

In general, choose the data type that uses the smallest number of bytes but can still handle all the data the program assigns to it.

When VBA is working with data, execution speed depends in part on the number of bytes VBA must handle. The fewer bytes used by the data, the faster VBA can access and manipulate the data.

Declaring and scoping variables

You now know about variables and data types. In this section, you discover how to declare a variable as a certain data type.

If you don't declare the data type for a variable you use in a VBA routine, VBA uses the default data type, variant. Data stored as a variant acts like a chameleon; it changes type depending on what you do with it. For example, if a variable is a variant data type and contains a text string that looks like a number (such as "143"), you can use this variable for string manipulations as well as numeric calculations. VBA automatically handles the conversion. This may seem like an easy way out, but remember that you sacrifice speed and memory.

Before you use variables in a procedure, it's an excellent practice to *declare* your variables — that is, tell VBA each variable's data type. Declaring your variables makes your program run faster and use memory more efficiently. The default data type, variant, causes VBA to repeatedly

perform time-consuming checks and reserve more memory than necessary. If VBA knows a variable's data type, it doesn't have to investigate,
and it can reserve just enough memory to store the data.

To force yourself to declare all the variables you use, include the following
as the first statement in your VBA module:

```
Option Explicit
```

This statement causes your program to stop whenever VBA encounters a
variable name that has not been declared. VBA displays an error message,
and you must declare the variable before you can proceed.

Suppose that you use an undeclared variable (that is, a variant) named
CurrentRate. At some point in your routine, you insert the following
statement

```
CurentRate = .075
```

This misspelled variable, which is difficult to spot, will probably cause your
routine to give incorrect results. If you use Option Explicit at the beginning
of your module (and declare the CurrentRate variable), Excel generates an
error if it encounters a misspelled variation of that variable.

To ensure that the Option Explicit statement is inserted automatically
whenever you insert a new VBA module, enable the Require Variable Declaration option in the Editor tab of the Options dialog box (in the VBE, choose
Tools➪Options). I highly recommend doing so.

You now know the advantages of declaring variables, but *how* do you do
this? Before getting into the mechanics, I need to discuss one other topic: a
variable's scope.

Recall that a workbook can have any number of VBA modules. And a VBA
module can have any number of procedures (that is, subroutines and
functions). A variable's *scope* determines which modules and procedures
can use the variable. A variable's scope can be any of the following:

Scope	*How the Variable Is Declared*
Single procedure only	By using a Dim or a Static statement in the procedure that uses the variable.
Module only	By using a Dim statement before the first Sub or Function statement in the module.
All procedures in all modules	By using a Public statement before the first Sub or Function statement in a module.

If you're completely confused at this point, don't despair. I discuss each of these in the following sections.

Procedure-only variables

The lowest level of scope for a variable is at the procedure level. (A *procedure* is either a subroutine or a function.) Variables declared with this scope can be used only in the procedure in which they are declared. When the procedure ends, the variable no longer exists, and Excel frees up its memory. If you execute the procedure again, the variable comes back to life, but its previous value is lost.

The most common way to declare a procedure-only variable is with a Dim statement placed between a Sub statement and an End Sub statement (or between a Function and an End Function statement). You usually place Dim statements immediately after the Sub or Function statement, before the procedure's code.

The following examples show some procedure-only variables declared by using Dim statements:

```
Sub MySub()
    Dim x As Integer
    Dim First As Long
    Dim InterestRate As Single
    Dim TodaysDate As Date
    Dim UserName As String * 20
    Dim MyValue
'    ... [The procedure's code goes here] ...
End Sub
```

A note about the examples in this chapter

This chapter contains many examples of VBA code, usually presented in the form of simple subroutine procedures. I provide these examples to demonstrate various concepts as simply as possible. Most of these examples do not perform any particularly useful task; in fact, you can often perform the task using a different method. In other words, don't use these examples in your own work. Subsequent chapters provide many more code examples that *are* useful.

Notice that the last Dim statement in the preceding example doesn't declare a data type; it declares only the variable itself. The effect is that the variable MyValue is a variant.

By the way, you can also declare several variables with a single Dim statement, as in the following example:

```
Dim x as Integer, y as Integer, z as Integer
Dim First as Long, Last as Double
```

Unlike some languages, VBA doesn't allow you to declare a group of variables to be a particular data type by separating the variables with commas. For example, the following statement, though valid, does *not* declare all the variables as integers:

```
Dim i, j, k as Integer
```

In this example, only k is declared to be an integer; the other variables are declared variants.

If you declare a variable with procedure-only scope, other procedures in the same module can use the same variable name, but each instance of the variable is unique to its own procedure. In general, variables declared at the procedure level are the most efficient because VBA frees up the memory they use when the procedure ends.

Another way of data-typing variables

Like most other dialects of BASIC, VBA lets you append a character to a variable's name to indicate the data type. For example, you can declare the MyVar variable as an integer by tacking % onto its name:

```
MyVar% = 189
```

Most VBA data types have type-declaration characters. Here are the type-declaration characters for VBA's data types (data types not listed don't have type-declaration characters):

Integer: %
Long: &
Single: !

Double: #
Currency: @
String: $

If your module contains an Option Explicit statement, you still need to declare your variables, even if you use a type declaration character. This method of data-typing variables is a holdover from older versions of BASIC. In general, it's better to declare your variables using the procedures described in this chapter. I present this information just in case you run across some code that has these strange characters appended to variable names.

Module-only variables

Sometimes, you want a variable to be available to all procedures in a module. If so, just declare the variable *before* the module's first Sub or Function statement — that is, outside any procedures.

In the following example, the Dim statement is the first statement in the module:

```
Dim CurrentValue as Integer

Sub MySub()
'    ... [Code goes here] ...
End Sub

Sub YourSub()
'    ... [Code goes here] ...
End Sub
```

Both MySub and YourSub have access to the CurrentValue variable, and its value does not change when a procedure ends.

Public variables

If you need to make a variable available to all the procedures in all your VBA modules in a workbook, declare the variable at the module level by using the Public keyword rather than Dim. Here's an example:

```
Public CurrentRate as Long
```

The Public keyword makes the CurrentRate variable available to any procedure in the workbook, even those in other VBA modules. You must insert this statement before the first Sub or Function statement in a module.

If you would like a variable to be available to modules in other workbooks, you must declare the variable as Public and establish a reference to the workbook that contains the variable declaration. You set up a reference by using the Tools⇨References command in VBE.

Static variables

Static variables are a special case because they retain their value even when the procedure ends. You declare a static variable at the procedure level. Using a static variable may be useful if you need to keep track of the number of times you execute a subroutine. You can declare a static variable and increment it each time you run the subroutine.

As shown in the following example, you declare static variables by using the Static keyword:

```
Sub MySub()
    Static Counter as Integer
    Counter = Counter + 1
    Msg = "Number of executions: " & Counter
    MsgBox Msg
End Sub
```

The preceding subroutine keeps track of the number of times the subroutine was called. The value of Counter is not reset when the subroutine ends.

Working with constants

A variable's value may — and usually does — change while your procedure is executing (that's why they call it a variable). Sometimes, you need to refer to a value or string that never changes — that is, a *constant*. A constant is a named element (like a variable) but its value doesn't change.

As shown in the following examples, you declare constants by using the Const statement:

```
Const NumQuarters as Integer = 4
Const Rate = .0725, Period = 12
Const ModName as String = "Budget Macros"
Public Const AppName as String = "Budget Application"
```

Like variables, constants have a scope. Following are some points to keep in mind about constants:

✔ To make a constant available within only a single procedure, declare the constant after the procedure's Sub or Function statement.

✔ To make a constant available to all procedures in a module, declare the constant before the first Sub or Function statement in the module.

✔ To make a constant available to all modules in the workbook, use the Public keyword and declare the constant before the first Sub or Function statement in a module.

If you attempt to change the value of a constant in a VBA routine, you get an error — this is not surprising because a constant is constant. If you need to change the value of a constant, what you really need is a variable.

Using constants in place of hard-coded values or strings is an excellent programming practice. For example, if your procedure needs to refer to a specific value (such as an interest rate) several times, it's better to declare the value as a constant and refer to the constant's name rather than the value. This makes your code more readable and easier to change; should the need for changes arise, you have to change only one statement rather than several.

Excel and VBA contain many predefined constants, which you can use without declaring. In general, you don't need to know the value of these constants to use them. The macro recorder usually uses constants rather than actual values.

The following simple procedure uses a built-in constant (xlManual) to change the Calculation property of the Application object. (In other words, this changes the Excel recalculation mode to manual.)

```
Sub CalcManual()
    Application.Calculation = xlManual
End Sub
```

I discovered the xlManual constant by recording a macro that changed the calculation mode. I also could have looked in the online help under Calculation Property; as shown in Figure 7-2, the online help lists all relevant constants for this property.

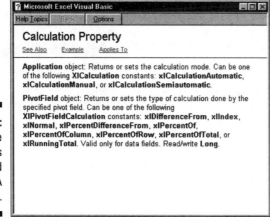

Figure 7-2:
The online help lists Excel and VBA constants.

The actual value of the built-in xlManual constant is –4135. Obviously, it's easier to use the constant's name than to look up the value (even if you knew where to look). By the way, the constant for changing to automatic calculation mode is xlAutomatic; its value is –4105. As you can see, many of the built-in constants are just arbitrary numbers that have special meaning to VBA.

To find the actual value of a built-in constant, execute a statement such as the following:

```
MsgBox xlAutomatic
```

Working with strings

Excel can manipulate both numbers and text, so it should come as no surprise that VBA has this same power. You can work with two types of strings in VBA:

- **Fixed-length strings** are declared with a specified number of characters. The maximum length is about 65,526 characters.
- **Variable-length strings** theoretically can hold as many as two billion characters.

Each character in a string takes one byte of storage. In addition, a variable-length string consumes an additional 16 bytes. Therefore, if you're striving for efficiency, it's better to use fixed-length strings if possible.

When you declare a string variable with a Dim statement, you can specify the maximum length if you know it (that is, a fixed-length string) or let VBA handle it dynamically (a variable-length string). The following example declares the MyString variable as a string with a maximum length of 50 characters. (Use an asterisk to specify the number of characters, up to the 65,526 character limit.) YourString is also declared as a string, but its length is unspecified:

```
Dim MyString as String * 50
Dim YourString as String
```

In general, using fixed-length strings is more efficient in terms of memory usage.

Working with dates

Another data type you may find useful is the date data type. You can use a string variable to store dates, but you can't perform date calculations on strings. Using the date data type gives your routines greater flexibility. For example, you might need to calculate the number of days between two dates — which would be impossible if you used strings to hold your dates.

A variable defined as a date uses 8 bytes of storage and can hold dates ranging from January 1, 0100 to December 31, 9999. That's a span of nearly 10,000 years — more than enough for even the most aggressive financial forecast. You can use the date data type also to work with time data, accurate to whole seconds only.

Here are some examples of declaring variables and constants as a date data type:

```
Dim Today As Date
Dim StartTime As Date
Const FirstDay As Date = #1/1/95#
Const Noon = #12:00:00#
```

In VBA, you specify dates and times by placing them between two pound signs, as shown in the preceding.

Date variables display dates according to your system's short date format, and display times according to your system's time format (either 12- or 24-hour). These system settings are stored in the Windows Registry, and you can modify them by using the Regional Settings dialog box in the Windows Control Panel. Therefore, the date or time format displayed using VBA may vary, depending on the settings for the system on which the application is running.

Using Assignment Statements

An *assignment statement* is a VBA statement that assigns the result of an expression to a variable or an object. Excel's online help defines the term *expression* as

> ". . . a combination of keywords, operators, variables, and constants that yields a string, number, or object. An expression can be used to perform a calculation, manipulate characters, or test data."

I couldn't have said it better myself.

Much of your work in VBA involves developing (and debugging) expressions. If you know how to create formulas in Excel, you'll have no trouble creating expressions. With a worksheet formula, Excel displays the result in a cell. A VBA expression, on the other hand, can be assigned to a variable.

Assignment statement examples

Here are a few examples of assignment statements (the expressions are to the right of the equal sign):

```
x = 1
x = x + 1
x = (y * 2) / (z  * 2)
FileOpen = True
FileOpen = Not FileOpen
Range("TheYear").Value = 1995
```

Expressions can be as complex as you need; use the line continuation character (a space followed by an underscore) to make lengthy expressions easier to read.

Often, expressions use functions — VBA's built-in functions, Excel's worksheet functions, or functions that you develop using VBA. I discuss functions in Chapter 9.

About that equal sign

As you can see in the preceding examples, VBA uses the equal sign as its assignment operator. This may be confusing at first, because you're probably accustomed to using an equal sign as a mathematical symbol for equality. Therefore, an assignment statement like the following may cause you to raise your eyebrows:

```
z = z + 1
```

How can z be equal to itself plus 1? Answer: It can't. In this case, the assignment statement is increasing the value of z by 1. Just remember that an assignment uses the equal sign as an operator, not a symbol of equality.

Other operators

Operators play a major role in VBA. Besides the equal sign operator (discussed in the previous section), VBA provides several other operators to describe mathematical operations such as addition (+), multiplication (*), division (/), subtraction (-), exponentiation (^), and string concatenation (&). You already know these operators from your experience with worksheet formulas. VBA uses a few other, less familiar operators, including the backslash operator (\ ) for integer division (the result is always an integer) and the Mod operator for modulo arithmetic (this returns the remainder of a division operation).

As shown in Table 7-2, VBA also provides a full set of logical operators. Consult the online help for complete details.

Table 7-2	VBA's Logical Operators
Operator	*What It Does*
Not	Performs a logical negation on an expression
And	Performs a logical conjunction on two expressions
Or	Performs a logical disjunction on two expressions
XoR	Performs a logical exclusion on two expressions
Eqv	Performs a logical equivalence on two expressions
Imp	Performs a logical implication on two expressions

The order of precedence for operators in VBA is exactly the same as in Excel formulas. Exponentiation has the highest precedence. Multiplication and division come next, followed by addition and subtraction. You can use parentheses to change the natural order of precedence.

Working with Arrays

All programming languages support arrays. An *array* is a group of variables that have a common name; you refer to a specific variable in the array by using the array name and an index number. For example, you may define an array of 12 string variables to hold the names of the months of the year. If you name the array *MonthNames*, you can refer to the first element of the array as MonthNames(1), the second element as MonthNames(2), and so on.

Declaring arrays

You declare an array with a Dim or a Public statement, just like you declare a regular variable. However, you also need to specify the number of elements in the array. You do this by specifying the first index number, the keyword *to*, and the last index number — all inside parentheses. The following example shows how to declare an array of 100 integers:

```
Dim MyArray(1 to 100) as Integer
```

When you declare an array, you can specify only the upper index. VBA assumes that 0 is the lower index. Therefore, the following statements both declare the same array:

```
Dim MyArray(0 to 100) as Integer
Dim MyArray(100) as Integer
```

If you want VBA to assume that 1 is the lower index for your arrays, simply include the following statement before any Sub or Function statements in your module:

```
Option Base 1
```

This statement forces VBA to use 1 as the first index number for arrays that declare only the upper index. If this statement is present, the following statements are identical:

```
Dim MyArray(1 to 100) as Integer
Dim MyArray(100) as Integer
```

Multidimensional arrays

The arrays created in the previous examples are all one-dimensional arrays. Arrays you create in VBA can have as many as 60 dimensions — although you rarely need more than three dimensions in an array. The following example declares a 100-integer array with two dimensions:

```
Dim MyArray(1 to 10, 1 to 10) as Integer
```

You can think of this array as occupying a 10 by 10 matrix. To refer to a specific element in this array, you need to specify two index numbers. The following example shows how you can assign a value to an element in this array:

```
MyArray(3, 4) = 125
```

This statement assigns a value to a single element in the array. If you're thinking of the array in terms of a 10 by 10 matrix, this assigns 125 to the element located in the third row and fourth column of the matrix.

You can think of a three-dimensional array as a cube. I can't tell you how to visualize the data layout of an array of more than three dimensions. (Sorry, I haven't yet mastered the fourth dimension and beyond.)

You can also create *dynamic* arrays. A dynamic array doesn't have a preset number of elements. You declare a dynamic array with a blank set of parentheses:

```
Dim MyArray() as Integer
```

Before you can use this array, you must use the ReDim statement to tell VBA how many elements the array has. You can use the ReDim statement any number of times, changing the array's size as often as you need.

When you redimension an array by using ReDim, you wipe out the values stored in the array elements. You can avoid this by using the Preserve keyword. The following example shows how you can preserve an array's values when you redimension the array:

```
ReDim Preserve MyArray(200)
```

If MyArray has 100 elements and you execute the preceding statement, the first 100 elements will remain intact, and the array will have room for 100 more elements.

The topic of arrays comes up again in Chapter 10, when I discuss looping.

Using Labels

In early versions of BASIC, every line of code required a label. For example, if you were writing a BASIC program in the '70s (dressed, of course, in your bell-bottoms) it may look something like this:

```
010: LET X=5
020: LET Y=3
030: LET Z=X*Y
040: PRINT Z
050: END
```

VBA permits the use of such line numbers, or labels. You don't typically use a label for each line, but you may occasionally need to use a label. For example, if you use a GoTo statement (which I discuss in Chapter 10), you need to insert a label. A label must begin with the first nonblank character in a line and end with a colon.

Here's an example of code with one label. This useful VBA function determines whether a particular path exists:

```
Private Function PathExists(PathName As String) As Boolean
'    Returns True if PathName is a valid path
    On Error GoTo NoPath
    x = Dir(PathName & "\*.*")
    If x = "" Then GoTo NoPath
    PathExists = True
    Exit Function
NoPath:
    PathExists = False
End Function
```

In this example, NoPath is a label. If the path does not exist, execution jumps to this label. Otherwise, execution ends before it gets to the label.

The information in this chapter becomes clearer as you read subsequent chapters. If you want to find out more about VBA language elements, I refer you to the online help. You'll find as much detail as you need, or care to know.

Chapter 8

Working with Range Objects

In Chapter 4, I run the risk of overwhelming you with an introduction to Excel's object model. In that chapter, I also cover the basics of properties and methods. Now you get to dig a bit deeper and take a close look at Range objects. Why do you need to know so much about Range objects? Because much of the programming work you do in Excel focuses on Range objects. You'll thank me later.

A Quick Review

I start this chapter with a brief review. Recall that a Range object is a range contained in a Worksheet object. A Range object can be as small as a single cell or as large as every cell on a worksheet (A1:IV65536, or 16,777,216 cells).

You can refer to a range object like this:

```
Range("A1:C5")
```

Or if the range has a name, you can use an expression like this:

```
Range("PriceList")
```

Unless you tell Excel otherwise, it assumes you're referring to a range on the active worksheet. If anything other than a worksheet is active (such as a chart sheet), the range reference fails and your macro displays an error message.

As shown in the following example, you can refer to a range that is not on the active sheet by qualifying the range reference with a worksheet name from the active workbook:

```
Worksheets("Sheet1").Range("A1:C5")
```

And if you need to refer to a range in a different workbook (that is, any workbook other than the active workbook), you can use a statement like this:

```
Workbooks("Budget").Worksheets("Sheet1").Range("A1:C5")
```

A range object can consist of one or more entire rows or columns. You can refer to an entire row (in this case, row 3) by using syntax like this:

```
Range("3:3")
```

And, you can refer to an entire column (column 4 in this example) like this:

```
Range("D:D")
```

To further confuse matters, you can even work with noncontiguous ranges. (In Excel, you select noncontiguous ranges by holding down the Ctrl key while you select various ranges in a worksheet.) The following expression refers to a two-area noncontiguous range. Notice that a comma separates the two areas.

```
Range("A1:B8,D9:G16")
```

Finally, recall that Range objects (like all other objects) have properties (which you can examine and change) and methods (which perform actions on the object).

Other Ways to Refer to a Range

The more you work with VBA, the more you realize that it's a well-conceived language and is really quite logical (despite what you may be thinking). Often, VBA provides multiple ways of performing an action. You can choose the most appropriate method for your problem.

The Cells property

Instead of using the VBA Range keyword, you can refer to a range by using the Cells property.

Notice that I wrote Cells *property* — not Cells *object*. Although Cells certainly may seem like an object, it's really not. Rather, Cells is a property that is evaluated by VBA and then returns an object (more specifically, a Range object). If this seems strange, don't worry. Even Microsoft appears to be confused about this issue. In prior versions of Excel, the Cells property was known as the Cells method. Regardless of what it is, just understand that Cells is a handy way to refer to a range.

The Cells property takes two arguments: the row and the column. For example, the following expression refers to cell C2 on Sheet1:

```
Worksheets("Sheet1").Cells(2,3)
```

You can use the Cells property also to refer to a larger range — that is, a range containing more than a single cell. The following example demonstrates the syntax you use:

```
Range(Cells(1, 1), Cells(10, 10))
```

This refers to a range that extends from cell A1 (row 1, column 1) to cell J10 (row 10, column 10).

The following statements both produce the same result; they enter a value of 99 into a 10-by-10 range of cells. More specifically, these statements set the Value property of the Range object:

```
Range("A1:J10").Value = 99
Range(Cells(1, 1), Cells(10, 10)).Value = 99
```

The advantage of using the Cells method to refer to ranges becomes apparent when you use variables rather than actual numbers as the Cells arguments. And things really start to click when you understand looping, which I cover in Chapter 10.

The Offset property

The Offset property provides another handy means for referring to ranges. This property, which operates on a Range object and returns another Range object, lets you refer to a cell that is a particular number of rows and columns away from another cell.

Like the Cells property, the Offset property takes two arguments. The first argument represents the number of rows to offset; the second represents the number of columns to offset.

The following expression refers to a cell that is one row below cell A1 and two columns to the right of cell A1. In other words, this refers to the cell commonly known as C2:

```
Range("A1").Offset(1, 2)
```

The Offset method can also use negative arguments. A negative row offset refers to a row above the range. A negative column offset refers to a column to the left of the range. The following example refers to cell A1:

```
Range("C2").Offset(-1, -2)
```

And, as you may expect, you can use zero as one or both of the arguments for Offset. The following expression refers to cell A1:

```
Range("A1").Offset(0, 0)
```

The Offset method is most useful when you use variables instead of actual values for the arguments. In Chapter 10, I present some examples that demonstrate this.

Referring to entire columns and rows

If you need to refer to a range that consists of one or more entire columns, you can use an expression like the following:

```
Columns("A:C")
```

And to refer to one or more complete rows, use an expression like this:

```
Rows("1:5")
```

Some Useful Range Object Properties

I checked the online help, and discovered that a Range object has 84 properties. You can write Excel programs nonstop for the next century, and I guarantee that you will never need to use all 84 properties. In this section, I briefly describe some of the more commonly used Range properties. For complete details, consult the online help (search for *Range object*, and then click *Properties*).

Some Range properties are *read-only* properties, which means you can't change them. For example, every Range object has an Address property (which holds the range's address). You can access this read-only property, but you can't change it.

The examples that follow are typically statements rather than complete subroutines. If you'd like to try any of these (which you should), you'll need to create a subroutine to do so. Also, many of these statements will work properly only if a worksheet is the active sheet.

The Value property

The Value property represents the value contained in a cell. It's a read-write property, so your VBA code can either read the value or change it.

The following statement displays a message box that shows the value in cell A1 on Sheet1:

```
MsgBox Worksheets("Sheet1").Range("A1").Value
```

It stands to reason that you would read the Value property only for a single-cell Range object. For example, the following statement generates an error:

```
MsgBox Worksheets("Sheet1").Range("A1:C3").Value
```

You can, however, change the Value property for a range of any size. The following statement enters 123 into a range of cells:

```
Worksheets("Sheet1").Range("A1:C3").Value = 123
```

Value is the default property for a Range object. In other words, if you omit a property for a Range, Excel uses its Value property. The following statements have the same effect:

```
Worksheets("Sheet1").Range("A1").Value = 75
Worksheets("Sheet1").Range("A1") = 75
```

The Text property

The Text property returns a string that represents the text as displayed in a cell — the formatted value. The Text property is read-only. For example, suppose that cell A1 contains the value 12.3 and is formatted to display two decimals and a dollar sign ($12.30). The following statement displays a message box containing $12.30:

```
MsgBox Worksheets("Sheet1").Range("A1").Text
```

But the next statement displays a message box containing 12.3:

```
MsgBox Worksheets("Sheet1").Range("A1").Value
```

The Count property

The Count property returns the number of cells in a Range. It's a read-only property. The following statement accesses the Count property of a range and displays the result (9) in a message box:

```
MsgBox Range("A1:C3").Count
```

The Column and Row properties

The Column property returns the column number of a single-cell range, and the Row property returns the row number of a single-cell range. Both are read-only properties. For example, the following statement displays 6 because the cell is in the sixth column:

```
MsgBox Sheets("Sheet1").Range("F3").Column
```

The next expression displays 3 because cell F3 is in the third row:

```
MsgBox Sheets("Sheet1").Range("F3").Row
```

If the Range object consists of more than one cell, the Column property returns the column number of the first column in the range, and the Row property returns the row number of the first row in the range.

Don't confuse the Column and Row properties with the Columns and Rows properties (discussed earlier in this chapter). The Column and Row properties return a single value, and the Columns and Rows properties return a Range object.

The Address property

The Address property (a read-only property) displays the cell address for a Range object. The following statement displays the message box shown in Figure 8-1.

```
MsgBox Range(Cells(1, 1), Cells(5, 5)).Address
```

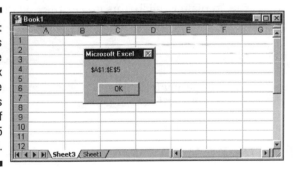

Figure 8-1: This message box displays the Address property of a 1-by-5 range.

The HasFormula property

The HasFormula property (which is read-only) returns True if the single-cell Range contains a formula or False if the cell does not have a formula. If the range consists of more than one cell, accessing this property results in an error unless all the cells in the range have a formula or all the cells in the range don't have a formula.

For example, assume that cell A1 contains a value and cell A2 contains a formula. The following statement generates an error because the range doesn't consist of all formula or all non-formulas:

```
Range("A1:A2").HasFormula
```

The Font property

As I note earlier in this chapter (see "The Cells property"), a property can return an object. Here's another example: The Font property of a Range object returns a Font object.

A Font object, as you may expect, has many properties that you can access. To change some aspect of a range's font, you must first access the range's Font object, and then manipulate the properties of that Font object. This might be confusing at first, but it eventually makes sense.

The following expression returns a Font object for a range:

```
Range("A1").Font
```

The following statement sets the Bold property of the Font object contained in the Range object to True. In plain English, this makes the cell display in boldface:

```
Range("A1").Font.Bold = True
```

To see other examples of manipulating font objects, record your actions while you modify some of the font attributes of a range.

The Interior property

Here's another example of a property that returns an object. The Interior property of a Range object returns an Interior object. This works the same way as the Font property (which I describe in the preceding section).

For example, the following statement sets the ColorIndex property of the Interior object contained in the Range object to True:

```
Range("A1").Interior.ColorIndex = 3
```

In other words, this changes the cell's background to red.

The ColorIndex values correspond to the default color palette for Excel 5 and Excel 95 — which has changed in Excel 97! In other words, the ColorIndex values do not correspond to the order of the colors in the Excel 97 color palette. The easiest way to determine the ColorIndex for a particular color is to record your actions while you change a cell's color. If you need to use standard colors, use the Color property along with a built-in constant: vbBlack, vbRed, vbGreen, vbYellow, vbBlue, vbMagenta, vbCyan, or vbWhite. For example, the following statement makes cell A1 yellow:

```
Range("A1").Interior.Color = vbYellow
```

The Formula property

The Formula property represents the formula in a cell. This is a read-write property, so you can access it to insert a formula into a cell. For example, the following statement enters a SUM formula into cell A13:

```
Range("A13").Formula = "=SUM(A1:A12)"
```

If a cell doesn't have a formula, the Formula property returns the cell's Value property.

The NumberFormat property

The NumberFormat property represents the number format (expressed as a string) of the Range object. This is a read-write property, so your VBA code can change the number format. The following statement changes the number format of column A to percent with two decimal places:

```
Columns("A:A").NumberFormat = "0.00%"
```

To see a list of other number formats, activate a worksheet and then access the Format Cells dialog box (press Ctrl+1). Click the Number tab, and then select the Custom category to view some additional number format strings.

Some Useful Range Object Methods

As you know, a VBA method performs an action. You can use 70 methods to do things with a Range object. But again, you will never need most of these. In this section, I point out some of the more commonly used Range object methods.

The Select method

You use the Select method to select a range of cells. The following statement selects a range on the active worksheet:

```
Range("A1:C12").Select
```

Before you select a range, make sure that you have activated the range's worksheet; otherwise, you get an error or the wrong range will be selected. For example, if Sheet1 contains the range you want to select, you can use the following statements to select the range:

```
Sheets("Sheet1").Activate
Range("A1:C12").Select
```

Contrary to what you may expect, the following statement generates an error if Sheet1 is not the active sheet:

```
Sheets("Sheet1").Range("A1:C12").Select
```

The Copy and Paste methods

You can perform copy and paste operations in VBA by using the Copy method and the Paste method. This short subroutine copies range A1:A12 and pastes it to the range beginning at cell C1:

```
Sub CopyRange()
    Range("A1:A12").Select
    Selection.Copy
    Range("C1").Select
    ActiveSheet.Paste
End Sub
```

Notice that the preceding example, which the macro recorder generated, selects the range before copying it. However, you don't have to select a range before doing something with it. In fact, the following subroutine accomplishes the same task as the preceding example by using a single statement:

```
Sub CopyRange2()
    Range("A1:A12").Copy Range("C1")
End Sub
```

This routine takes advantage of the fact that the Copy method can use an argument that corresponds to the destination range for the copy operation.

The Clear method

The Clear method deletes the *contents* of a range and all of the cell formatting. For example, if you want to zap everything in column D, the following statement does the trick:

```
Columns("D:D").Clear
```

You should be aware of two related methods. The ClearContents method deletes the contents of the range but leaves the formatting intact. The ClearFormats method deletes the formatting in the range but not the cell contents.

The Delete method

Clearing a range differs from deleting a range. When you delete a range, Excel shifts the remaining cells around to fill up the range you deleted.

The following example uses the Delete method to delete row 6:

```
Rows("6:6").Delete
```

When you delete a range that's not a complete row or column, Excel needs to know how to shift the cells. (To see how this works, experiment with the Excel Edit⇨Delete command.)

The following statement deletes a range and then fills the resulting gap by shifting the other cells to the left:

```
Range("C6:C10").Delete xlToLeft
```

The Delete method uses an argument that indicates how Excel should shift the remaining cells. In this case, I use a built-in constant (xlToLeft) for the argument. I could also use xlUp, another named constant.

This chapter gives you greater insight into Excel's object model. You now know about the Range object, as well as some of the more useful properties and methods for this object. This chapter, however, barely scratches the surface. As you work with VBA, you'll probably need to access other properties and methods. The online help is the best place to find out about them, but it's also helpful to simply record your actions and examine the code that Excel generates.

Chapter 9

Using VBA Functions and Excel Functions

In This Chapter

▶ Using functions to make your VBA expressions more powerful

▶ Examples of using the VBA built-in functions

▶ Examples of using the Excel worksheet functions in your VBA code

▶ An introduction to writing custom functions

*I*n previous chapters, I allude to the fact that you can use functions in your VBA expressions. In this chapter, I explain myself. Functions can make your VBA code perform some powerful feats, with little or no programming effort required. If you like that idea, this chapter's for you.

What Is a Function?

All Excel users beyond rank beginners use worksheet functions in their formulas. The most common worksheet function is the SUM function, and you have hundreds of others at your disposal.

A function essentially performs a calculation and returns a single value. The SUM function, of course, returns the sum of a range of values. The same holds true for functions used in your VBA expressions: Each function does its thing and returns a single value.

The functions you use in VBA can come from three sources:

- ✔ Built-in functions provided by VBA
- ✔ Worksheet functions provided by Excel
- ✔ Custom functions that you (or someone else) writes in VBA

The rest of this chapter clarifies the differences and — I hope — convinces you of the value of using functions in your VBA code.

Using VBA Functions

VBA provides numerous built-in functions. Some of these functions take arguments, and some do not.

VBA function examples

In this section, I present a few examples of using VBA functions in code. You can enter these short subroutines and try them out. In many of these examples, I use the MsgBox function to display a value in a message box.

Yes, MsgBox is a VBA function — a rather unusual one, but a function nonetheless. This useful function displays a message in a pop-up dialog box. For more details about the MsgBox function, see Chapter 15.

Displaying the system date

The first example uses VBA's Date function to display the current system date in a message box:

```
Sub ShowDate()
    MsgBox Date
End Sub
```

Notice that the Date function doesn't use an argument. Unlike worksheet functions, a VBA function with no argument doesn't require an empty set of parentheses (but you can provide empty parentheses if you like).

To get the system date and time, use the Now function instead of the Date function. Or to get only the time, use the Time function.

Finding the length of a string

The following subroutine uses the VBA Len function, which returns the length of a string. (The function takes one argument.) When you execute this subroutine, the message box displays 11 because there are 11 characters in the argument:

```
Sub GetLength()
    MyString = "Hello World"
    StringLength = Len(MyString)
    MsgBox StringLength
End Sub
```

Excel also has a LEN function, which you can use in your worksheet formulas. The Excel version and the VBA function work the same.

Displaying the integer part of a number

The following subroutine uses the Fix function, which returns the integer part of a value — the value without any decimal digits:

```
Sub GetIntegerPart()
    MyValue = 123.456
    IntValue = Fix(MyValue)
    MsgBox IntValue
End Sub
```

In this case, the message box displays 123.

Determining the size of a file

The following subroutine displays the size, in bytes, of the Excel executable file. It finds this value by using the FileLen function.

```
Sub GetFileSize()
    TheFile = "C:\MSOFFICE\EXCEL\EXCEL.EXE"
    MsgBox FileLen(TheFile)
End Sub
```

Notice that this routine *hard codes* the filename, which isn't a good idea because the file might not be on the C drive, or the Excel folder may have a different name. The following statement shows a better approach:

```
TheFile = Application.Path & "\EXCEL.EXE"
```

Path is a property of the Application object. It simply returns the folder in which the application is installed (without a trailing backslash).

Identifying the type of a selected object

The following subroutine uses the TypeName function, which returns the type of the selected object (as a string):

```
Sub ShowSelectionType()
    SelType = TypeName(Selection)
    MsgBox SelType
End Sub
```

This could be a Range, a ChartObject, a TextBox, or any other type of object that can be selected.

VBA functions that do more than return a value

A few VBA functions go above and beyond the call of duty. Rather than simply return a value, these functions have some useful side effects:

Function	What It Does
MsgBox	Displays a handy dialog box containing a message and buttons. The function returns a code that identifies which button the user clicks. See Chapter 15 for details.
InputBox	Displays a simple dialog box that asks the user for some input. The function returns whatever the user enters into the dialog box. I discuss this in Chapter 15.
Shell	Executes another program. The function returns the *task ID* (a unique identifier) of the other program (or an error if the function can't start the other program).

Discovering VBA functions

So, how do you find out which functions VBA provides? Good question. The best source is the Excel Visual Basic online help. I compiled a semicomplete list of functions, which I share with you in the form of Table 9-1. I omit some of the more obscure functions that you will probably never need.

For complete details on a particular function, type the function name into a VBA module, move the cursor anywhere in the text, and press F1.

Table 9-1	VBA's Most Useful Built-In Functions
Function	*What It Does*
Abs	Returns the absolute value of a number
Array	Returns a variant containing an array
Asc	Converts the first character of a string to its ASCII value
Atn	Returns the arctangent of a number
Choose	Returns a value from a list of items
Chr	Converts an ANSI value to a string
Cos	Returns the cosine of a number
CurDir	Returns the current path
Date	Returns the current system date
DateAdd	Returns a date to which a specified time interval has been added — for example, one month from a particular date
DateDiff	Returns a date to which a specified time interval has been subtracted — for example, one month prior to a particular date
DatePart	Returns an integer containing the specified part of a given date — for example, the day of the year for a date
DateSerial	Converts a date to a serial number
DateValue	Converts a string to a date
Day	Returns the day of the month from a date value
Dir	Returns the name of a file or a directory that matches a pattern
EOF	Returns True if the end of a text file has been reached
Erl	Returns the line number that caused an error
Err	Returns the error number of an error condition
Error	Returns the error message that corresponds to an error number
Exp	Returns the base of the natural logarithm (*e*) raised to a power
FileAttr	Returns the file mode for a text file
FileDateTime	Returns the date and time when a file was last modified
FileLen	Returns the number of bytes in a file
Fix	Returns the integer portion of a number
Format	Displays an expression in a particular format
FreeFile	Returns the next available file number when working with text files

(continued)

Table 9-1 *(continued)*

Function	What It Does
GetAttr	Returns a code representing a file attribute
GetSetting	Returns a value from the Windows registry
Hex	Converts from decimal to hexadecimal
Hour	Returns the hours portion of a time
Input	Returns characters from a sequential text file
InputBox	Displays a box to prompt a user for input
InStr	Returns the position of a string within another string
Int	Returns the integer portion of a number
IPmt	Returns the interest payment for an annuity or loan
IsArray	Returns True if a variable is an array
IsDate	Returns True if a variable is a date
IsEmpty	Returns True if a variable has been initialized
IsError	Returns True if an expression is an error value
IsMissing	Returns True if an optional argument was not passed to a procedure
IsNull	Returns True if an expression contains no valid data
IsNumeric	Returns True if an expression can be evaluated as a number
IsObject	Returns True if an expression references an OLE Automation object
LBound	Returns the smallest subscript for a dimension of an array
LCase	Returns a string converted to lowercase
Left	Returns a specified number of characters from the left of a string
Len	Returns the number of characters in a string
Loc	Returns the current read or write position of a text file
LOF	Returns the number of bytes in an open text file
Log	Returns the natural logarithm of a number to base e
LTrim	Returns a copy of a string, with any leading spaces removed
Mid	Returns a specified number of characters from a string
Minute	Returns the minutes portion of a time
Month	Returns the month from a date value

Function	**What It Does**
MsgBox	Displays a modal message box
Now	Returns the current system date and time
RGB	Returns a numeric RGB value representing a color
Right	Returns a specified number of characters from the right of a string
Rnd	Returns a random number between 0 and 1
RTrim	Returns a copy of a string, with any trailing spaces removed
Second	Returns the seconds portion of a time
Seek	Returns the current position in a text file
Sgn	Returns an integer that indicates the sign of a number
Shell	Runs an executable program
Sin	Returns the sine of a number
Space	Returns a string with a specified number of spaces
Spc	Positions output when printing to a file
Sqr	Returns the square root of a number
Str	Returns a string representation of a number
StrComp	Returns a value indicating the result of a string comparison
String	Returns a repeating character or string
Tab	Positions output when printing to a file
Tan	Returns the tangent of a number
Time	Returns the current system time
Timer	Returns the number of seconds since midnight
TimeSerial	Returns the time for a specified hour, minute, and second
TimeValue	Converts a string to a time serial number
Trim	Returns a string without leading or trailing spaces
TypeName	Returns a string that describes the data type of a variable
UBound	Returns the largest available subscript for a dimension of an array
UCase	Converts a string to uppercase
Val	Returns the numbers contained in a string
VarType	Returns a value indicating the subtype of a variable
Weekday	Returns a number representing a day of the week
Year	Returns the year from a date value

Using Worksheet Functions in VBA

Although VBA offers a decent assortment of built-in functions, you might not always find exactly what you need. Fortunately, you can also use Excel's worksheet functions in your VBA procedures. The only worksheet functions that you cannot use are those that have an equivalent VBA function.

VBA makes Excel's worksheet functions available through the WorksheetFunction object, which is contained in the Application object. (Remember, the Application object is Excel.) Therefore, any statement that uses a worksheet function must use the Application.WorksheetFunction qualifier. In other words, you must precede the function name with **Application.WorksheetFunction** (with a dot separating the two).

Actually, you can omit the WorksheetFunction part of the expression and VBA will still be able to determine that you want to use an Excel worksheet function. It's a good idea, however, to use WorksheetFunction to make it perfectly clear that the code is using an Excel function.

Worksheet function examples

In this section, I demonstrate how to use worksheet functions in your VBA expressions.

Finding the maximum value in a range

Here's an example showing how to use the MAX worksheet function in a VBA procedure. This subroutine displays the maximum value in the range named NumberList on the active worksheet:

```
Sub ShowMax()
TheMax = Application.WorksheetFunction. _
    Max(Range("NumberList"))
MsgBox TheMax
End Sub
```

You can use the MIN function to get the smallest value in a range. And, as you might expect, you can use other worksheet functions in a similar manner. For example, you can use the LARGE function to determine the kth-largest value in a range. The following expression demonstrates this:

```
SecondHighest = Application.WorksheetFunction. _
    Large(Range("NumberList"),2)
```

Notice that the LARGE function uses two arguments; the second argument represents the *k*th part — in this case, 2 (the second-largest value).

Calculating a mortgage payment

The next example uses the PMT worksheet function to calculate a mortgage payment. In this example, I use three variables to store the data that's passed to the PMT function as arguments. A message box displays the calculated payment.

```
Sub PmtCalc()
    IntRate = 0.0825 / 12
    Periods = 30 * 12
    LoanAmt = 150000
    MsgBox Application.WorksheetFunction. _
        Pmt(IntRate, Periods, -LoanAmt)
End Sub
```

As the following statement shows, you can also insert the values directly as the function arguments:

```
MsgBox Application.Pmt(0.0825 /12, 360, -150000)
```

However, using variables to store the parameters makes the code easier to read.

Using a lookup function

The following example uses the simple lookup table shown in Figure 9-1. Range A1:B15 is named PriceList.

```
Sub GetPrice()
    PartNum = InputBox("Enter the Part Number")
Sheets("Prices").Activate
    Price = Application.WorksheetFunction. _
        VLookup(PartNum, Range("PriceList"), 2, False)
    MsgBox PartNum & " costs " & Price
End Sub
```

The subroutine starts by using VBA's InputBox function to ask the user for a part number. Figure 9-2 shows the dialog box Excel displays when this statement is executed. This statement assigns the part number the user enters to the PartNum variable. Then I use the VBA Val function to convert PartNum to a value (the InputBox function always returns a string). The next statement simply activates the Prices worksheet — just in case it's not already the active sheet.

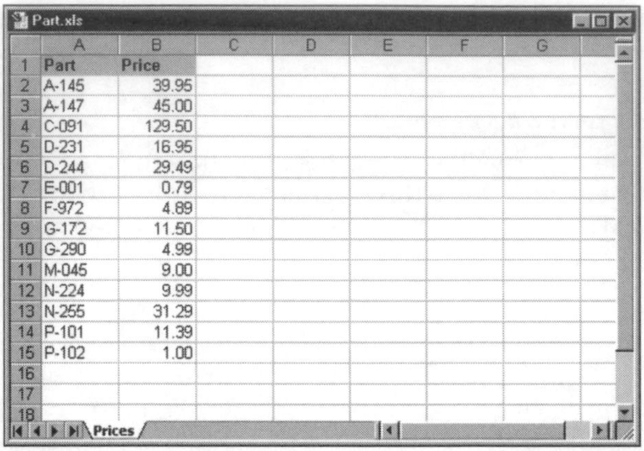

Figure 9-1:
This range, named PriceList, contains prices for parts.

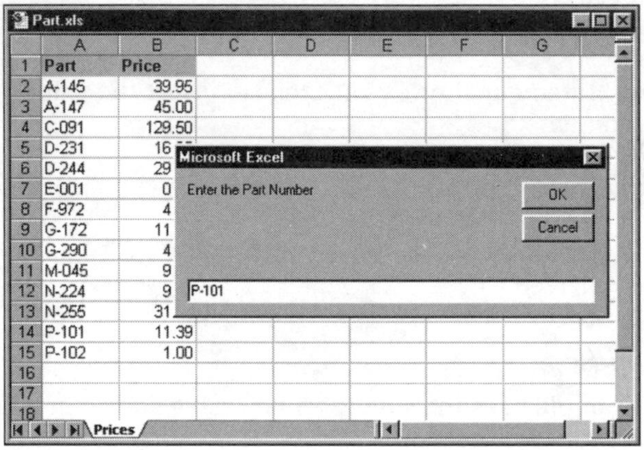

Figure 9-2:
Using the InputBox function to get input from the user.

Next, the subroutine uses the VLOOKUP function to find the part number in the table. Notice that the arguments you use in this statement are the same as the ones you would use with the function in a worksheet formula. This statement assigns the result of the function to the Price variable. Finally, the subroutine displays the price for the part by using the MsgBox function.

This subroutine fails if you enter a nonexistent part number (try it). For a more robust subroutine, you need to add some error-handling statements. I discuss error handling in Chapter 12.

Entering worksheet functions

You can't use the Excel Paste Function dialog box to insert a worksheet function into a VBA module. Instead, you enter such functions the old-fashioned way: by hand. However, you *can* use the Paste Function dialog box to identify the function you want to use and find out about its arguments. Just activate a worksheet, and use the Insert⇔Function command as you normally would. Then, when you figure out how the function works, you can enter it into your module.

The Auto List Members option in the VBE displays a drop-down list of all worksheet functions after you type Application.WorksheetFunction. If this feature isn't working, choose VBE's Tools⇔Options command, click the Editor tab, and place a check mark next to Auto List Members.

More about Using Worksheet Functions

Newcomers to VBA often confuse VBA's built-in functions and Excel's workbook functions. A good rule of thumb is that VBA doesn't try to reinvent the wheel. For the most part, VBA doesn't duplicate Excel worksheet functions.

Bottom line? If you need to use a function, first determine whether VBA has something that meets your needs. If not, check out the worksheet functions. If all else fails, you may be able to write a custom function by using VBA.

The WorksheetFunction object contains the worksheet functions available to VBA procedures. To see a list of these functions, you can use the Object Browser, as shown in Figure 9-3. Follow these steps to display a complete list of worksheet functions available in VBA:

1. **In the VBE, press F2.**

   The Object Browser appears.

2. **In the first drop-down list, select Excel.**

3. **In the list labeled Classes, select WorksheetFunction.**

   The Members of list shows all the worksheet functions you can use in your code.

For most worksheet functions that are not available as methods of the Application object, you can use an equivalent VBA built-in operator or function. For example, the MOD worksheet function is not available in the WorksheetFunction object because VBA has an equivalent, built-in Mod operator. This is by design — a VBA operator works faster than an Excel function in a VBA module.

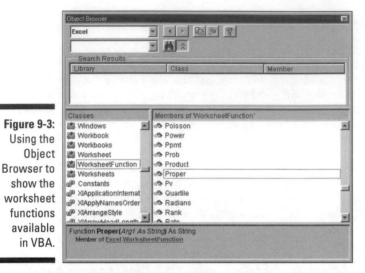

Figure 9-3:
Using the
Object
Browser to
show the
worksheet
functions
available
in VBA.

Using Custom Functions

The third category of functions you can use in your VBA procedures is custom functions. A custom function is one you develop yourself using (what else?) VBA. To use a custom function, you must define it in the workbook in which you use it.

Here's an example of defining a simple custom function, and then using it in a VBA subroutine:

```
Function MultiplyTwo(firstnum, secondnum)
    MultiplyTwo = firstnum * secondnum
End Function

Sub ShowResult()
    ValOne = 123
    ValTwo = 544
    Result = MultiplyTwo(ValOne, ValTwo)
    MsgBox Result
End Sub
```

The custom function MultiplyTwo has two arguments. The ShowResult subroutine uses this custom function by passing two arguments to it (in parentheses). The ShowResult subroutine then displays a message box showing the value returned by the MultiplyTwo function.

You can use custom functions also in your worksheet formulas. I devote an entire chapter to this important and useful topic (see Chapter 21).

Chapter 10

Controlling Program Flow and Making Decisions

. . . .

. . . .

Some VBA procedures start at the beginning and progress line by line to the end, never deviating from this top-to-bottom program flow. Macros you record always work like this. In many cases, however, you need to control the flow of your routines by skipping over some statements, executing some statements multiple times, and testing conditions to determine what the routine does next. Ready or not, you find out how to do all that stuff in this chapter.

Go with the Flow, Dude

Some programming newbies can't understand how a dumb computer can make intelligent decisions. The secret lies in several programming constructs that most programming languages support. Table 10-1 provides a quick summary of these constructs. (I explain all of these later in this chapter.)

Table 10-1	Programming Constructs for Making Decisions
Construct	**How It Works**
The GoTo statement	Jumps to a particular statement
The If-Then structure	Does something if something else is true
The Select Case structure	Does any of several things, depending on the value of something
The For-Next loop	Executes a series of statements a specified number of times
The Do-While loop	Does something as long as something else remains true
The Do-Until loop	Does something until something else becomes true

The GoTo Statement

A GoTo statement offers the most straightforward means for changing the flow of a program. The GoTo statement simply transfers program control to a new statement, which is preceded by a label.

Your VBA routines can contain as many labels you like. A label is just a text string followed by a colon. (See "Using Labels" in Chapter 7.)

The following subroutine shows how a GoTo statement works:

```
Sub GoToDemo()
    UserName = InputBox("Enter Your Name: ")
    If UserName <> "Bill Gates" Then GoTo WrongName
    MsgBox ("Welcome Bill...")
'   ...[More code here] ...
    Exit Sub
WrongName:
    MsgBox "Sorry. Only Bill Gates can run this."
End Sub
```

The subroutine uses the InputBox function to get the user's name. If the user enters a name other than Bill Gates, the program flow jumps to the WrongName label, displays an apologetic message, and the subroutine ends. On the other hand, if Mr. Gates signs on, the procedure displays a welcome message and then executes some additional code (not shown in the example). The Exit Sub statement ends the routine before the MsgBox function has a chance to work.

This simple routine works, but VBA provides several better alternatives than using GoTo. In general, you should use the GoTo statement only when you have no other way to perform an action. In VBA, you need to use a GoTo statement only for trapping errors. (I cover this in Chapter 12.)

Many hard-core programming types have a deep-seated dislike for GoTo statements. Therefore, you should avoid this subject when talking with other programmers.

What is structured programming? Does it matter?

If you hang around with programmers, sooner or later you'll hear the term *structured programming*. This term has been around for decades, and programmers generally agree that structured programs are superior to unstructured programs. So, what is structured programming? And can you write structured programs using VBA?

The basic premise of structured programming is that a routine or a code segment should have only one entry point and only one exit point. In other words, a block of code should be a stand-alone unit, and program control cannot jump into the middle of this unit, nor can it exit at any point except the single exit point. When you write structured code, your program progresses in an orderly manner and is easy to follow — unlike a program that jumps around in a haphazard fashion. This pretty much rules out the GoTo statement.

In general, a structured program is easier to read and understand. More important, it's also easier to modify.

VBA is indeed a structured language. It offers standard structured constructs such as If-Then-Else, For-Next loops, Do-Until loops, Do-While loops, and Select Case structures. Furthermore, it fully supports modular code construction. If you're new to programming, you should try to develop good structured programming habits early. End of lecture.

Decisions, Decisions

In this section, I discuss two programming structures that can empower your VBA procedures with some impressive decision-making capabilities: If-Then and Select Case.

The If-Then structure

Okay, I'll say it: If-Then is VBA's most important control structure. You'll probably use this command on a daily basis (at least *I* do). As in many other aspects of life, effective decision making is the key to success in writing programs. If this book has the effect I intended, you'll soon share my philosophy that a successful Excel application boils down to making decisions and acting upon them.

The If-Then structure has this basic syntax:

```
If condition Then statements [Else elsestatements]
```

You use the If-Then structure when you want to execute one or more statements conditionally. The optional Else clause, if included, lets you execute one or more statements if the condition you're testing is not true. Sound confusing? Don't worry, a few examples will make this crystal clear.

If-Then examples

The following routine demonstrates the use of the If-Then structure without the optional Else clause:

```
Sub GreetMe()
    If Time < 0.5 Then MsgBox "Good Morning"
End Sub
```

This uses VBA's Time function to get the system time. If the current system time is less than .5 (in other words, before noon), the routine displays a message. If Time is greater than or equal to .5, the routine ends and nothing happens.

To display a different greeting if Time is greater than or equal to .5, add another If-Then statement after the first one, like this:

```
Sub GreetMe()
    If Time < 0.5 Then MsgBox "Good Morning"
    If Time >= 0.5 Then MsgBox "Good Afternoon"
End Sub
```

Notice that I used >= (greater than or equal to) for the second If-Then statement. This covers the extremely remote chance that the time is precisely 12:00 noon.

An If-Then-Else example

Another approach to the preceding problem uses the Else clause. Here's the same routine recoded to use the If-Then-Else structure:

```
Sub GreetMe()
    If Time < 0.5 Then MsgBox "Good Morning" Else _
       MsgBox "Good Afternoon"
End Sub
```

Notice that I use the line continuation character in the preceding example. The If-Then-Else statement is actually a single statement.

What if you need to expand this routine to handle three conditions: morning, afternoon, and evening? You have two options: use three If-Then statements, or use a *nested* If-Then-Else structure. The first approach is the simplest:

```
Sub GreetMe2()
   If Time < 0.5 Then Msg = "Morning"
   If Time >= 0.5 And Time < 0.75 Then Msg = "Afternoon"
   If Time >= 0.75 Then Msg = " Evening"
   MsgBox "Good " & Msg
End Sub
```

The following routine performs the same action but uses a nested If-Then-Else structure:

```
Sub GreetMe3()
   If Time < 0.5 Then Msg = "Morning" Else
     If Time >= 0.5 And Time < 0.75 Then Msg = "Afternoon"
           Else
        If Time >= 0.75 Then Msg = "Evening"
   MsgBox "Good " & Msg
End Sub
```

The preceding example works fine, but it could be simplified a bit by omitting the last If-Then part. Because the routine has already tested for two conditions (morning and afternoon), the only remaining condition is evening. Here's the modified subroutine:

```
Sub GreetMe4()
  If Time < 0.5 Then Msg = "Morning" Else
    If Time >= 0.5 And Time < 0.75 Then _
      Msg = "Afternoon" Else Msg = "Evening"
  MsgBox "Good " & Msg
End Sub
```

Using ElseIf

In both of the previous examples, every statement in the routine is executed — even in the morning. A more efficient structure would exit the routine as soon as a condition is found to be true. In the morning, for example, the procedure should display the "Good Morning" message and then exit — without evaluating the other superfluous conditions.

With a tiny routine like this, you don't have to worry about execution speed. But for larger applications that you must optimize for speed, you should know about another syntax for the If-Then structure, the ElseIf syntax:

```
If condition Then
    [statements]
[ElseIf condition-n Then
    [elseifstatements]] . . .
[Else
    [elsestatements]]
End If
```

Here's how you can rewrite the GreetMe routine using this syntax:

```
Sub GreetMe5()
  If Time < 0.5 Then
    Msg = "Morning"
      ElseIf Time >= 0.5 And Time < 0.75 Then
        Msg = "Afternoon"
          Else
            Msg = "Good Evening"
  End If
  MsgBox "Good " & Msg
End Sub
```

When a condition is true, VBA executes the conditional statements, and the If structure ends. In other words, VBA doesn't waste time evaluating the extraneous conditions, which makes this routine a bit more efficient than the previous examples. The trade-off (there are always trade-offs) is that the code is more difficult to understand (of course, you already knew that).

Another If-Then example

Here's another example that uses the simple form of the If-Then structure. This routine prompts the user for a Quantity, and then displays the appropriate discount, based on the quantity the user enters:

```
Sub ShowDiscount()
    Quantity = InputBox("Enter Quantity: ")
    If Quantity >= 0 Then Discount = 0.1
    If Quantity >= 25 Then Discount = 0.15
    If Quantity >= 50 Then Discount = 0.2
    If Quantity >= 75 Then Discount = 0.25
    MsgBox "Discount: " & Discount
End Sub
```

Notice that each If-Then statement in this routine is executed, and the value for Discount can change as the statements are executed. However, the routine ultimately displays the correct value for Discount.

The following routine performs the same tasks by using the alternative ElseIf syntax. In this case, the routine ends immediately after executing the statements for a true condition.

```
Sub ShowDiscount2()
  Quantity = InputBox("Enter Quantity: ")
  If Quantity >= 0 And Quantity < 25 Then
    Discount = 0.1
      ElseIf Quantity >= 25 And Quantity < 50 Then
        Discount = 0.15
          ElseIf Quantity >= 50 And Quantity < 75 Then
            Discount = 0.2
              ElseIf Quantity >= 75 Then
                Discount = 0.25
  End If
  MsgBox "Discount: " & Discount
End Sub
```

Personally, I find these multiple If-Then structures rather cumbersome. I generally use the If-Then structure for only simple binary decisions. When a decision involves three or more choices, the Select Case structure offers a simpler, more efficient approach than using multiple If-Then structures.

The Select Case structure

The Select Case structure is useful for decisions involving three or more options (although it also works with two options, providing a good alternative to the If-Then-Else structure).

The syntax for the Select Case structure is

```
Select Case testexpression
[Case expressionlist-n
    [statements-n]] . . .
[Case Else
    [elsestatements]]
End Select
```

Don't be scared off by this official syntax. As you see next, using the Select Case structure is quite easy.

A Select Case example

The following example shows how you use the Select Case structure. This also shows another way to code the examples presented in the previous section:

```
Sub ShowDiscount3()
    Quantity = InputBox("Enter Quantity: ")
    Select Case Quantity
        Case 0 To 24
            Discount = 0.1
        Case 25 To 49
            Discount = 0.15
        Case 50 To 74
            Discount = 0.2
        Case Is >= 75
            Discount = 0.25
    End Select
    MsgBox "Discount: " & Discount
End Sub
```

In this example, the Quantity variable is being evaluated. The routine is checking for four different cases (0 to 24, 25 to 49, 50 to 74, and 75 or greater).

Any number of statements can follow each Case statement, and they all are executed if the case is true. If you use only one statement, as in this example, you can put the statement on the same line as the Case keyword, preceded by a colon — the VBA statement separator character. In my opinion, this makes the code more compact and a bit clearer. Here's how the routine looks using this format:

```
Sub ShowDiscount4 ()
Quantity = InputBox("Enter Quantity: ")
    Select Case Quantity
        Case  0 To 24: Discount = 0.1
        Case 25 To 49: Discount = 0.15
        Case 50 To 74: Discount = 0.2
        Case Is >= 75: Discount = 0.25
    End Select
    MsgBox "Discount: " & Discount
End Sub
```

When VBA executes a Select Case structure, the structure is exited as soon as VBA finds a true case.

A nested Select Case example

As demonstated in the following example, you can nest Select Case structures. Nesting means placing a Select Case structure within another Select Case structure. This routine examines the active cell, and displays a message describing the cell's contents. Notice that the subroutine has three Select Case structures, and each has its own End Select statement.

```
Sub CheckCell()
    Select Case ActiveCell
        Case Empty
            Msg = "is blank."
        Case Else
            Select Case ActiveCell.HasFormula
                Case True
                    Msg = "has a formula"
                Case False
                    Select Case IsNumeric(ActiveCell)
                        Case True
```

(continued)

(continued)

```
                     Msg = "has a number"
              Case Else
                     Msg = "has text"
           End Select
        End Select
    End Select
    MsgBox "Cell " & ActiveCell.Address & " " & Msg
End Sub
```

The logic goes something like this:

1. Find out whether the cell is empty.

2. If it's not empty, see whether it contains a formula.

3. If not, find out whether it contains a numeric value or text.

When the routine ends, the Msg variable contains a string that describes the cell's contents. As shown in Figure 10-1, the MsgBox function displays that message.

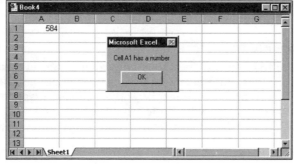

Figure 10-1: A message displayed by the CheckCell procedure.

You can nest Select Case structures as deeply as you need, but make sure that each Select Case statement has a corresponding End Select statement.

As you can see, indenting makes this potentially confusing code much more understandable. If you don't believe me, take a look at the same procedure without any indentation:

```
Sub CheckCell()
Select Case ActiveCell
Case Empty
Msg = "is blank."
Case Else
```

```
Select Case ActiveCell.HasFormula
Case True
Msg = "has a formula"
Case False
Select Case IsNumeric(ActiveCell)
Case True
Msg = "has a number"
Case Else
Msg = "has text"
End Select
End Select
End Select
MsgBox "Cell " & ActiveCell.Address & " " & Msg
End Sub
```

Fairly incomprehensible, eh?

Knocking Your Code for a Loop

The term *looping* refers to the process of repeating a block of VBA state-ments numerous times. You may know how many times your program needs to loop, or this might be determined by the current values of variables in your program.

There are two types of loops: good loops and bad loops. The following code demonstrates a bad loop. The procedure simply enters consecutive num-bers into a range. It starts by prompting the user for two values: a starting value and the total number of cells to fill. (Because InputBox returns a string, I convert the strings to integers by using the CInt function.) This loop uses the GoTo statement to control the flow. The CellCount variable keeps track of how many cells are filled. If this value is less than the number requested by the user, program control loops back to DoAnother.

```
Sub BadLoop()
    StartVal = CInt(InputBox("Enter the starting value: "))
    NumToFill = CInt(InputBox("How many cells? "))
    ActiveCell = StartVal
    CellCount = 1
DoAnother:
    ActiveCell.Offset(CellCount, 0) = StartVal + CellCount
    CellCount = CellCount + 1
    If CellCount < NumToFill Then GoTo DoAnother Else Exit _
        Sub
End Sub
```

This routine works as intended, so why is it an example of bad looping? As I mention earlier in this chapter, avoid using a GoTo statement unless it's absolutely necessary. Using GoTo statements to perform looping

- Is contrary to the concept of structured programming (see the sidebar earlier in this chapter, "What is structured programming? Does it matter?")
- Makes the code more difficult to read
- Is more prone to errors than using structured looping procedures

VBA has enough structured looping commands that you almost never have to rely on GoTo statements for your decision making. The exception, as I mention earlier, is for error handling.

Now you can move on to a discussion of the good looping structures.

For-Next loops

The simplest type of loop is a For-Next loop. Here's the syntax for this structure:

```
For counter = start To end [Step stepval]
    [statements]
    [Exit For]
    [statements]
Next [counter]
```

The looping is controlled by a counter variable, which starts at one value and stops at another value. The statements between the For statement and the Next statement are the statements in the loop. To see how this works, keep reading.

A For-Next example

The following example shows a For-Next loop that doesn't use the optional Step value or the optional Exit For statement. This routine loops 100 times, and uses the VBA Rnd function to enter a random number into 100 cells:

```
Sub FillRange()
    For Count = 1 To 100
        ActiveCell.Offset(Count - 1, 0) = Rnd
    Next Count
End Sub
```

In this example, Count (the loop counter variable) starts with a value of 1, and increases by 1 each time through the loop. Because I didn't specify a Step value, VBA uses the default value (1). The Offset method uses the value of Count as an argument. The first time through the loop, the procedure enters a number into the active cell offset by zero rows. The second time through (Count = 2), the procedure enters a number into the active cell offset by one row, and so on.

Because the loop counter is a normal variable, you can change its value within the block of code between the For and the Next statements. This, however, is a *bad* practice. Changing the counter within the loop can have unpredictable results. You should take special precautions to ensure that your code does not change the value of the loop counter.

A For-Next example with a Step

You can use a Step value to skip some values in a For-Next loop. Here's the same procedure as in the preceding section, but rewritten to insert random numbers into every *other* cell:

```
Sub FillRange()
    For Count = 1 To 100 Step 2
        ActiveCell.Offset(Count - 1, 0) = Rnd
    Next Count
End Sub
```

This time, Count starts out as 1, and then takes on a value of 3, 5, 7, and so on. The final value of Count is 99.

Earlier in this chapter, the introduction to looping presents the BadLoop example, which uses a GoTo statement. Here's the same example, but I convert a bad loop into a good loop by using the For-Next structure:

```
Sub FillRange()
    StartVal = CInt(InputBox("Enter the starting value: "))
    NumToFill = CInt(InputBox("How many cells? "))
    For CellCount = 1 To NumToFill
        ActiveCell.Offset(CellCount - 1, 0) = _
            StartVal + CellCount - 1
    Next CellCount
End Sub
```

A For-Next example with an Exit For statement

A For-Next loop can also include one or more Exit For statements within the loop. When VBA encounters this statement, the loop terminates immediately.

The following example demonstrates the Exit For statement. This routine identifies which cell in column A of the active worksheet has the largest value:

```
Sub ExitForDemo()
  MaxVal = Application.WorksheetFunction. _
    Max(Range("A:A"))
  For Row = 1 To 65536
    If Range("A1").Offset(Row - 1, 0).Value = MaxVal Then
        Range("A1").Offset(Row - 1, 0).Activate
        MsgBox "Max value is in Row " & Row
        Exit For
    End If
  Next Row
End Sub
```

The routine calculates the maximum value in the column by using Excel's MAX function, and assigns the result to the MaxVal variable. Then, the For-Next loop checks each cell in the column. If the cell being checked is equal to MaxVal, the routine doesn't need to continue looping (its job is finished), so the Exit For statement terminates the loop. Before terminating the loop, the procedure activates the cell with the maximum value and informs the user of its location.

Notice that the number of rows (65536) is hard-coded in the preceding subroutine. In previous versions of Excel, a worksheet had only 16384 rows. To make this routine compatible with with earlier versions of Excel, substitute the following, which calculates the number of rows in the worksheet:

```
For Row = 1 to Range("A:A").Rows.Count
```

A nested For-Next example

So far, all the examples in this chapter use relatively simple loops. However, you can have any number of statements in the loop, and you can nest For-Next loops inside other For-Next loops.

The following example uses a nested For-Next loop to insert random numbers into a 12-row by 5-column range of cells, as shown in Figure 10-2. Notice that the routine executes the inner loop (the loop with the Row counter) once for each iteration of the outer loop (the loop with the Col counter). In other words, the routine executes the Cells(Row, Col) = Rnd statement 60 times.

```
Sub FillRange()
    For Col = 1 To 5
        For Row = 1 To 12
            Cells(Row, Col) = Rnd
        Next Row
    Next Col
End Sub
```

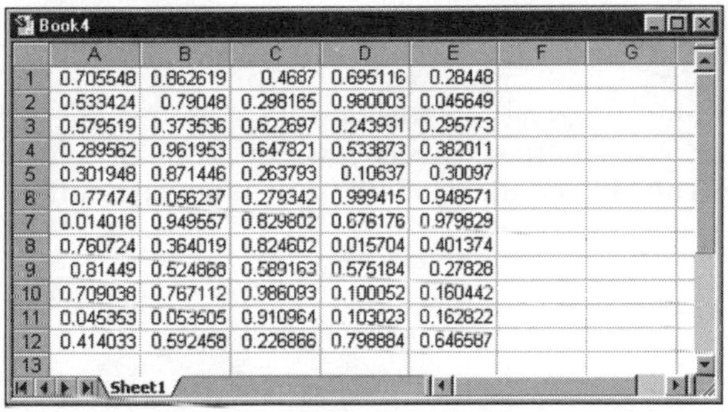

	A	B	C	D	E	F	G
1	0.705548	0.862619	0.4687	0.695116	0.28448		
2	0.533424	0.79048	0.298165	0.980003	0.045649		
3	0.579519	0.373536	0.622697	0.243931	0.295773		
4	0.289562	0.961953	0.647821	0.533873	0.382011		
5	0.301948	0.871446	0.263793	0.10637	0.30097		
6	0.77474	0.056237	0.279342	0.999415	0.948571		
7	0.014018	0.949557	0.829802	0.676176	0.979829		
8	0.760724	0.364019	0.824602	0.015704	0.401374		
9	0.81449	0.524868	0.589163	0.575184	0.27828		
10	0.709038	0.767112	0.986093	0.100052	0.160442		
11	0.045353	0.053505	0.910964	0.103023	0.162822		
12	0.414033	0.592458	0.226866	0.798884	0.646587		
13							

Figure 10-2: These cells were filled using a nested For-Next loop.

The next example uses nested For-Next loops to initialize a three-dimensional array with zeros. This routine executes the statement in the middle of all the loops (the assignment statement) 1000 times, each time with a different combination of values for i, j, and k:

```
Sub NestedLoops()
    Dim MyArray(10, 10, 10)
    For i = 1 To 10
        For j = 1 To 10
            For k = 1 To 10
                MyArray(i, j, k) = 0
            Next k
        Next j
    Next i
End Sub
```

Refer to Chapter 7 for information about arrays.

Do-While loop

VBA supports another type of looping structure known as a Do-While loop. Unlike a For-Next loop, a Do-While loop continues until a specified condition is met. Here's the Do-While loop syntax:

```
Do [While condition]
    [statements]
    [Exit Do]
    [statements]
Loop
```

The following example uses a Do-While loop. This routine uses the active cell as a starting point, and then travels down the column, multiplying each cell's value by 2. The loop continues until the routine encounters an empty cell.

```
Sub DoWhileDemo()
    Do While ActiveCell.Value <> Empty
        ActiveCell.Value = ActiveCell.Value * 2
        ActiveCell.Offset(1, 0).Select
    Loop
End Sub
```

Some people prefer to code a Do-While loop as a Do-Loop While loop. The example below performs exactly as the previous subroutine but uses a different syntax for the loop.

```
Sub DoLoopWhileDemo()
    Do
        ActiveCell.Value = ActiveCell.Value * 2
        ActiveCell.Offset(1, 0).Select
    Loop While ActiveCell.Value <> Empty
End Sub
```

Do-Until loop

The Do-Until loop structure is similar to the Do-While structure. The two structures differ in their handling of the tested condition. A program continues to execute a Do-While loop *while* the condition remains true. In a Do-Until loop, the program executes the loop *until* the condition is true.

Here's the Do-Until syntax:

```
Do [Until condition]
    statements]
    [Exit Do]
    [statements]
Loop
```

The following example is the same one presented for the Do-While loop, but recoded to use a Do-Until loop:

```
Sub DoUntilDemo()
    Do Until ActiveCell.Value = Empty
        ActiveCell.Value = ActiveCell.Value * 2
        ActiveCell.Offset(1, 0).Select
    Loop
End Sub
```

You may encounter a different form of the Do-Until loop — a Do-Loop Until loop. The following example below, which has the same effect as the preceding subroutine, demonstrates an alternate syntax for this type of loop:

```
Sub DoLoopUntilDemo()
    Do
        ActiveCell.Value = ActiveCell.Value * 2
        ActiveCell.Offset(1, 0).Select
    Loop Until ActiveCell.Value = Empty
End Sub
```

Looping through a Collection

VBA supports yet another type of looping — looping through each object in a collection. Recall that a collection consists of a number of objects of the same type. For example, each workbook has a collection of worksheets (the Worksheets collection), and Excel has a collection of all open workbooks (the Workbooks collection).

When you need to loop through each object in a collection, use the For Each-Next structure. The syntax is

```
For Each element In collection
    [statements]
    [Exit For]
    [statements]
Next [element]
```

The following example loops through each worksheet in a workbook named MyBook.xls, and deletes the first row of each worksheet.

```
Sub DeleteRow1()
    For Each Sht In Workbooks("MyBook.xls").Worksheets
        Sht.Rows(1).Delete
    Next sht
End Sub
```

In this example, the variable Sht is an object variable that represents each worksheet in the workbook. Nothing is special about the variable name Sht — you can use any variable name that you like.

Here's another example that loops through each chart on Sheet1 (that is, the ChartObjects collection) and changes each chart to a line chart. In this example, Cht is a variable that represents each ChartObject. If Sheet1 has no ChartObjects, nothing happens.

```
Sub ChangeCharts()
    For Each Cht In Sheets("Sheet1").ChartObjects
        Cht.Chart.ChartType = xlLine
    Next Cht
End Sub
```

Chapter 11

Automatic Procedures and Events

. . . .

In This Chapter

▶ The types of events that can trigger the execution of a subroutine

▶ Finding out where to place your event-handler VBA code

▶ Executing a subroutine when a workbook is opened or closed

▶ Executing a subroutine when a workbook or worksheet is activated

▶ All about other events, including double-clicking a cell, entering data into a cell, and saving a file

. . . .

*W*ay back in Chapter 5, I mentioned that subroutines can be executed automatically. In this chapter, I cover the ins and outs of this potentially useful feature. I explain how to set things up so that a subroutine is executed automatically when a particular event occurs. (No, this chapter is not about capital punishment.)

Preparing for the Big Event

Okay, what types of events am I talking about here? Good question. Excel can recognize many events, but it can't recognize quite a few others.

Following are a few examples of the types of events that Excel can deal with:

- ✔ A workbook is opened or closed
- ✔ A window is activated
- ✔ A worksheet is activated or deactivated
- ✔ Data is entered into a cell, or the cell is edited
- ✔ A workbook is saved
- ✔ A worksheet is calculated

- ✔ An object is clicked

- ✔ A particular key or key combination is pressed

- ✔ A cell is double-clicked

- ✔ A particular time of day occurs

- ✔ An error occurs

Most Excel programmers never need to worry about most of the events in this list. You should, however, at least know that these events exist because they may come in handy someday. In this chapter, I discuss the most commonly used events.

Although previous versions of Excel supported some events, Excel 97 takes this concept to a new level by supporting lots of additional events.

Table 11-1 lists all of the workbook-related and worksheet-related events. These events are listed in the drop-down event list in the Code window for a ThisWorkbook item.

Table 11-1	Workbook and Worksheet Events
Event	*When It's Triggered*
Workbook Events	
AddinUninstall	The add-in is uninstalled (relevant only for add-ins).
BeforeClose	The workbook is closed.
BeforePrint	The workbook is printed.
BeforeSave	The workbook is saved.
Deactivate	The workbook is deactivated.
NewSheet	A new sheet is added to the workbook.
Open	The workbook is opened.
SheetActivate	A sheet in the workbook is activated.
SheetBeforeDoubleClick	A cell in the workbook is double-clicked.
SheetBeforeRightClick	A cell in the workbook is right-clicked.
SheetCalculate	The workbook is recalculated.
SheetChange	A change is made to a cell in the workbook.
SheetDeactivate	A sheet in the workbook is deactivated.
SheetSelectionChange	The selection is changed.
WindowActivate	The workbook window is activated.
WindowDeactivate	The workbook window is deactivated.
WindowResize	The workbook window is resized.

Event	When It's Triggered
Worksheet Events	
Activate	The worksheet is activated.
BeforeDoubleClick	A cell in the worksheet is double-clicked.
BeforeRightClick	A cell in the worksheet is right-clicked.
Calculate	The worksheet is recalculated.
Change	A change is made to a cell in the worksheet.
Deactivate	The worksheet is deactivated.
SelectionChange	The selection is changed.

Is this stuff useful?

You may wonder how this event business can be useful. Here's a quick example.

Suppose you have a workbook that other people use for data entry. Any values entered into this worksheet must be greater than 1000. You can write a simple macro that Excel automatically executes whenever someone enters data into a cell (entering data is an event). If the user enters a value less than 1000, the macro displays a dialog box reprimanding the user.

The new Excel 97 Data⇨Validation command provides another way to perform this type of data entry checking — without even using VBA. However, as you see later in this chapter (see the section "A data validation example"), using VBA for data validation offers some distinct advantages.

That's just one example of how you can take advantage of an event. Keep reading for some more examples.

More about programming automatic events

Programming these events is relatively straightforward after you understand how the process works. It all boils down to a few steps, all of which I explain later:

1. **Identify the event you want to trap.**
2. **Activate the Visual Basic Editor (Alt+F11).**

3. **In the Project Window of the VBE, double-click the appropriate object listed under Microsoft Excel Objects.**

   The object will be either ThisWorkbook (for a workbook-related event) or a sheet (for a sheet-related event).

4. **Write the subroutine that is executed when the event occurs.**

   This subroutine will have a special name that identifies it as an event-handler subroutine.

These steps become clearer as you progress through the chapter. Trust me.

Where Does the VBA Code Go?

Event-handler subroutines do not go in a normal VBA module. They must reside in the Code window of an Object module. Figure 11-1 shows the VBE window with one project displayed in the Project window. (Refer to Chapter 3 for some background on the VBE.) Notice that the project consists of several items:

- One item for each sheet in the workbook (in this case, three Sheet objects)
- An item labeled ThisWorkbook
- A VBA module that I inserted manually using the Insert⇨Module command

When you double-click any of these items, the Code window displays the code associated with the item, if any.

The event-handler subroutines that you write will go into the Code window for the ThisWorkbook item (for workbook-related events) or one of the Sheet objects (for worksheet-related events).

Writing an Event-Handler Subroutine

The VBE helps you out when you're ready to write an event-handler subroutine because it displays a list of all events that Excel can recognize.

Figure 11-2 shows a Code window for the ThisWorkbook object. To display this empty Code window, double-click the ThisWorkbook object in the Project window. This Code window has two drop-down lists at the top.

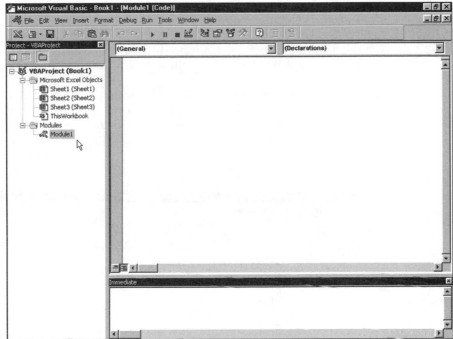

Figure 11-1:
The VBE
window,
displaying
items for a
single
project.

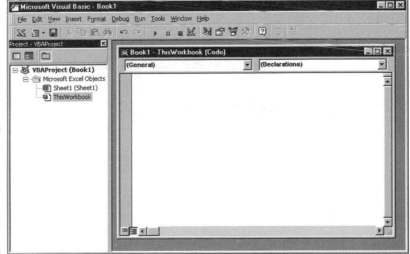

Figure 11-2:
An empty
Code
window
for the
ThisWorkbook
object.

By default, the left drop-down list in the Code window displays General. To write an event-handler subroutine, you need to select Workbook from this list (Workbook is the only other item in the list). If the event-handler is for a worksheet, double-click the appropriate Sheet item in the Project window before you select Worksheet from the list.

Figure 11-3 shows the right drop-down list, which consists of all the workbook-related events that Excel recognizes. When you select an event from the list, VBE automatically starts creating an event-handler subroutine for you. Figure 11-4 shows the Code window after I selected Open from the list of events.

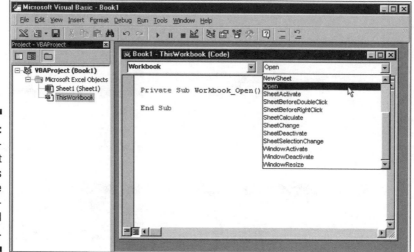

Figure 11-3:
The drop-down list displays all the workbook-related events.

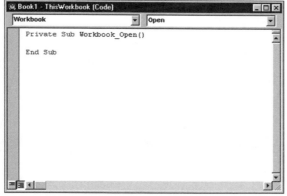

Figure 11-4:
When you select an item from the event list, VBE writes a Sub statement for you.

VBE's help goes only so far, however. It writes the Sub statement and the End statement. Writing the VBA code that goes in between these two statements is your job.

Some event-handler subroutines use one or more arguments in the Sub statement. For example, if you select SheetActivate from the event list for a Workbook object, VBE writes the following Sub statement:

```
Private Sub Workbook_SheetActivate(ByVal Sh As Object)
```

In this case, Sh is the argument passed to the subroutine and is a variable that represents the sheet in the workbook that is activated. Examples later in this chapter will clarify this point.

Introductory Examples

In this section, I provide a few simple examples so that you can get the hang of this event-handling business.

The Open event for a workbook

For the first example, assume that you have a workbook that you use every day. The subroutine in this example is executed every time the workbook is opened. The procedure checks the day of the week; if it's Friday, the procedure displays a reminder message for you.

To create the subroutine that is executed whenever the Open event for the workbook occurs, follow these steps:

1. **Open the workbook.**

   Any workbook will do.

2. **Press Alt+F11 to activate the VBE.**

3. **Locate the workbook in the Project window.**

4. **Double-click the project to display its items.**

5. **Double-click the ThisWorkbook item.**

   The VBE displays an empty Code window for the ThisWorkbook object.

6. **In the Code window, select Workbook from the left drop-down list.**

   The VBE enters the beginning and ending statements for a Workbook_Open subroutine.

7. Enter the following statements:

```
Private Sub Workbook_Open()
  If WeekDay(Now) = 6 Then
      Msg = "Today is Friday. Make sure that you "
      Msg = Msg & "do your weekly backup!"
      MsgBox Msg
  End If
End Sub
```

The Code window should look like Figure 11-5.

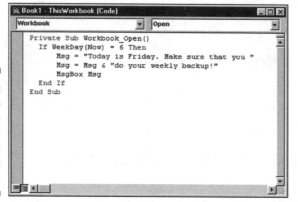

Figure 11-5:
This subroutine is executed when the workbook is opened.

Workbook_Open is executed automatically whenever the workbook is opened. It uses VBA's Weekday function to determine the day of the week. If it's Friday, a message box appears reminding the user to perform a weekly file backup. If it's not Friday, nothing happens.

Note: If today isn't Friday, you might have a hard time testing this subroutine. Here's a chance to test your own skill at VBA. You can modify this subroutine any way you like. For example, the following version displays a message every time the workbook is opened. This will get annoying after a while, trust me.

```
Private Sub Workbook_Open()
    Msg = "This is Frank's cool workbook!"
    MsgBox Msg
End Sub
```

A Workbook_Open subroutine can do almost anything. These subroutines are often used for

- ✔ Displaying welcome messages
- ✔ Opening other workbooks
- ✔ Activating a particular worksheet in the workbook
- ✔ Setting up custom menus
- ✔ Displaying (or hiding) toolbars

The BeforeClose event for a workbook

Here's an example of the Workbook_BeforeClose macro, which is automatically executed immediately before the workbook is closed. This subroutine is located in the Code window for a ThisWorkbook object.

```
Private Sub Workbook_BeforeClose(Cancel As Boolean)
Msg = "Would you like to make a backup of this file?"
    Ans = MsgBox(Msg, vbYesNo)
    If Ans = vbYes Then
        FName = "F:\BACKUP\" & ThisWorkbook.Name
        ThisWorkbook.SaveCopyAs FName
    End If
End Sub
```

A new way of handling events

Excel 97 introduces a new way of dealing with workbook- and worksheet-related events. As I describe in this chapter, event-handler subroutines are stored in the Code window for a ThisWorkbook object or a Sheet object. Previous versions of Excel supported some events, but not nearly as many as Excel 97. In previous versions of Excel, event-handler subroutines were stored in a regular VBA module. If you open an older Excel file, you may find a subroutine named Auto_Open or Auto_Activate. These specially named subroutines are event handlers. Excel 97 still supports these events; but for new applications you develop, use the techniques described in this chapter.

This routine uses a message box to ask the user if he or she would like to make a backup copy of the workbook. If the answer is yes, the routine uses the SaveCopyAs method to save a backup copy of the file on drive F. If you adapt this subroutine for your own use, you will probably need to change the drive and path.

Excel programmers often use a Workbook_BeforeClose subroutine to clean up after themselves. If you use a Workbook_Open subroutine to change some settings when you open a workbook (hiding the status bar, for example), it's only appropriate that you return the settings to their original state when you close the workbook. You can perform this electronic house-keeping with a Workbook_BeforeClose subroutine.

The BeforeSave event for a workbook

The BeforeSave event, as its name implies, is triggered before a workbook is saved. This event occurs when you use either the File⇨Save or File⇨Save As command.

The following subroutine, which is placed in the Code window for a ThisWorkbook object, demonstrates the BeforeSave event. The routine updates the value in a cell (cell A1 on Sheet1) every time the workbook is saved. In other words, cell A1 serves as a counter to keep track of the number of times the file was saved.

```
Private Sub Workbook_BeforeSave(ByVal SaveAsUI _
    As Boolean, Cancel As Boolean)
    Sheets("Sheet1").Range("A1").Value = _
        Sheets("Sheet1").Range("A1").Value +1
End Sub
```

Notice that the Workbook_BeforeSave subroutine has two arguments, SaveAsUI and Cancel.

To demonstrate how these arguments work, examine the following subroutine, which is executed before the workbook is saved. This subroutine prevents the user from saving the workbook with a different name. If the user chooses the File⇨Save As command, the SaveAsUI argument is True. If SaveAsUI is True, the procedure displays a message and sets Cancel to True — which cancels the Save operation.

```
Private Sub Workbook_BeforeSave(ByVal SaveAsUI _
    As Boolean, Cancel As Boolean)
    If SaveAsUI Then
        MsgBox "You cannot save a copy of this workbook!"
```

```
            Cancel = True
            Exit Sub
        End If
End Sub
```

Examples of Activation Events

Another category of events consists of activating and deactivating objects — specifically, sheets and windows.

Activate and Deactivate events in a sheet

Excel can detect when a particular sheet is activated or deactivated and execute a macro when either of these events occurs. These event-handler subroutines go in the Code window for a Sheet object.

The following example shows a simple subroutine that is executed whenever a particular sheet is activated. This subroutine simply pops up a message box that displays the name of the active sheet:

```
Private Sub Worksheet_Activate()
    MsgBox "You just activated " & ActiveSheet.Name
End Sub
```

Here's another example that activates cell A1 whenever the sheet is activated:

```
Private Sub Worksheet_Activate()
    Range("A1").Activate
End Sub
```

Although the code in these two subroutines is about as simple as it gets, event-handler subroutines can be as complex as you like.

The following subroutine (which is stored in the Code window for the Sheet1 object) uses the Deactivate event to prevent a user from activating any other sheet in the workbook. If Sheet1 is deactivated (that is, another sheet is activated), the user gets a message and Sheet1 is activated.

```
Private Sub Worksheet_Deactivate()
    MsgBox "You must stay on Sheet1"
    Sheets("Sheet1").Activate
End Sub
```

Activate and Deactivate events in a workbook

The previous examples use events associated with a worksheet. The ThisWorkbook object also handles events that deal with sheet activation and deactivation. The following subroutine, which is stored in the Code window for the ThisWorkbook object, is executed whenever *any* sheet in the workbook is activated. The subroutine displays a message with the name of the activated sheet.

```
Private Sub Workbook_SheetActivate(ByVal Sh As Object)
    MsgBox Sh.Name
End Sub
```

You'll notice that the Workbook_SheetActivated subroutine uses the Sh argument. Sh is a variable that represents the active Sheet object. The message box displays the Name property of the Sheet object.

The next example is contained in a ThisWorkbook Code window. It consists of two event-handler subroutines. Workbook_SheetDeactivate is executed when a sheet is deactivated. It stores the sheet that is deactivated in an object variable. (The Set keyword is used to create an object variable.) The Workbook_SheetActivate subroutine checks the type of sheet that is activated (using the TypeName function). If the sheet is a chart sheet, the user gets a message and the *previous* sheet (which is stored in the OldSheet variable) is reactivated. The effect is that users cannot activate a chart sheet (and are always returned to the previous sheet if they try).

```
Dim OldSheet As Object

Private Sub Workbook_SheetDeactivate(ByVal Sh As Object)
    Set OldSheet = Sh
End Sub

Private Sub Workbook_SheetActivate(ByVal Sh As Object)
    If TypeName(Sh) = "Chart" Then
        MsgBox "Sorry, you can't activate any charts."
        OldSheet.Activate
    End If
End Sub
```

Workbook activation events

Excel also recognizes the event that occurs when you activate or deactivate a particular workbook. The following code, which is contained in the Code window for a ThisWorkbook object, is executed whenever the workbook is activated. The subroutine simply maximizes the workbook's window.

```
Private Sub Workbook_Activate()
    ActiveWindow.WindowState = xlMaximized
End Sub
```

The Workbook_Deactivate subroutine, shown next, is executed when a workbook is deactivated. This subroutine minimizes the workbook's window.

```
Private Sub Workbook_Deactivate()
    ThisWorkbook.Windows(1).WindowState = xlMinimized
End Sub
```

Notice that I didn't use ActiveWindow in this code. That's because the workbook will no longer be the active window when it's deactivated. Therefore, I used ThisWorkbook, which refers to the workbook that contains the subroutine.

Other Worksheet-Related Events

In the preceding section, I present examples for worksheet activation and deactivation events. In this section, I discuss three additional events that occur in worksheets: double-clicking a cell, right-clicking a cell, and changing a cell.

The BeforeDoubleClick event

You can set up a subroutine to be executed when the user double-clicks a cell. In the following example (which is stored in the Code window for a Sheet object), double-clicking a cell makes the cell bold (if it's not bold) or not bold (if it is bold):

```
Private Sub Worksheet_BeforeDoubleClick _
  (ByVal Target As Excel.Range, Cancel As Boolean)
    Target.Font.Bold = Not Target.Font.Bold
    Cancel = True
End Sub
```

The Worksheet_BeforeDoubleClick subroutine has two arguments, Target and Cancel. Target represents the cell (a Range object) that was double-clicked. If Cancel is set to True, the default double-click action doesn't occur.

In the preceding subroutine, notice that I set the Cancel argument to True. This causes the default action to not occur. In other words, double-clicking the cell won't put Excel into cell edit mode.

The BeforeRightClick event

The BeforeRightClick event is similar to the BeforeDoubleClick event, except it consists of right-clicking a cell. The following subroutine checks to see whether the cell that was right-clicked contains a numeric value. If so, the subroutine displays the Format Number dialog box and sets the Cancel argument to True (avoiding the normal shortcut menu display). If the cell does not contain a numeric value, nothing special happens — the shortcut menu is displayed as usual.

```
Private Sub Worksheet_BeforeRightClick _
  (ByVal Target As Excel.Range, Cancel As Boolean)
    If IsNumeric(Target) Then
        Application.Dialogs(xlDialogFormatNumber).Show
        Cancel = True
    End If
End Sub
```

The Change event

The Change event occurs whenever a cell (any cell) on the worksheet is changed. In the following example, Worksheet_Change subroutine effectively prevents a user from entering a non-numeric value into cell A1. This subroutine is stored in the Code window for the Sheet object.

```
Private Sub Worksheet_Change(ByVal Target As Excel.Range)
    If Target.Address = "$A$1" Then
        If Not IsNumeric(Target) Then
            MsgBox "Enter a number in cell A1."
            Range("A1").ClearContents
        End If
    End If
End Sub
```

The single argument for the Worksheet_Change subroutine represents the range that was changed. The first statement checks to see whether the cell's address is A1. If so, the subroutine uses the IsNumeric function to determine whether the cell contains a numeric value. If not, a message appears and the cell's value is erased. If the change occurs in any cell except A1, nothing happens.

Why not use the Excel Data⇨Validation command?

You may be familiar with the Data⇨Validation command — a new feature in Excel 97 that makes it easy to ensure that only data of the proper type is entered into a particular cell or range. Although the Data⇨Validation command is useful, it's definitely not foolproof. To demonstrate, start with a blank worksheet and perform the following steps:

1. **Select the range A1:C12.**

2. **Choose Data⇨Validation.**

3. **Set up your validation criteria to accept only whole numbers between 1 and 12 (see Figure 11-6).**

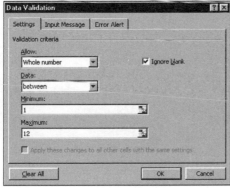

Figure 11-6:
These settings allow only whole numbers between 1 and 12.

Now, enter some values in the range A1:C12. You'll find that the data validation works as it should. But to see it fall apart at the seams, try this:

1. **Enter -1 into any cell outside the validation range (that is, any cell not in A1:C12).**

2. **Choose Edit⇨Copy to copy the negative number to the Clipboard.**

3. **Select any cell in the validation range.**

4. **Choose Edit⇨Paste.**

You'll find that the paste operation is allowable. Look a little closer, however, and you'll find that the cell into which you pasted the negative value no longer has any validation criteria. Pasting wipes out the data validation criteria! The severity of this flaw depends on your application. In the next section, I describe how to use the Change event to provide a better way of validating data.

A data validation example

The next subroutine demonstrates a better alternative to the Excel Data⇨ Validation command. It ensures that only positive values are entered into the range A1:C12.

```
Private Sub Worksheet_Change(ByVal Target As Excel.Range)
    Set ValRange = Range("A1:C12")
    Dim cell As Range
    DataOK = True
    For Each cell In Target
        If Union(cell, ValRange).Address = ValRange.Address
            Then
            If cell.Value < 0 Then
                cell.ClearContents
                DataOK = False
            End If
        End If
    Next cell
    If Not DataOK Then
        Msg = "Only positive values are acceptable in "
        Msg = Msg & ValRange.Address
        MsgBox Msg, vbCritical
    End If
End Sub
```

The subroutine starts by creating an object variable (ValRange) that represents the range to be validated. DataOK is a Boolean variable that is initially set to True. The For-Next loop examines each cell in Target (which is the cell or range that was changed). I use the Union function to determine whether the cell is contained in ValRange. If so, an If statement determines whether the cell's value is less than zero. If so, the contents are erased and DataOK is set to False.

When all the cells have been checked, another If statement checks the value of DataOK. If it was set to False, one or more cells in the changed range were negative. Therefore, a message is displayed to the user. You'll find that this routine works even when data is copied and pasted to the validation range.

Events Not Associated with Objects

The events that I discuss previously in this chapter are associated with either a workbook object or a worksheet object. In this section, I discuss two types of events that are not associated with objects: time and keypresses.

Because time and keypresses aren't associated with a particular object such as a workbook or a worksheet, you program these events in a normal VBA module (unlike the other events discussed in this chapter).

The OnTime event

The OnTime event occurs when a particular time of day occurs. The following example demonstrates how to program Excel so that it beeps and then displays a message at 3:00 p.m.:

```
Sub SetAlarm()
    Application.OnTime 0.625, "DisplayAlarm"
End Sub

Sub DisplayAlarm()
    Beep
    MsgBox "Wake up. It's time for your afternoon break!"
End Sub
```

In this example, I use the OnTime method of the Application object. This method takes two arguments: the time (0.625, or 3:00 p.m.) and the subroutine to execute when the time occurs (DisplayAlarm).

This subroutine is quite useful if you tend to get so wrapped up in your work that you forget about meetings and appointments. Just set an OnTime event to remind yourself.

Most people (this author included) find it difficult to think of time in terms of the Excel numbering system. Therefore, you may want to use the VBA TimeValue function to represent the time. TimeValue converts a string that looks like a time into a value that Excel can handle. The following statement shows an easier way to program an event for 3:00 p.m.:

```
Application.OnTime TimeValue("3:00:00 pm"), "DisplayAlarm"
```

If you want to schedule an event relative to the current time — for example, 20 minutes from now — you can use a statement like this:

```
Application.OnTime Now + TimeValue("00:20:00"), _
        "DisplayAlarm"
```

You can also use the OnTime method to schedule a subroutine on a particular day. You must make sure that your computer keeps running and that the workbook with the procedure is open. The following statement runs the DisplayAlarm procedure at 5:00 a.m. on December 25, 1997:

```
Application.OnTime DateValue("12/25/97 5:00 am"), _
        "DisplayAlarm"
```

The OnTime method has two additional arguments. If you plan to use this method, you should refer to the online help for complete details.

Keypress events

While you work, Excel constantly monitors what you type. Because of this, you can set up a keystroke or a key combination to execute a subroutine.

Here's an example that reassigns the PgDn and PgUp keys:

```
Sub Setup_OnKey()
    Application.OnKey "{PgDn}", "PgDn_Sub"
    Application.OnKey "{PgUp}", "PgUp_Sub"
End Sub

Sub PgDn_Sub()
    On Error Resume Next
    If TypeName(ActiveSheet) = "Worksheet" _
      Then ActiveCell.Offset(1, 0).Activate
End Sub

Sub PgUp_Sub()
    On Error Resume Next
    If TypeName(ActiveSheet) = "Worksheet" _
      Then ActiveCell.Offset(-1, 0).Activate
End Sub
```

After setting up the OnKey events in the Setup_OnKey procedure, pressing PgDn moves down one row. Pressing PgUp moves up one row.

Notice that the key codes are enclosed in brackets, not parentheses. For a complete list of keyboard codes, consult the online help. Search for *OnKey*.

In this example, I use On Error Resume Next to ignore any errors that are generated. For example, if the active cell is in the first row, trying to move up one row causes an error that can safely be ignored. Also, notice that the subroutines check to see which type of sheet is active. The routine reassigns the PgUp and PgDn keys only when a worksheet is the active sheet.

By executing the following routine, you cancel the OnKey events:

```
Sub Cancel_OnKey()
    Application.OnKey "{PgDn}"
    Application.OnKey "{PgUp}"
End Sub
```

Using an empty string as the second argument for the OnKey method does *not* cancel the OnKey event. Rather, it causes Excel to simply ignore the keystroke and do nothing. For example, the following statement tells Excel to ignore Alt+F4 (the percent sign represents the Alt key):

```
    Application.OnKey "%{F4}", ""
```

Although you can use the OnKey method to assign a shortcut key for executing a macro, you should use the Macro Options dialog box for this task. For more details, see "Assigning a shortcut key" in Chapter 5.

Chapter 12

Error-Handling Techniques

● ●

● ●

*W*hen working with VBA, you should be aware of two broad classes of errors: programming errors (aka *bugs*, which I cover in the next chapter), and *run-time* errors (which I cover right here). A well-written program handles errors like Fred Astaire dances: gracefully. Fortunately, VBA includes several tools to help you identify errors — and then handle them gracefully.

Types of Errors

If you've tried any of the examples in this book, you have probably encountered one or more error messages. Some of these errors result from bad VBA code. For example, you may spell a keyword incorrectly or type a statement with the wrong syntax. If you make such an error, you won't even be able to execute the procedure until you correct it.

This chapter does not deal with those types of errors. Instead, I discuss run-time errors — the errors that occur while Excel executes your VBA code. More specifically, this chapter covers

✔ Identifying errors

✔ Doing something about the errors that occur

✔ Recovering from errors

✔ Creating intentional errors (yes, sometimes an error can be a good thing)

The ultimate goal of error handling is to write code that avoids Excel's error messages as much as possible. In other words, you want to anticipate potential errors and deal with them before Excel has a chance to rear its ugly head with a (usually) less-than-informative error message.

An Erroneous Example

To get things started, I developed a short subroutine. Activate the VBE, insert a module, and enter the following subroutine:

```
Sub EnterSquareRoot()
'    Prompt for a value
     Num = InputBox("Enter a value")

'    Insert the square root
     ActiveCell.Value = Sqr(Num)
End Sub
```

As shown in Figure 12-1, this subroutine asks the user for a value. It then enters the square root of that value into the active cell.

You can execute this subroutine directly from the VBE by pressing F5. Or you may want to add a button to a worksheet (use the Forms toolbar to do this) and then attach the macro to the button (Excel prompts you for the macro to attach). Then you can run the procedure by simply clicking the button.

Error handling: Why bother?

Error handling involves trapping run-time errors and handling them in some way. If you write programs for only your own use, you might find error handling unnecessary. If a run-time error occurs, you simply deal with it. Because you wrote the code, you'll know if the error is serious or not.

Error handling becomes important if other people — especially inexperienced users — use your programs. For example, suppose you were running someone's macro and the macro suddenly stopped. Wouldn't you want to see a friendly message that tells you how to proceed, rather than a techno-babble error message that states *Object variable not set*?

Figure 12-1:
The
InputBox
function
displays a
dialog box
that asks
the user for
a value.

Not quite perfect

After entering this subroutine, try it out. It works pretty well, doesn't it? Now try entering a negative number when you are prompted for a value. Oops. Trying to calculate the square root of a negative number is illegal on this planet. Excel responds with the message shown in Figure 12-2, indicating that your procedure generated a run-time error. For now, just click the End button. Or click the Debug button, and Excel will suspend the macro so that you can use the debugging tools. I describe the debugging tools in Chapter 13.

Figure 12-2:
Excel
displays
this
message
when the
procedure
attempts to
calculate
the square
root of a
negative
number.

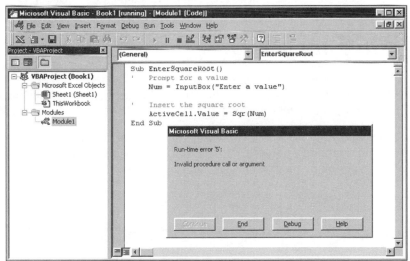

Most folks don't find the Excel error messages (for example, *Invalid proce-dure call or argument*) very helpful. To improve the subroutine, you need to anticipate this error and handle it more gracefully.

Here's a modified version of EnterSquareRoot:

```
Sub EnterSquareRoot2()
'   Prompt for a value
    Num = InputBox("Enter a value")

'   Make sure the number is nonnegative
    If Num < 0 Then
        MsgBox "You must enter a positive number."
        Exit Sub
    End If

'   Insert the square root
    ActiveCell.Value = Sqr(Num)
End Sub
```

An If statement checks the value contained in the Num variable. If Num is less than zero, the subroutine displays a message box containing a message that humans can actually understand. Then the subroutine ends with the Exit Sub statement, so the error never has a chance to occur.

Still not perfect

So the modified EnterSquareRoot subroutine is perfect, right? Not really. Try entering text instead of a value. Or try clicking the Cancel button. Both of these actions generate an error (*Type mismatch*).

The following modified code uses the IsNumeric function to make sure that Num contains a numeric value. If the user doesn't enter a number, the subroutine displays a message and then stops:

```
Sub EnterSquareRoot3()
'   Prompt for a value
    Num = InputBox("Enter a value")

'   Make sure Num is a number
    If Not IsNumeric(Num) Then
        MsgBox "You must enter a number."
```

```
        Exit Sub
    End If

'   Make sure the number is nonnegative
    If Num < 0 Then
        MsgBox "You must enter a positive number."
        Exit Sub
    End If

'   Insert the square root
    ActiveCell.Value = Sqr(Num)
End Sub
```

Is it perfect yet?

Now this subroutine is absolutely perfect, right? Not quite. Try running the subroutine while the active sheet is a Chart sheet. As shown in Figure 12-3, Excel displays another message that's as illuminating as the other error messages you've seen. This error occurs because there is no active cell on a Chart sheet.

Figure 12-3:
Running the EnterSquare-Root procedure when a chart is selected generates this error.

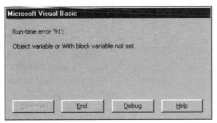

The following listing uses the TypeName function to make sure the selection is a range. If anything other than a range is selected, this subroutine displays a message and then exits:

```
Sub EnterSquareRoot4()
'   Make sure a worksheet is active
    If TypeName(Selection) <> "Range" Then
```

(continued)

(continued)

```
        MsgBox "Select a range first."
        Exit Sub
    End If

'   Prompt for a value
    Num = InputBox("Enter a value")

'   Make sure Num is a number
    If Not IsNumeric(Num) Then
        MsgBox "You must enter a number."
        Exit Sub
    End If

'   Make sure the number is nonnegative
    If Num < 0 Then
        MsgBox "You must enter a positive number."
        Exit Sub
    End If

'   Insert the square root
    ActiveCell.Value = Sqr(Num)
End Sub
```

Ready to give up on perfection?

By now, this subroutine simply *must* be perfect. Think again, pal. Protect the worksheet (using the <u>T</u>ools⇨<u>P</u>rotection⇨<u>P</u>rotect Sheet command), and then run the subroutine and see what happens. Yep, a protected worksheet generates yet another error. And I probably haven't thought of all the other errors that can occur. Keep reading for another way to deal with errors — even those you can't anticipate.

Another Way to Handle Errors

From the previous examples, you probably have a better idea of the types of errors that can occur. The question is: *How can you identify and handle every possible error?* The answer is: Often you can't. Fortunately, VBA provides another way to deal with errors.

The EnterSquareRoot subroutine, revisited

Examine the following subroutine. I modified the routine from the previous
section by adding an On Error statement to trap all errors and checking to
see whether the InputBox was cancelled.

```
Sub EnterSquareRoot5()
'    Set up error handling
     On Error GoTo BadEntry

'    Prompt for a value
     Num = InputBox("Enter a value")

'    Exit if cancelled
     If Num = "" Then Exit Sub

'    Insert the square root
     ActiveCell.Value = Sqr(Num)

     Exit Sub
BadEntry:
     Msg = "An error occurred." & VBCrLf
     Msg = Msg & "Make sure that a range is selected "
     Msg = Msg & "and you enter a nonnegative value."
     MsgBox Msg
End Sub
```

This routine traps any type of run-time error. After trapping a run-time error,
the revised EnterSquareRoot subroutine displays the message box shown in
Figure 12-4.

Figure 12-4:
Any error
in the
EnterSquare-
Root
subroutine
generates
this helpful
error
message.

The code uses the concatenation operator (&) to build the error message and assigns it to the Msg variable. VBCrLf is a built-in constant that represents a carriage return and a line feed and causes the text to skip to the next line.

About the On Error statement

Using an On Error statement in your VBA code causes Excel to bypass its built-in error handling and use your own error-handling code. In the previous example, a run-time error causes macro execution to jump to the statement labeled BadEntry. As a result, you avoid Excel's unfriendly error messages, and you can display your own (friendly, I hope) message to the user.

Notice that the example uses an Exit Sub statement right before the BadEntry label. This statement is necessary because you don't want to execute the error-handling code if an error does *not* occur.

On Error not working?

If an On Error statement doesn't seem to be working as advertised, you need to change one of your settings. Activate the VBE, choose the Tools⇨Options command, and click the General tab of the Options dialog box. Make sure the Break on All Errors setting is *not* checked. If this setting is checked, Excel essentially ignores any On Error statements. You'll normally want to keep this set to Break on Unhandled Errors.

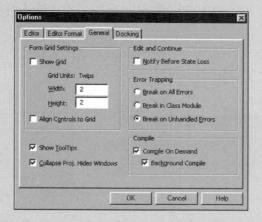

Handling Errors: The Details

You can use the On Error statement in three ways:

Syntax	What It Does
On Error GoTo *line*	After executing this statement, VBA resumes execution at the specified line. The value you enter for *line* can be a label or a line number. In either case, you must include a colon so that it is recognized as a label.
On Error Resume Next	After executing this statement, VBA simply ignores all errors and resumes execution with the next statement. I present an example of how this works in the next section.
On Error GoTo 0	After executing this statement, VBA resumes its normal error-checking behavior. Use this statement after you use one of the other On Error statements.

Resuming after an error

In some cases, you simply want your routine to end gracefully when an error occurs. For example, you may display a message describing the error and then exit the subroutine. (The EnterSquareRoot5 example uses this technique.) In other cases, you want to recover from the error, if possible.

To recover from an error, you must use a Resume statement. This clears the error condition and lets you continue execution at some location. You can use the Resume statement in three ways:

Syntax	What It Does
Resume	Execution resumes with the statement that caused the error. Use this if your error-handling code corrects the problem and it's okay to continue.
Resume Next	Execution resumes with the statement immediately following the statement that caused the error. This essentially ignores the error.
Resume *line*	Execution resumes at the line you specify, which must be a line label or a line number.

The following example uses a Resume statement after an error occurs:

```
Sub EnterSquareRoot6()
TryAgain:
'    Set up error handling
    On Error GoTo BadEntry

'    Prompt for a value
    Num = InputBox("Enter a value")
    If Num = "" Then Exit Sub

'    Insert the square root
    ActiveCell.Value = Sqr(Num)

    Exit Sub
BadEntry:
    Msg = "An error occurred. Try again?"
    Ans = MsgBox(Msg, vbYesNo)
    If Ans = vbYes Then Resume TryAgain
End Sub
```

This subroutine has another label, TryAgain. If an error occurs, execution continues at the BadEntry label, and the subroutine displays the message shown in Figure 12-5. If the user responds by clicking Yes, the Resume statement kicks in, and execution jumps back to the TryAgain label. If the user clicks No, the subroutine ends.

Figure 12-5:
If an error occurs, the user can decide whether to try again.

Remember that the Resume statement clears the error condition before continuing. To see what I mean, try substituting the following statement for the second-to-last statement in the preceding example:

```
If Ans = vbYes Then GoTo TryAgain
```

If you use GoTo instead of Resume, the subroutine doesn't work correctly. To demonstrate, enter a negative number. You'll get the error prompt. Click Yes to try again, and then enter *another* negative number. You'll find that this second error is not trapped because the original error condition was not cleared.

Error handling in a nutshell

To help you keep all this error-handling business straight, I've prepared a quick-and-dirty summary. An error-handling routine has the following characteristics:

- ✔ It begins immediately after the label specified in the On Error statement.
- ✔ It should be reached by your macro only if an error occurs. This means that you need to use a statement such as Exit Sub or Exit Function right before the label.
- ✔ If you choose not to abort the procedure when an error occurs, you must execute a Resume statement before returning to the main code.

Knowing when to ignore errors

In some cases, it's perfectly okay to ignore errors. That's when the On Error Resume Next statement comes into play.

The following example loops through each cell in the selection and converts the value to its square root. This procedure generates an error message if any cell in the selection contains a nonpositive number:

```
Sub SelectionSqrt()
    For Each cell In Selection
        cell.Value = Sqr(cell.Value)
    Next cell
End Sub
```

In this case, you may want to simply skip any cell that contains a value you can't convert to a square root. You *could* create all sorts of error-checking capabilities by using If statements. But you can devise a better (and simpler) solution by simply ignoring the errors that occur.

The following routine accomplishes this by using the On Error Resume Next statement:

```
Sub SelectionSqrt()
    On Error Resume Next
    For Each cell In Selection
        cell.Value = Sqr(cell.Value)
    Next cell
End Sub
```

In general, you can use an On Error Resume Next statement if you consider the errors inconsequential to your task.

Identifying specific errors

All errors are not created equally. Some are serious and some are less serious. Although you may ignore errors you consider inconsequential, you must deal with other, more serious errors. In some cases, you need to identify the specific error that occurred.

When an error occurs, Excel stores the error number in a variable named Err. You can get a description of the error by using the VBA Error function. For example, the following statement displays the error number and a description:

```
MsgBox Err & ": " & Error(Err)
```

Figure 12-6 shows an example of this. Keep in mind, however, that the Excel error messages are not always very useful.

Figure 12-6:
Displaying
an error
number
and a
description.

The following subroutine demonstrates how to determine which error occurred. In this case, you can safely ignore errors caused by trying to get the square root of a nonpositive number (that is, error 13). On the other hand, you need to inform the user if the worksheet is protected and the selection contains one or more locked cells. (Otherwise, the user may think the macro worked when it really didn't.) This event causes error 1005.

```
Sub SelectionSqrt()
    On Error GoTo ErrorHandler
    For Each cell In Selection
        cell.Value = Sqr(cell.Value)
    Next cell
    Exit Sub

ErrorHandler:
    Select Case Err
        Case 13 'Type mismatch
            Resume Next
        Case 1005 'Locked cell, protected sheet
            MsgBox "The cell is locked. Try again."
            Exit Sub
        Case Else
            ErrMsg= Error(Err)
            MsgBox "ERROR: " & ErrMsg
            Exit Sub
    End Select
End Sub
```

When a run-time error occurs, execution jumps to the ErrorHandler label. The Select Case structure tests for two common error numbers. If the error number is 13, execution resumes at the next statement (in other words, the error is ignored). But if the error number is 1005, the routine advises the user and then ends. The last case, a catch-all, traps all other errors and displays the actual error message.

An Intentional Error

Sometimes you can use an error to your advantage. For example, suppose you have a macro that works only if a particular workbook is open. How can you determine whether that workbook is open? Perhaps the best solution is to write a general-purpose function that accepts one argument (a workbook name) and returns True if the workbook is open and False if it's not.

Here's the function:

```
Function WorkbookOpen(book) As Boolean
    On Error GoTo NotOpen
    x = Workbooks(book).Name
    WorkbookOpen = True
    Exit Function
NotOpen:
    WorkbookOpen = False
End Function
```

This function takes advantage of the fact that Excel generates an error if you refer to a workbook that is not open. For example, the following statement generates an error if a workbook named MyBook.xls is not open:

```
x = Workbooks("MyBook.xls").Name
```

In the WorkbookOpen function, the On Error statement tells VBA to resume the macro at the NotOpen statement if an error occurs. Therefore, an error means the workbook is not open, and the function returns False. If the workbook is open, no error occurs and the function returns True.

The following example demonstrates how to use this function in a subroutine:

```
Sub Macro1()
    If Not WorkbookOpen("Prices.xls") Then
        MsgBox "Please open the Prices workbook first!"
        Exit Sub
    End If
'   Other code goes here
End Sub
```

The Macro1 subroutine calls the WorkbookOpen function and passes the workbook name (Prices.xls) as an argument. The WorkbookOpen function returns either True or False. Therefore, if the workbook is not open, the subroutine informs the user of that fact. If the workbook is open, the macro continues.

Error handling can be a tricky proposition — after all, many different errors can occur, and it's not always possible to anticipate them all. In general, you should trap errors and correct the situation before Excel intervenes, if possible. Writing effective error-trapping code requires a thorough knowledge of Excel, and a clear understanding of how the VBA error handling works. Subsequent chapters contain more examples of error handling.

Chapter 13
Bug Extermination Techniques

● ●

In This Chapter

▶ The definition of a bug, and why you should squash it

▶ Types of program bugs you may encounter

▶ Tips for identifying bugs

▶ Techniques for debugging your code

▶ Details on using the Excel built-in debugging tools

● ●

*I*f the word *bugs* conjures up an image of a cartoon rabbit, this chapter can set you straight. I cover the topic of programming bugs — how to identify them and how to wipe them off the face of your module.

Species of Bugs

Welcome to Entomology 101. The term *program bug*, as you probably know, refers to a problem with software. In other words, if software doesn't perform as expected, it has a bug. Fact is, all major software has bugs — lots of bugs. It has been said that software that doesn't contain bugs is probably so trivial that it's not worth using. Excel itself has hundreds (if not thousands) of bugs. Fortunately, the vast majority of these bugs are relatively obscure and appear in only very unusual circumstances.

When you write VBA programs, your code probably will have bugs — this is a fact of life and not necessarily a reflection of your programming ability. The bugs may fall into any of the following categories:

✔ **Logic flaws in your code.** You can often avoid these bugs by carefully thinking through the problem your program addresses.

✔ **Incorrect context bugs.** This type of bug surfaces when you attempt to do something at the wrong time. For example, you may try to write data to cells in the active sheet when the active sheet is not a worksheet.

✔ **Extreme-case bugs.** These bugs rear their ugly heads when you encounter data you didn't anticipate, such as very large or very small numbers.

✔ **Wrong data type bugs.** This type of bug occurs when you try to process data of the wrong type, such as attempting to take the square root of a text string.

✔ **Wrong version bugs.** This type of bug involves incompatibilities between different versions of Excel. For example, you may develop a worksheet using Excel 97, and then find out that the worksheet doesn't work with Excel 95. You can usually correct such problems by avoiding features specific to Excel 97 and by testing your work using both versions of Excel.

✔ **Beyond-your-control bugs.** These are the most frustrating. An example occurs when Microsoft upgrades Excel and makes a minor, undocumented change that causes your macro to bomb.

Debugging is the process of identifying and correcting bugs in your program. In the following section, I discuss some debugging techniques you can use. Developing debugging skills takes time, so don't be discouraged if this process is difficult at first.

It's important to understand the distinction between *bugs* and *syntax errors*. A syntax error is a language error. For example, you might misspell a keyword, omit the Next statement in a For-Next loop, or enter a set of mismatched parentheses. Before you can even execute the procedure, you must correct these syntax errors. A program bug is much subtler. You can execute the routine, but it doesn't perform as expected.

Identifying Bugs

Before you can do any debugging, you must determine whether a bug actually exists. You can tell that your macro contains a bug if it doesn't work the way it should. (Gee, this book is just filled with insight, isn't it?) Usually, but not always, you can easily discern this.

A bug often (but not always) becomes apparent when Excel displays a run-time error message. Figure 13-1 shows an example. Notice that this error message includes a button labeled Debug. More about this later in the section named "About the Debugger."

It's important to remember that bugs often appear when you least expect them. For example, just because your macro works fine with one set of data, you can't assume that it will work equally as well with all sets of data. The best debugging approach is thorough testing, under a variety of real-life conditions.

Figure 13-1:
An error
message
like this
usually
means your
VBA code
contains a
bug.

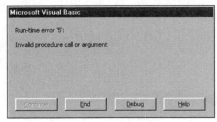

Debugging Techniques

In this section, I discuss the three most common methods for debugging Excel VBA code:

- ✔ Examining the code
- ✔ Inserting MsgBox functions at various locations in your code
- ✔ Using the Excel built-in debugging tools

Examining your code

Perhaps the most straightforward debugging technique is simply taking a close look at your code to see whether you can find the problem. If you're lucky, the error jumps right out and you can quickly correct it.

Using the MsgBox function

A common problem in many programs involves one or more variables that don't take on the values you expect. In such cases, a helpful debugging technique is to monitor the variable (or variables) while your code runs. You can do this by inserting temporary MsgBox functions in your routine. For example, if you have a variable named CellCount, you can insert the following statement:

```
MsgBox CellCount
```

When you execute the routine, the MsgBox function displays the value of CellCount.

It's often helpful to display the values of two or more variables in the message box. The following statement displays the current value of LoopIndex and CellCount, as shown in Figure 13-2:

```
MsgBox LoopIndex & " " & CellCount
```

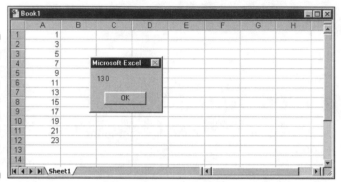

Figure 13-2:
Using a message box to display the values of two variables.

Notice that I combine the two variables with the concatenation operator (&) and insert a space character between them. Otherwise, the message box strings the two values together, making them look like a single value. You can also use the built-in constant, vbCrLf, in place of the space character. vbCrLf inserts a carriage return and line feed, which causes the text to display on a new line. The following statement displays three variables, each on a separate line:

```
MsgBox LoopIndex & vbCrLf & CellCount & vbCrLf & MyVal
```

This technique isn't limited to monitoring variables. You can use a message box to display all sorts of useful information while your code is running. For example, if your code loops through a series of sheets, you can use the following statement to display the name and type of the active sheet:

```
MsgBox ActiveSheet.Name & " " & TypeName(ActiveSheet)
```

I use MsgBox functions frequently when I debug my code. Just make sure that you remove them after you identify and correct the problem.

Using the Excel debugger

The Excel designers are intimately familiar with the concept of bugs. Consequently, Excel includes a set of debugging tools that can help you correct problems in your VBA code. The Excel debugger is the topic of the next section.

About the Debugger

In this section, I discuss the gory details of using the Excel debugging tools.

Setting breakpoints in your code

Earlier in this chapter, I discuss using MsgBox functions in your code to monitor the values of certain variables. Displaying a message box essentially halts your code in mid-execution, and clicking the OK button resumes execution.

Wouldn't it be nice if you could halt the execution of a routine, take a look at some variables, and then continue execution? Well, that's exactly what you can do by setting a breakpoint.

To set a breakpoint in your code, move the cursor to the line at which you want execution to stop, and press F9. Or just click in the gray margin to the left of the statement. As shown in Figure 13-3, Excel highlights the line to remind you that you set a breakpoint there and also inserts a large dot in the gray margin.

When you execute the procedure, Excel goes into *Break mode* when the line with the breakpoint is executed. In Break mode, the word [Break] is displayed in the VBE title bar. To get out of Break mode and continue execution, press F5 or click the Run Sub/UserForm button in the VBE toolbar. Refer to "Stepping through your code" (later in this chapter) to find out what else you can do in Break mode.

To remove a breakpoint, click the large dot in the gray margin, or move the cursor to the highlighted line and press F9. To remove all breakpoints in the module, press Ctrl+Shift+F9.

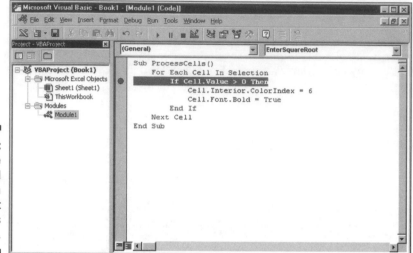

Figure 13-3: The highlighted line marks a breakpoint in this procedure.

So, what is Break mode? You can think of it as a state of suspended animation. Your VBA code stops running, and the current statement is highlighted in bright yellow. In Break mode, you can

✔ Type VBA statements in the Immediate window (see the next section for details)

✔ Step through your code one line at a time so that you can check various things while the program is paused

In Break mode, you can move the mouse pointer over a variable in your code, and the variable's value will be displayed in a small pop-up window. Figure 13-4 shows an example.

Figure 13-4: In Break mode, move the mouse pointer over a variable to display its current value.

Using the Immediate window

The Immediate window may or may not be visible in the VBE. You can view or hide the VBE's Immediate window at any time by pressing Ctrl+G.

In Break mode, the Immediate window (see Figure 13-5) is particularly useful for finding the current value of any variable in your program. For example, if you want to know the current value of a variable named CellCount, enter the following in the Immediate window, and press Enter:

```
Print CellCount
```

You can save a few milliseconds by using a question mark in place of the word *Print,* like this:

```
? CellCount
```

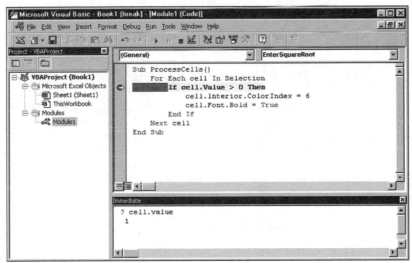

Figure 13-5:
The Immediate window in action.

The Immediate window lets you do other things besides checking the values of variables. For example, you can change the value of a variable, activate a different sheet, or even open a new workbook. Just make sure that the command you enter is a valid VBA statement.

You can also use the Immediate window when Excel is not in Break mode. I often use the Immediate window to test small code snippets before incorporating them into my procedures.

Stepping through your code

While in Break mode, you can also step through your code, line by line. You do this by using the following keystrokes:

Keystroke	What It Does
F8	Executes the next statement
F5	Resumes normal execution of the code
F9	Makes the current line a breakpoint, or removes the breakpoint if it already has one

Throughout this line-by-line execution of your code, you can activate the Immediate window at any time to check the status of your variables.

Using the Watch window

In some cases, you may want to know whether a certain variable or expression takes on a particular value. For example, suppose a procedure loops through 1000 cells. You notice that a problem occurs during the 900th iteration of the loop. Well, you *could* insert a breakpoint in the loop, but that would mean responding to 899 prompts before the code finally gets to the iteration you want to see (and that gets boring real fast). A more efficient solution involves setting a *watch expression*.

For example, you can create a watch expression that puts the procedure into Break mode whenever a certain variable takes on a specific value — for example, Counter=900. To create a watch expression, choose <u>D</u>ebug↔<u>A</u>dd Watch to display the Add Watch dialog box (see Figure 13-6).

The Add Watch dialog has three parts:

- **Expression:** Enter a valid VBA expression or a variable here. For example, *Counter=900* or just *Counter*.
- **Context:** Select the procedure and the module you want to watch. Note that you can select All procedures and All modules.
- **Watch Type:** Select the type of watch by clicking an option button. Your choice here depends on the expression you enter. The first choice, Watch Expression, does not cause a break; it simply displays the expression's value when a break occurs.

Figure 13-6:
The Add
Watch
dialog box
lets you
specify a
condition
that will
cause a
break.

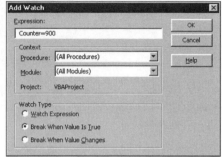

After setting up your watch expression(s), execute your procedure. Things run normally until your watch expression is satisfied (based on the Watch Type you specified). When that happens, Excel enters Break mode (unless the Watch Type is set to Watch Expression). From there, you can step through the code or use the Immediate pane to debug your code.

When you create a watch, VBE displays the Watches window, shown in Figure 13-7. This window displays the value of all watches that you've defined.

The best way to understand how this Watch business works is to use it and try various options. Before long, you'll realize what a useful tool it is.

Figure 13-7:
The
Watches
window
displays all
watches.

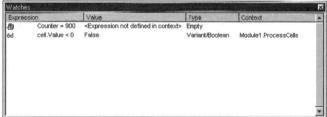

Bug Reduction Tips

I can't tell you how to completely eliminate bugs in your programs, but I can provide a few tips to help you keep those bugs to a minimum:

✓ **Use an Option Explicit statement at the beginning of your modules.**
This statement requires you to define the data type for every variable you use. This creates a bit more work, but you avoid the common error of misspelling a variable name. And, it has a nice side benefit: Your routines run faster.

✔ **Format your code with indentation.** Using indentations helps delineate different code segments. If your program has several nested For-Next loops, for example, consistent indentation helps you keep track of them all.

✔ **Be careful with the On Error Resume Next statement.** As I discuss in Chapter 12, this statement causes Excel to ignore any errors and continue executing the routine. In some cases, using this statement causes Excel to ignore errors that it shouldn't ignore. Your code may have bugs and not even realize it.

✔ **Use lots of comments.** Nothing is more frustrating than revisiting code you wrote six months ago and not having a clue as to how it works. By adding a few comments to describe your logic, you can save lots of time down the road.

✔ **Keep your subroutines and functions simple.** By writing your code in small modules, each of which has a single, well-defined purpose, you simplify the debugging process.

✔ **Use the macro recorder to help you identify properties and methods.** When I can't remember the name or the syntax of a property or a method, I often simply record a macro and look at the recorded code.

✔ **Understand Excel's debugger.** Although it can be a bit daunting at first, the Excel debugger is a useful tool. Invest some time and get to know it.

Debugging code is not one of my favorite activities (it ranks right up there with getting audited by the IRS), but it's a necessary evil that goes along with programming. As you gain more experience with VBA, you'll spend less time debugging, and you'll find that it gets easier to do.

Chapter 14

VBA Programming Examples

In This Chapter

▶ Short VBA examples that you may find helpful or instructive

▶ Some tips on how to make your VBA code run as fast as possible

My philosophy for finding out how to write Excel macros places heavy emphasis on examples. I find that a well-thought-out example often communicates a concept much better than a lengthy description of the underlying theory — and because you bought this book, you probably agree with me. This chapter presents several examples that demonstrate common VBA techniques.

I organize these examples into the following categories:

- Working with ranges
- Changing Excel settings
- Working with charts
- Speeding up your VBA code

Although you might be able to use some of the examples directly, in most cases, you need to adapt them to your own needs.

Working with Ranges

Most of your VBA programming will probably involve worksheet ranges. (For a refresher course on working with Range objects, refer to Chapter 8.) When you work with Range objects, keep the following points in mind:

- Your VBA doesn't need to select a range to work with it.
- If your code does select a range, its worksheet must be active.
- The macro recorder doesn't always generate the most efficient code. Often, you can create your macro by using the recorder, and then edit the code to make it more efficient.

✔ It's a good idea to use named ranges in your VBA code. For example, Range("Total") is better than Range("D45"). In the latter case, if you add a row above row 45, you need to modify the macro so that it uses the correct range address (D46).

✔ The macro recorder doesn't record keystrokes used to select a range. For example, if you press Ctrl+Shift+→ to select to the end of a row, Excel records the actual range selected.

✔ When running a macro that works on the current range selection, the user might select entire columns or rows. In most cases, you don't want to loop through every cell in the selection. Your macro should create a subset of the selection consisting of only the nonblank cells.

✔ Excel allows multiple selections. For example, you can select a range, press Ctrl, and select another range. You can test for this in your macro and take appropriate actions.

The examples in this section demonstrate these points.

To try any of the examples in this section, press Alt+F11 to activate the VBE. Then insert a VBA module and type the code. Make sure the workbook is set up properly. For example, if the example uses two sheets named Sheet1 and Sheet2, make sure the workbook has sheets with those names.

Copying a range

Copying a range is right up there in the Top Ten list of favorite Excel activities. When you turn on the macro recorder and copy a range from A1:A5 to B1:B5, you get this VBA macro:

```
Sub CopyRange()
    Range("A1:A5").Select
    Selection.Copy
    Range("B1").Select
    ActiveSheet.Paste
    Application.CutCopyMode = False
End Sub
```

This macro works fine, but you can copy a range more efficiently than this. You can produce the same result with the following one-line macro, which doesn't select any cells:

```
Sub CopyRange2()
    Range("A1:A5").Copy Range("B1")
End Sub
```

This subroutine takes advantage of the fact that the Copy method can use an argument that specifies the destination. This example also demonstrates that the macro recorder doesn't always generate the most efficient code.

Copying a variable-sized range

In many cases, you need to copy a range of cells but you don't know the exact row and column dimensions. For example, you might have a workbook that tracks weekly sales. The number of rows changes weekly as you add new data.

Figure 14-1 shows a range on a worksheet. This range consists of several rows, and the number of rows can change from day to day. Because you don't know the exact range address at any given time, writing a macro to copy the range can be challenging. Are you up for the challenge?

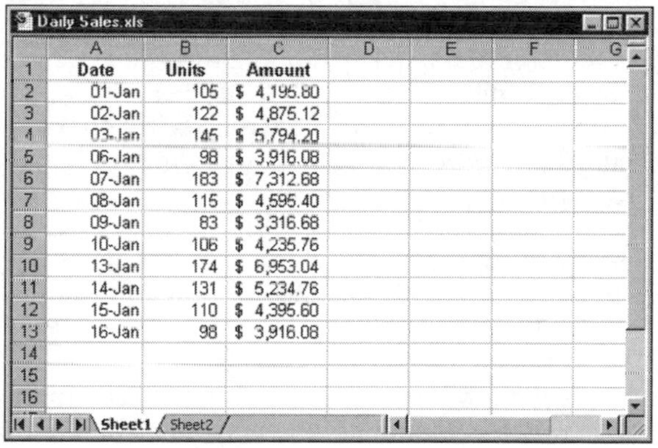

Figure 14-1: This range can consist of any number of rows.

The following macro demonstrates how to copy this range from Sheet1 to Sheet2 (beginning at cell A1). It uses the CurrentRegion property, which returns a Range object that corresponds to the block of cells around a particular cell (in this case, A1):

```
Sub CopyCurrentRegion()
    Range("A1").CurrentRegion.Copy
    Sheets("Sheet2").Select
    Range("A1").Select
    ActiveSheet.Paste
    Sheets("Sheet1").Select
    Application.CutCopyMode = False
End Sub
```

Using the CurrentRegion property is equivalent to choosing the Edit⇨Go To command, clicking the Special button, and selecting the Current Region option. To see how this works, record your actions while you issue that command. Generally, the CurrentRegion consists of a rectangular block of cells surrounded by one or more blank rows or columns.

You can make this macro even more efficient by not selecting the destination. The following macro takes advantage of the fact that the Copy method can use an argument for the destination range:

```
Sub CopyCurrentRegion2()
    Range("A1").CurrentRegion.Copy _
           Sheets("Sheet2").Range("A1")
    Application.CutCopyMode = False
End Sub
```

Selecting to the end of a row or column

You're probably in the habit of using key combinations such as Ctrl+Shift+→ and Ctrl+Shift+↓ to select a range that consists of the active cell to the end of a row or a column. You might be surprised to discover that the macro recorder doesn't record this type of keystroke combination. Instead, it records the address of the range you selected.

As I describe in the preceding section, you can use the CurrentRegion property to select an entire block of cells. But what if you want to select, say, one column from a block of cells?

Fortunately, VBA can accommodate this type of action. The following VBA subroutine selects the range beginning at the active cell and extending down to the cell just above the first blank cell in the column. After selecting the range, you can do whatever you want with it — copy it, move it, format it, and so on.

```
Sub SelectDown()
    Range(ActiveCell, ActiveCell.End(xlDown)).Select
End Sub
```

This example uses the End method of the Range object, which returns a Range object. The End method takes one argument, which can be any of the following constants:

✓ xlUp

✓ xlDown

🖊 xlToLeft

🖊 xlToRight

It's not necessary to select a range before you do something with it. The following subroutine applies bold formatting to a variable-sized range without selecting the range:

```
Sub MakeBold()
    Range(ActiveCell, ActiveCell.End(xlDown)).Font.Bold = _
        True
End Sub
```

Selecting a row or column

The following subroutine demonstrates how to select the column containing the active cell. It uses the EntireColumn property, which returns a Range object that consists of a column:

```
Sub SelectColumn()
    ActiveCell.EntireColumn.Select
End Sub
```

As you may expect, VBA also offers an EntireRow property, which returns a Range object that consists of a row.

Moving a range

You move a range by cutting it to the Clipboard and then pasting it in another area. If you record your actions while performing a move operation, the macro recorder generates code like the following:

```
Sub MoveRange()
    Range("A1:C6").Select
    Selection.Cut
    Range("A10").Select
    ActiveSheet.Paste
End Sub
```

As with the copying example earlier in this chapter, this is not the most efficient way to move a range of cells. In fact, you can move a range with a single VBA statement, as follows:

```
Sub MoveRange2()
    Range("A1:C6").Cut Range("A10")
End Sub
```

This macro takes advantage of the fact that the Cut method can use an argument that specifies the destination. Notice also that the range was not selected. The cell pointer remains in its original position.

Looping through a range efficiently

Many macros perform an operation on each cell in a range, or they might perform selected actions based on the content of each cell. These macros usually include a For-Next loop that processes each cell in the range.

The following example demonstrates how to loop through a range. In this case, the range is the current selection. An object variable named *Cell* refers to the cell being processed. Within the For-Next loop, the single statement evaluates the cell and changes its interior color if the cell contains a positive value.

```
Sub ProcessCells()
    For Each Cell In Selection
        If Cell.Value > 0 Then Cell.Interior.ColorIndex = 6
    Next Cell
End Sub
```

This example works, but what if the selection consists of an entire column or an entire row? (This is not uncommon because Excel lets you perform operations on entire columns or rows.) The macro seems to take forever because it loops through each cell in the selection — even the blank cells. To make the macro more efficient, you need a means for processing only the nonblank cells.

The following routine does just that by using the SpecialCells method. (Refer to the online help for specific details about its arguments.) This routine uses the Set keyword to create two new objects: the subset of the selection that consists of cells with constants, and the subset of the selection that consists of cells with formulas. The routine processes each of these subsets, with the net effect of skipping all blank cells. Pretty slick, eh?

```
Sub SkipBlanks()
'    Ignore errors
    On Error Resume Next

'    Process the constants
    Set ConstantCells = Selection.SpecialCells(xlConstants, _
        23)
    For Each cell In ConstantCells
        If cell.Value > 0 Then cell.Interior.ColorIndex = 6
    Next cell

'    Process the formulas
    Set FormulaCells = Selection.SpecialCells(xlFormulas, _
        23)
    For Each cell In FormulaCells
        If cell.Value > 0 Then cell.Interior.ColorIndex = 6
    Next cell
End Sub
```

The SkipBlanks subroutine works equally fast, regardless of what you select. For example, you can select the range, all columns in the range, all rows in the range, or even the entire worksheet. It's a vast improvement over the ProcessCells subroutine presented earlier in this section.

Notice that I use the following statement in this subroutine:

```
On Error Resume Next
```

This statement tells Excel to ignore any errors that occur and simply process the next statement (see Chapter 12 for a discussion of error handling). This is necessary because the SpecialCells method produces an error if no cells qualify.

Using the SpecialCells method is equivalent to choosing the Edit⇨Go To command, clicking the Special button, and selecting the Constants or Formulas option. To get a feel for how this works, record your actions while you issue that command and select various options.

Prompting for a cell value

As shown in Figure 14-2, you can use VBA's InputBox function to get a value from the user. Then you can insert that value into a cell. The following subroutine demonstrates how to ask the user for a value and place the value in cell A1 of the active worksheet, using only one statement:

```
Sub GetValue()
    Range("A1").Value = InputBox("Enter the value for cell _
            A1")
End Sub
```

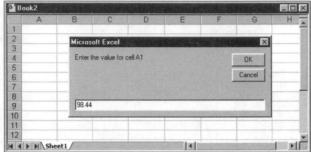

Figure 14-2:
Using
the VBA
InputBox
function to
get a value
from the
user.

If you try out this example, you'll find that clicking the Cancel button in the Input Box erases the current value in cell A1. The following subroutine demonstrates a better approach: using a variable (x) to store the value entered by the user. If the value is not empty (that is, the user didn't click Cancel), the value of x is placed into cell A1. Otherwise, nothing happens.

```
Sub GetValue2()
    x = InputBox("Enter the value for cell A1")
    If x <> "" Then Range("A1").Value = x
End Sub
```

Determining the type of selection

If you design your macro to work with a range selection, the macro must be able to determine whether a range is actually selected. If something other than a range is selected (such as a chart), the macro will probably bomb. The following subroutine uses the VBA TypeName function to identify the type of object that is currently selected:

```
Sub SelectionType()
    MsgBox TypeName(Selection)
End Sub
```

If a Range object is selected, the MsgBox displays *Range*. If your macro works only with ranges, you can use an If statement to ensure that a range is selected. Here's an example that beeps, displays a message, and exits the subroutine if the current selection is not a Range object:

```
Sub CheckSelection()
    If TypeName(Selection) <> "Range" Then
        Beep
        MsgBox "Select a range."
        Exit Sub
    End If
'   ... [Other statements go here]
End Sub
```

Identifying a multiple selection

As you know, Excel allows you to make a multiple selection by pressing Ctrl while you select objects or ranges. This can cause problems with some macros. For example, you can't copy a multiple selection that consists of nonadjacent ranges. (Try it, if you don't believe me.)

The following macro demonstrates how to determine whether the user made a multiple selection:

```
Sub MultipleSelection()
    If Selection.Areas.Count > 1 Then
        MsgBox "Multiple selections not allowed."
        Exit Sub
    End If
'   ... [Other statements go here]
End Sub
```

This example uses the Areas method, which returns a collection of all objects in the selection. The Count property returns the number of objects in the collection.

Changing Excel Settings

Some of the most useful macros are simple subroutines that change one or more of Excel's settings. For example, simply changing the recalculation mode from automatic to manual requires numerous steps. You can save yourself some keystrokes and menu choices (not to mention time) by creating a macro that automates this task.

This section presents two examples that show you how to change settings in Excel. You can apply the general principles demonstrated by these examples to other operations.

Changing Boolean settings

Like a light switch, a *Boolean* setting is either on or off. For example, you might want to create a macro that turns the row and column headings on and off. With the headings turned on, if you record your actions while you access the Options dialog box, Excel generates the following code:

```
ActiveWindow.DisplayHeadings = False
```

On the other hand, if the headings are turned off, Excel generates the following code:

```
ActiveWindow.DisplayHeadings = True
```

This may lead you to suspect that you need two macros: one to turn the headings on, and one to turn them off. Not true. The following subroutine uses the Not operator to effectively toggle the heading display from True to False and from False to True:

```
Sub ToggleHeadings()
    If TypeName(ActiveSheet) <> "Worksheet" Then Exit Sub
    ActiveWindow.DisplayHeadings = Not _
            ActiveWindow.DisplayHeadings
End Sub
```

The first statement ensures that the active sheet is a worksheet and that the subroutine ends if a worksheet is not active. Attempting to change the headings on a chart sheet causes an error. You can use this technique with any settings that have Boolean (True or False) values.

Changing Non-Boolean Settings

For non-Boolean settings, you can use a Select Case structure. This example toggles the calculation mode and displays a message indicating the current mode:

```
Sub ToggleCalcMode()
    Select Case Application.Calculation
        Case xlManual
            Application.Calculation = xlAutomatic
            MsgBox "Automatic Calculation Mode"
        Case xlAutomatic
            Application.Calculation = xlManual
            MsgBox "Manual Calculation Mode"
    End Select
End Sub
```

Working with Charts

Because charts are simply packed with different objects, manipulating charts with VBA can be quite confusing. To get a feel for this, turn on the macro recorder, create a chart, and perform some routine chart-editing tasks. You may be surprised by the amount of code Excel generates. After you understand the objects in a chart, however, you can create some useful macros.

To write macros that manipulate charts, you must understand some terminology. An embedded chart on a worksheet is a ChartObject object. You can activate a ChartObject much like you activate a sheet. The following statement activates the ChartObject named Chart 1:

```
ActiveSheet.ChartObjects("Chart 1").Activate
```

After you activate the chart, you can refer to it in your VBA code as the ActiveChart. If the chart is on a separate chart sheet, it becomes the active chart as soon as you activate that chart sheet.

If you've used previous versions of Excel, you may have noticed that Excel 97 works a bit differently with charts. With previous versions, clicking an embedded chart selected the Chart object. With Excel 97, clicking an embedded chart selects an object *inside* the Chart object. You can, however, still select the Chart object itself. To do so, press Ctrl while you click the embedded chart. You'll need to select the Chart object if you want to change the name of an embedded chart; after selecting the Chart object, use the Name box (the control to the left of the formula bar) to change the chart's name.

Modifying the chart type

A ChartObject object acts as a container for a Chart object. To modify a chart with VBA, you don't have to activate it. Rather, you can use the Chart method to return the chart contained in the ChartObject. This is confusing, I admit. The following two subroutines have the same effect — they change the chart named Chart 1 to an area chart. The first subroutine activates the chart first; the second one doesn't. The built-in constant xlArea represents an area chart.

```
Sub ModifyChart1()
    ActiveSheet.ChartObjects("Chart 1").Activate
    ActiveChart.Type = xlArea
    ActiveWindow.Visible = False
End Sub

Sub ModifyChart2()
    ActiveSheet.ChartObjects("Chart 1").Chart.Type = xlArea
End Sub
```

Looping through the ChartObjects collection

This example changes the chart type of every embedded chart on the active sheet. The subroutine uses a For-Next loop to cycle through each object in the ChartObjects collection and then accesses the Chart object in each and changes its Type property.

```
Sub ChartType()
    For Each cht In ActiveSheet.ChartObjects
        cht.Chart.Type = xlArea
    Next cht
End Sub
```

The following macro performs the same function, but works on all the chart sheets in the active workbook:

```
Sub ChartType2()
    For Each cht In ActiveWorkbook.Charts
        cht.Type = xlArea
    Next cht
End Sub
```

Modifying properties

The following example changes the legend font for all charts on the active
sheet. It uses a For-Next loop to process all ChartObject objects:

```
Sub LegendMod()
    For Each cht In ActiveSheet.ChartObjects
        With cht.Chart.Legend.Font
            .Name = "Arial"
            .FontStyle = "Bold"
            .Size = 12
        End With
    Next cht
End Sub
```

Note that the Font object is contained in the Legend object, which is contained in the Chart object, which is contained in the ChartObjects collection. Now do you understand why it's called an object hierarchy?

Applying chart formatting

This example applies several different types of formatting to the active
chart:

```
Sub ChartMods()
    ActiveChart.Type = xlArea
    ActiveChart.ChartArea.Font.Name = "Arial"
    ActiveChart.ChartArea.Font.FontStyle = "Regular"
    ActiveChart.ChartArea.Font.Size = 9
    ActiveChart.PlotArea.Interior.ColorIndex = xlNone
    ActiveChart.Axes(xlValue).TickLabels.Font.Bold = True
    ActiveChart.Axes(xlCategory).TickLabels.Font.Bold = _
            True
    ActiveChart.Legend.Position = xlBottom
End Sub
```

Before executing this macro, you must activate a chart. You activate an
embedded chart by clicking it. To activate a chart on a chart sheet, activate
the chart sheet.

To ensure that a chart is selected, you can add some error-handling code (see Chapter 12 for details about error handling). Here's the modified macro, which displays a message if a chart is not selected:

```
Sub ChartMods2()
    On Error GoTo ErrorHandler
    ActiveChart.Type = xlArea
    ActiveChart.ChartArea.Font.Name = "Arial"
    ActiveChart.ChartArea.Font.FontStyle = "Regular"
    ActiveChart.ChartArea.Font.Size = 9
    ActiveChart.PlotArea.Interior.ColorIndex = xlNone
    ActiveChart.Axes(xlValue).TickLabels.Font.Bold = True
    ActiveChart.Axes(xlCategory).TickLabels.Font.Bold = _
            True
    ActiveChart.Legend.Position = xlBottom
    Exit Sub
ErrorHandler:
    MsgBox "Select a chart first."
End Sub
```

I created this macro by recording my actions as I formatted a chart. Then I cleaned up the recorded code by removing irrelevant lines.

VBA Speed Tips

VBA is fast, but it's not always fast enough. (Computer programs are *never* fast enough.) This section presents some programming examples you can use to help speed up your macros.

Turning off screen updating

When executing a macro, you can watch everything that occurs in the macro. Although this can be instructive, after you get the macro working properly, it's often annoying and can slow things down considerably.

Fortunately, you can disable the screen updating that normally occurs when you execute a macro. To turn off screen updating, use the following statement:

```
Application.ScreenUpdating = False
```

If you want the user to see what's happening at any point during the macro, use the following statement to turn screen updating back on:

```
Application.ScreenUpdating = True
```

To demonstrate the difference in speed, execute this simple subroutine, which fills a range with numbers:

```
Sub FillRange()
    Number = 0
    For r = 1 To 50
        For c = 1 To 50
            Number = Number + 1
            Cells(r, c).Value = Number
        Next c
    Next r
End Sub
```

You'll see each value being entered into the cells. Now insert the following statement at the beginning of the subroutine and execute it again:

```
Application.ScreenUpdating = False
```

You'll find that the range is filled up *much* faster.

Turning off automatic calculation

If you have a worksheet with many complex formulas, you may find that you can speed things up considerably by setting the calculation mode to manual while your macro is executing. When the macro finishes, set the calculation mode back to automatic.

The following statement sets the Excel calculation mode to manual:

```
Application.Calculation = xlManual
```

Execute the next statement to set the calculation mode to automatic:

```
Application.Calculation = xlAutomatic
```

Eliminating those pesky alert messages

As you know, by using a macro, you cause Excel to perform a series of actions automatically. In many cases, you can start a macro and then go hang out at the water cooler while Excel does its thing. Some operations performed in Excel, however, display messages that require a response. For example, if your macro deletes a sheet, Excel displays the message shown in Figure 14-3. These types of messages mean you can't leave Excel unattended while it executes your macro.

Figure 14-3:
You can
instruct
Excel to not
display
these types
of alerts
while
running a
macro.

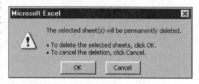

To avoid these alert messages, insert the following VBA statement in your macro:

```
Application.DisplayAlerts = False
```

When the subroutine ends, Excel automatically resets the DisplayAlerts property to True (its normal state).

Simplifying object references

As you probably already know, references to objects can become very lengthy. For example, a fully qualified reference to a Range object may look like this:

```
Workbooks("MyBook").Worksheets("Sheet1").Range("InterestRate")
```

If your macro frequently uses this range, you may want to create an object variable by using the Set command. For example, the following statement assigns this Range object to an object variable named *Rate*:

```
Set Rate = Workbooks("MyBook"). _
    Worksheets("Sheet1").Range("InterestRate")
```

After defining this object variable, you can use the variable *Rate* instead of the lengthy reference. For example, you can change the value of the cell named InterestRate by using a simple statement like this:

```
Rate.Value = .085
```

This is much easier to type (and understand) than the following statement:

```
Workbooks("MyBook").Worksheets("Sheet1"). _
    Range("InterestRate") = .085
```

In addition to simplifying your coding, using object variables also speeds up your macros considerably. After creating object variables, I've seen some macros execute twice as fast as before.

Declaring variable types

You don't usually have to worry about the *type* of data you assign to a variable. Excel handles all the details for you behind the scenes. For example, if you have a variable named *MyVar*, you can assign a number of any type to that variable. You can even assign a text string to it later in the procedure.

But if you want your procedures to execute as fast as possible, you should tell Excel what type of data will be assigned to each of your variables. This is known as *declaring* a variable's type. (Refer to Chapter 7 for complete details.)

In general, you should use the data type that requires the smallest number of bytes yet can still handle all the data assigned to it. When VBA works with data, execution speed depends on the number of bytes VBA has at its disposal. In other words, the fewer bytes used by data, the faster VBA can access and manipulate the data.

If you use an object variable (as described in the preceding section), you can declare the variable as a particular object type. Here's an example:

```
Dim Rate as Range
Set Rate = Workbooks("MyBook"). _
    Worksheets("Sheet1").Range("InterestRate")
```

To force yourself to declare all the variables you use, insert the following statement at the beginning of your module:

```
Option Explicit
```

If you use this statement, Excel displays an error message if it encounters a variable that hasn't been declared.

Part IV
Developing Custom Dialog Boxes

The 5th Wave
By Rich Tennant

Re·al Pro·gram·mers

©RICH TENNANT

Real Programmers either smoke two packs of cigarettes a day, or they don't smoke at all.

In this part . . .

The four chapters in this part show you how to develop custom dialog boxes (also known as UserForms). This VBA feature is fairly easy to use, after you get a few basic concepts under your belt. And, if you're like me, you may actually *enjoy* creating dialog boxes.

Chapter 15

Custom Dialog Box Alternatives

· ·

In This Chapter

▶ Saving time by using any of several alternatives to custom dialog boxes

▶ Using the InputBox and MsgBox functions to get information from the user

▶ Getting a filename and path from the user

▶ Writing VBA code to display any of the Excel built-in dialog boxes

· ·

You can't use Excel very long without being exposed to dialog boxes. They seem to pop up almost every time you select a command. Excel — like most Windows programs — uses dialog boxes to obtain information, clarify commands, and display messages. If you develop VBA macros, you can create your own dialog boxes that work just like the Excel built-in dialogs.

This chapter doesn't tell you anything about creating custom dialog boxes. Rather, it describes some techniques you can use in place of custom dialog boxes. (The next three chapters tell you everything you need to know to jazz up your applications with some award-winning dialogs.)

Why Create Dialog Boxes?

Some VBA macros you create behave the same every time you execute them. For example, you may develop a macro that enters a list of your employees into a worksheet range. This macro always produces the same result and requires no additional user input.

You might develop other macros, however, that behave differently under various circumstances, or that offer some options for the user. In such cases, the macro may benefit from a custom dialog box. A custom dialog box provides a simple means for getting information from the user. Your macro then uses that information to determine what it should do.

Do You Really Need a Custom Dialog Box?

Custom dialog boxes can be quite useful, but (as you'll soon see) creating them takes time. Before I cover the topic of creating custom dialog boxes, you need to know about some timesaving alternatives.

VBA lets you display four different types of dialog boxes that you can sometimes use in place of a custom dialog box. You can customize these built-in dialog boxes in some ways, but they certainly don't offer the options available in a custom dialog box. In some cases, however, they are just what the doctor ordered.

In this chapter, you learn about

- ✔ The MsgBox function
- ✔ The InputBox function
- ✔ The GetOpenFileName method
- ✔ The GetSaveAsFileName method

I also describe how to display the Excel built-in dialog boxes — the dialog boxes that Excel itself uses to get information from you.

The MsgBox Function

You're probably already familiar with the VBA MsgBox function — I use it quite a bit in the examples throughout this book. The MsgBox function provides a handy means for displaying information and getting simple input from users.

Here's a simplified version of the syntax for the MsgBox function:

```
MsgBox(prompt[,buttons][,title])
```

The MsgBox function accepts the following arguments:

Argument	What It Does
prompt	Supplies the text Excel displays in the message box
buttons	Specifies which buttons appear in the message box (optional)
title	Defines the text that appears in the message box's title bar (optional)

Displaying a simple message box

You can use the MsgBox function by itself or assign its result to a variable. If you use this function by itself, don't include parentheses around the arguments. The following example displays a message and does not return a result:

```
Sub MsgBoxDemo()
    MsgBox "Click OK to continue"
End Sub
```

Figure 15-1 shows how this message box looks.

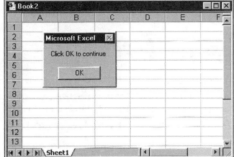

Getting a response from a message box

To get a response from a message box, you can assign the result of the MsgBox function to a variable. In the following code, I use some built-in constants (which I describe later in Table 15-1) that make it easy to work with the values returned by MsgBox:

```
Sub GetAnswer()
    Ans = MsgBox("Continue?", vbYesNo)
    Select Case Ans
        Case vbYes
'       ...[code if Ans is Yes]...
        Case vbNo
'       ...[code if Ans is No]...
    End Select
End Sub
```

When you execute this procedure, the Ans variable is assigned a value of either vbYes or vbNo — depending on which button the user clicks. The Select Case statement uses the value of Ans to determine which action the routine should perform.

You can also use the result of the MsgBox function without using a variable, as the following example demonstrates:

```
Sub GetAnswer()
    If MsgBox("Continue?", vbYesNo) = vbYes Then
'       ...[code if Yes is clicked]...
    Else
'       ...[code if Yes is not clicked]...
    End If
End Sub
```

Customizing message boxes

The flexibility of the *buttons* argument makes it easy to customize your message boxes. You can specify which buttons to display, whether an icon appears, and which button is the default. Table 15-1 lists the built-in constants you can use for the *buttons* argument. If you prefer, you can use the value instead of a constant.

Table 15-1	Constants Used in the MsgBox Function	
Constant	*Value*	*What It Does*
vbOKOnly	0	Displays OK button only
vbOKCancel	1	Displays OK and Cancel buttons
vbAbortRetryIgnore	2	Displays Abort, Retry, and Ignore buttons
vbYesNoCancel	3	Displays Yes, No, and Cancel buttons
vbYesNo	4	Displays Yes and No buttons
vbRetryCancel	5	Displays Retry and Cancel buttons
vbCritical	16	Displays Critical Message icon
vbQuestion	32	Displays Warning Query icon
vbExclamation	48	Displays Warning Message icon
vbInformation	64	Displays Information Message icon
vbDefaultButton1	0	First button is default

Constant	Value	What It Does
vbDefaultButton2	256	Second button is default
vbDefaultButton3	512	Third button is default
vbDefaultButton4	768	Fourth button is default
vbSystemModal	4096	System modal; all applications are suspended until the user responds to the message box

To use more than one of these constants as an argument, just connect them with a + operator. For example, to display a message box with Yes and No buttons and an exclamation icon, use the following expression as the second MsgBox argument:

```
vbYesNo + vbExclamation
```

Or, if you prefer to use values instead of constants, use a value of 52 (4 + 48).

The following example uses a combination of constants to display a message box with a Yes button and a No button (vbYesNo) as well as a question mark icon (vbQuestion). The constant vbDefaultButton2 designates the second button (the No button) as the default button — that is, the button Excel executes if the user presses Enter. For simplicity, I assign these constants to the Config variable and then use Config as the second argument in the MsgBox function:

```
Sub GetAnswer()
    Config = vbYesNo + vbQuestion + vbDefaultButton2
    Ans = MsgBox("Process the monthly report?", Config)
    If Ans = vbNo Then End
    If Ans = vbYes Then RunReport
End Sub
```

Figure 15-2 shows the message box Excel displays when you execute the GetAnswer subroutine. If the user clicks the No button (or presses Enter), the routine ends with no action. If the user clicks the Yes button, the routine executes the procedure named RunReport (which is not shown). Because I omitted the title argument in the MsgBox function, Excel uses the default title, *Microsoft Excel*.

Figure 15-2:
The buttons
argument of
the MsgBox
function
determines
what
appears
in the
message
box.

The following routine provides another example of using the MsgBox function:

```
Sub GetAnswer2()
    Msg = "Do you want to process the monthly report?"
    Msg = Msg & Chr(13) & Chr(13)
    Msg = Msg & "Processing the monthly report will take _
        approximately "
    Msg = Msg & "15 minutes. It will generate a 30-page _
        report for all "
    Msg = Msg & "sales offices for the current month."
    Title = "XYZ Marketing Company"
    Config = vbYesNo + vbQuestion
    Ans = MsgBox(Msg, Config, Title)
    If Ans = vbYes Then RunReport
    If Ans = vbNo Then End
End Sub
```

This example demonstrates an efficient way to specify a longer message in a message box. I use a variable (Msg) and the concatenation operator (&) to build the message in a series of statements. The Chr(13) function inserts a character that starts a new line. I also use the title argument to display a different title in the message box. Figure 15-3 shows the message box Excel displays when you execute this procedure.

Figure 15-3:
The dialog
box
displayed
by the
MsgBox
function.

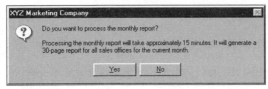

Previous examples have used constants (such as vbYes and vbNo) for the return value of a MsgBox function. Besides these two constants, there are a few others, listed in Table 15-2.

Table 15-2	Constants Used as Return Values for the MsgBox Function	
Constant	*Value*	*What It Means*
vbOK	1	User clicked OK
vbCancel	2	User clicked Cancel
vbAbort	3	User clicked Abort
vbRetry	4	User clicked Retry
vbIgnore	5	User clicked Ignore
vbYes	6	User clicked Yes
vbNo	7	User clicked No

The InputBox Function

The VBA InputBox function is useful for obtaining a single value from the user. This is a good alternative to developing a custom dialog box when you need to get only one value from a user.

InputBox syntax

Here's a simplified version of the syntax for the InputBox function:

```
InputBox(prompt[,title][,default])
```

The InputBox function accepts the following arguments:

Argument	What It Does
prompt	Supplies the text displayed in the input box
title	Specifies the text displayed in the input box's title bar (optional)
default	Defines the default value (optional)

An InputBox example

Here's an example showing how you can use the InputBox function:

```
TheName = InputBox("What is your name?","Greetings")
```

When you execute this VBA statement, Excel displays the dialog box shown in Figure 15-4. Notice that this example uses only the first two arguments and does not supply a default value. When the user enters a value and clicks OK, the routine assigns the value to the variable *TheName*.

Figure 15-4:
The
InputBox
function
displays
this
dialog box.

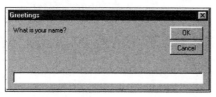

The following example uses the third argument and provides a default value. The default value is the username stored by Excel (that is, the UserName property of the Application object).

```
Sub GetName()
    DefName = Application.UserName
    TheName = InputBox("What is your name?", "Greetings", _
        DefName)
End Sub
```

VBA's InputBox function always returns a string, so you might need to convert the result to a value. You can convert a string to a value by using the Val function.

The following example uses the Val function to convert the user's entry to a value:

```
Sub GetName()
    Prompt = "How many sheets do you want to add?"
    Caption = "Tell me..."
    Default = 1
    NumSheets = Val(InputBox(Prompt, Caption, Default))
    If NumSheets > 0 then Sheets.Add Count:=NumSheets
End Sub
```

Figure 15-5 shows the dialog box this routine produces.

Figure 15-5:
Another
example of
using the
InputBox
function.

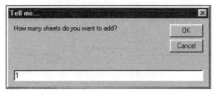

The GetOpenFilename Method

If your VBA procedure needs to get a filename from the user, you *could* use the InputBox function to ask the user to enter the filename. An InputBox usually isn't the best tool for this job, however, because most users find it difficult to remember paths and directory names, and typographic errors often result.

For a better solution to this problem, use the GetOpenFilename method of the Application object, which ensures that your application gets a valid filename (and its complete path).

The GetOpenFilename method displays the familiar Open dialog box (the same dialog box Excel displays when you choose File⇨Open). The GetOpenFilename method doesn't actually open the specified file. This method simply returns the filename selected by the user. Then you can write code to do whatever you want with the filename.

The syntax

The official syntax for this method is

```
object.GetOpenFilename([fileFilter],[filterIndex],[title],
[buttonText],[multiSelect])
```

The GetOpenFileName method takes the following arguments (all of them are optional):

Argument	What It Does
fileFilter	Determines the types of files that appear in the dialog box (for example, *.TXT). You can specify several different filters from which the user can choose.
filterIndex	Determines which of the file filters the dialog box displays by default.
title	Specifies the caption for the dialog box's title bar.
buttonText	Ignored (used only for the Macintosh version of Excel).
multiSelect	If True, the user can select multiple files.

An example

The fileFilter argument determines what appears in the dialog box's List files of type drop-down list. This argument consists of pairs of file filter strings followed by the wildcard file filter specification, with each part and each pair separated by commas. If omitted, this argument defaults to

```
User (*.*),*.*
```

Notice that this string consists of two parts:

```
User (*.*)
```

and

```
*.*
```

The first part of this string is the text displayed in the List files of type drop-down list. The second part determines which files the dialog box displays.

The following example pops up a dialog box that asks the user for a filename. The subroutine defines five file filters. Notice that I use the VBA line continuation sequence to set up the Filter variable; doing so helps simplify this rather complicated argument.

```
Sub GetImportFileName()
'    Set up list of file filters
     Filter = "Text Files (*.txt),*.txt," & _
              "Lotus Files (*.prn),*.prn," & _
              "Comma Separated Files (*.csv),*.csv," & _
              "ASCII Files (*.asc),*.asc," & _
              "All Files (*.*),*.*"

'    Display *.* by default
     FilterIndex = 5

'    Set the dialog box caption
     Title = "Select a File to Import"

'    Get the filename
     FileName = Application.GetOpenFilename(Filter, _
                    FilterIndex, Title)

'    Exit if dialog box canceled
     If FileName = False Then
         MsgBox "No file was selected."
         Exit Sub
     End If

'    Display full path and name of the file
     MsgBox "You selected " & FileName
End Sub
```

Figure 15-6 shows the dialog box Excel displays when you execute this procedure. In a real application, you would do something more meaningful with the filename. For example, you may want to open it using a statement such as

```
Workbooks.Open FileName
```

Figure 15-6:
The
GetOpen-
Filename
method
displays a
customizable
dialog box
and returns
the path
and name
of the
selected
file, but it
does not
open the
file.

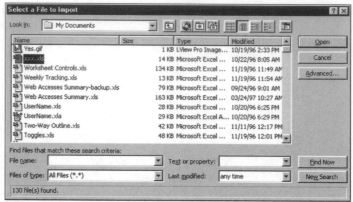

Selecting multiple files

If the MultiSelect argument for the GetOpenFilename method is True, the user can select multiple files in the dialog box. In this case, the GetOpenFilename method returns an array of filenames. Your code must loop through the array to identify each selected filename, as the following example demonstrates:

```
Sub GetImportFileName()
    Dim FileNames As Variant
    FileNames =
            Application.GetOpenFilename(MultiSelect:=True)

    If IsArray(FileNames) Then
'       Display full path and name of the files
        msg = "You selected:" & vbCrLf
        For i = 1 To UBound(FileNames)
            msg = msg & FileNames(i) & vbCrLf
        Next i
        MsgBox msg
    Else
'       Cancel button clicked
        MsgBox "No file was selected."
    End If
End Sub
```

Figure 15-7 shows the result of running this subroutine. The message box displays the filenames that were selected.

Figure 15-7:
Selecting
multiple
filenames
using the
GetOpen-
Filename
method.

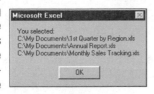

Notice that I used a named argument for the GetOpenFilename method. I set the MultiSelect argument to True. The other arguments are omitted, so they take on their default values. Using named arguments eliminates the need to specify arguments that aren't used.

The FileNames variable is defined as a variant data type. I use the IsArray function to determine whether FileName contains an array. If so, the code uses the VBA UBound function to determine the upper bound of the array and build a message that consists of each element of the array. If FileNames is not an array, the user clicked the Cancel button.

The GetSaveAsFilename Method

The Excel GetSaveAsFilename method works just like the GetOpenFilename method (but it displays the Excel Save As dialog box instead of its Open dialog box). The GetOpenFilename method gets a path and filename from the user but doesn't do anything with it.

The syntax for this method is

```
object.GetSaveAsFilename([initialFilename], [fileFilter], _
          [filterIndex], [title])
```

The GetSaveAsFilename method takes the following arguments (all of which are optional):

Argument	What It Does
initialFilename	Specifies a default filename that appears in the File name box.
fileFilter	Determines the types of files Excel displays in the dialog box (for example, *.TXT). You can specify several different filters from which the user can choose.
filterIndex	Determines which of the file filters Excel displays by default.
title	Defines a caption for the dialog box's title bar.

Displaying Excel's Built-In Dialog Boxes

You can write VBA code that executes the Excel menu commands. And, if a command leads to a dialog box, your code can make choices in the dialog box — although Excel doesn't actually display the dialog box.

For example, the following statement has the same effect as choosing the Edit⇨Go To command, specifying a range named InputRange, and clicking OK:

```
Application.Goto Reference:="InputRange"
```

When you execute this statement, the Go To dialog box does not appear. This is almost always what you want to happen; you don't want dialog boxes flashing across the screen while your macro executes.

In some cases, however, you may want to simply display one of Excel's many built-in dialog boxes and let the user make the choices in the dialog box. You can do this easily by using the Dialogs method of the Application object. Here's an example:

```
Result = Application.Dialogs(xlDialogFormulaGoto).Show
```

When executed, this statement displays the Go To dialog box, as shown in Figure 15-8. The user can specify a named range or enter a cell address. This dialog box works exactly as it does when you choose Edit⇨Go To (or press F5).

You may think that the value assigned to the Result variable is the range that the user selects in the Go To dialog box. Actually, the value assigned to Result is True if the user clicks OK and False if the user clicks Cancel or presses Escape.

Figure 15-8:
The Go To
dialog box,
displayed
by using
VBA code.

The preceding example uses the predefined constant xlDialogFormulaGoto. This constant determines which dialog box Excel displays.

You can get a list of dialog box constants by using the Object Browser:

1. In the VBE, press F2.

The Object Browser appears.

2. In the upper drop-down list, select Excel.

3. In the lower drop-down list type dialog.

4. Click the Search button (the button with the binoculars).

Figure 15-9 shows the Object Browser displaying a list of the dialog box constants.

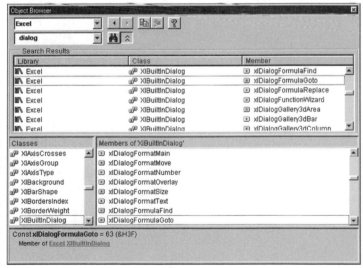

Figure 15-9:
Use the
Object
Browser to
get a list
of the
dialog box
constants.

If you try to display a built-in dialog box in an incorrect context, Excel displays an error message. For example, one of the dialog box constants is xlDialogAlignment. This dialog box is used to set the alignment of text in a cell. If you try to display this dialog box when something other than a range is selected, Excel displays an error message because that dialog box is appropriate only for worksheet cells.

Chapter 16

Custom Dialog Box Basics

● ●

In This Chapter

▶ Finding out when to use custom dialog boxes

▶ Understanding UserForm objects in the VBE

▶ Displaying a custom dialog box

▶ Creating a custom dialog box that works with a useful macro

● ●

*I*f your VBA macro needs to get only a few pieces of information from the user (for example, a Yes/No answer or a text string), the techniques I describe in Chapter 15 may do the job. But if you need to obtain more information, you must create a custom dialog box. In this chapter, you get the essential skills you need to create and work with custom dialog boxes.

 Compared to previous versions, Excel 97 uses a different method of creating custom dialog boxes. Dialog boxes created with previous versions of Excel will still work in Excel 97. Dialog boxes created using the new methods in Excel 97, however, will *not* work with older versions of Excel.

When a Custom Dialog Box Is Useful

The following macro changes the text in each cell in the selection to upper-case. It does this by using the VBA built-in UCase function.

```
Sub ChangeCase()
    If TypeName(Selection) <> "Range" Then Exit Sub
    For Each cell In Selection
        cell.Value = UCase(cell.Value)
    Next cell
End Sub
```

You can make this macro even more useful. For example, it would be nice if the macro could also change the cells to either lowercase or *proper* case (the first letter in each word is capitalized). One approach is to create two additional macros (one for lowercase and one for proper case). Another approach is to modify the macro — but you need some method of asking the user which type of change to make to the cells.

The solution is to display a dialog box like the one shown in Figure 16-1. You create this dialog box on a UserForm in the VBE, and you display it by using a VBA macro. Later in this chapter, I provide step-by-step instructions for creating this dialog box. But before I get into that, I need to set the stage with some introductory material.

Figure 16-1:
You can get information from the user by displaying a custom dialog box.

Creating Custom Dialog Boxes: An Overview

To create a custom dialog box, you usually take the following general steps:

1. **Determine exactly how the dialog box will be used and where it fits in your VBA macro.**

2. **Activate the VBE and insert a new UserForm object.**

   A UserForm object holds a single custom dialog box.

3. **Add controls to the dialog box.**

   Controls include items such as buttons, check boxes, and list boxes.

4. **Use the Properties window to modify the properties for the controls you add or for the dialog box itself.**

5. **Write event-handler subroutines for the controls (for example, a subroutine that executes when a dialog box button is clicked).**

   These subroutines are stored in the Code window for the UserForm object.

Is it a dialog box or a UserForm?

In Excel 97, the official name for a custom dialog box is a UserForm. But a UserForm is really an object that contains what's commonly known as a dialog box. This distinction isn't important, so I tend to use these terms interchangeably.

6. **Write a subroutine (stored in a VBA module) that displays the dialog box to the user.**

I provide more details in the following sections.

Working with UserForms

Each custom dialog box that you create is stored in its own UserForm object — one dialog box per UserForm. You create and access these UserForms in the Visual Basic Editor (VBE).

Inserting a new UserForm

To insert a UserForm object:

1. **Activate the VBE (press Alt+F11).**

2. **Select the workbook in the Project window.**

3. **Choose Insert⇨UserForm.**

   The VBE inserts a new UserForm object, which contains an empty dialog box.

Figure 16-2 shows a UserForm with an empty dialog box.

Adding controls to a dialog box

When you activate a UserForm object, the VBE displays the toolbox in a floating window. See Table 16-1. You use the tools in the toolbox to add controls to your custom dialog box. Just click the desired control in the toolbox, and then drag it into the dialog box to create the control. After you add a control, you can move and resize it using standard techniques.

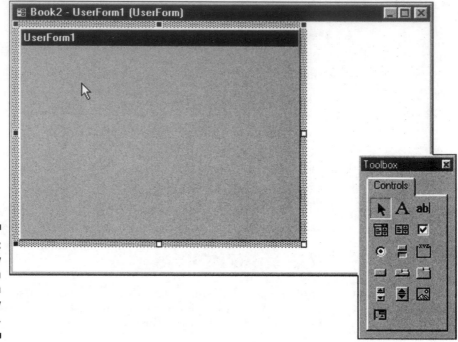

Figure 16-2:
A new
UserForm
object with
an empty
dialog box.

Table 16-1	Toolbox Controls
	Select Objects
A	Label
abl	TextBox
	ComboBox
	ListBox
	CheckBox
	OptionButton

🔲	ToggleButton	
🔲	Frame	
🔲	CommandButton	
🔲	TabStrip	
🔲	MultiPage	
🔲	ScrollBar	
🔲	SpinButton	
🔲	Image	
🔲	RefEdit	

Changing properties for a dialog box control

Every control you add to a dialog box has a number of properties that determine how it looks or behaves. You can change these properties with the Properties window, shown in Figure 16-3. This window appears when you press F4. To hide the Properties window, click the Close button in its title bar.

Properties for a control include its Name, Width, Height, Value, and Caption. Each control has its own set of properties (although many controls have many common properties). The next chapter tells you everything you need to know about working with dialog box controls.

If you select the dialog box itself (not a control on the dialog box), you can use the Properties window to adjust properties of the dialog box.

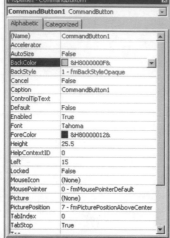

Figure 16-3:
Use the
Properties
window to
change the
properties
of a dialog
box control.

The UserForm Code window

Every UserForm object has a Code window that holds the VBA code (the event-handler subroutines) executed when the user works with the dialog box. To view the Code window, press F7. (The code window is empty until you add some subroutines.) Press Shift+F7 to return to the dialog box. (You find out more about the Code window in Chapter 17.)

Displaying a custom dialog box

The only way to display a custom dialog box is by using the UserForm's Show method in a VBA macro.

The macro that displays the dialog box must be in a VBA module — not in the Code window for the UserForm.

The following procedure displays the dialog box named UserForm1:

```
Sub ShowDialog()
    UserForm1.Show
'    Other statements can go here
End Sub
```

When Excel displays the dialog box, the macro halts until the user closes the dialog box (by clicking OK or Cancel). Then VBA executes any remaining statements in the procedure.

Using information from a custom dialog box

The VBE provides a name for each control you add to a dialog box. The control's name corresponds to its Name property. Use this name to refer to a particular control in your code. For example, if you add a CheckBox control to a dialog box, it is named CheckBox1 by default. The following statement makes this control appear with a check mark:

```
UserForm1.CheckBox1.Value = True
```

Your VBA code can also check various properties of the controls and take appropriate actions. The following statement executes a subroutine named PrintReport if the check box (named CheckBox1) is checked:

```
If UserForm1.CheckBox1.Value = True Then Call PrintReport
```

I discuss this topic in detail in the next chapter.

A Custom Dialog Box Example

In this section, I demonstrate how to develop a custom dialog box. The example is an enhanced version of the ChangeCase routine from the beginning of the chapter. Recall that the original version of this macro changes the text in the selected cells to uppercase. This modified version uses a custom dialog box to ask the user which type of case change to make: uppercase, lowercase, or proper case.

This dialog box needs to obtain one piece of information from the user: the type of change to make to the text. Because the user has three choices, your best bet is a custom dialog box with three OptionButton controls. The dialog box also needs two more buttons: an OK button and a Cancel button.

Creating the dialog box

Here are the steps required for creating the custom dialog box (start with an empty workbook):

1. **Press Alt+F11 to activate the VBE.**

2. **In the Project window, select the project that corresponds to the workbook you're using.**

3. Choose Insert⇨UserForm.

   The VBE inserts a new UserForm object with an empty dialog box.

4. Press F4 to display the Properties window.

5. In the Properties window, change the dialog box's Caption property to Change Case.

6. The dialog box is a bit too large, so you may want to click it and use the handles to make it smaller.

Adding the CommandButtons

In this section, I describe how to add two CommandButtons (OK and Cancel) to the dialog box:

1. **Make sure the toolbox is displayed. If it isn't, choose View⇨Toolbox.**

2. **In the toolbox, drag a CommandButton into the dialog box to create a button.**

   The button has a default name and caption: CommandButton1.

3. **If the Properties window isn't visible, press F4 to display it.**

4. **Make sure the CommandButton is selected. Then activate the Properties window and change the following properties:**

Property	Change To
Name	OKButton
Caption	OK
Default	True

5. **Add a second CommandButton object to the dialog box and change the following properties:**

Property	Change To
Name	CancelButton
Caption	Cancel
Cancel	True

6. **Adjust the size and position of the controls so that your dialog box looks something like Figure 16-4.**

Figure 16-4:
The custom
dialog box
with two
Command
Buttons.

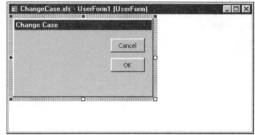

Adding the OptionButtons

In this section, you add three OptionButtons to the dialog box. Before adding the OptionButtons, you add a Frame object that will contain the OptionButtons. The Frame isn't necessary, but it makes the dialog box look better.

1. **In the toolbox, click the Frame tool and drag in the dialog box to create a frame to hold the options buttons.**

2. **Use the Properties window to change the frame's caption to Options.**

3. **In the Toolbox, click the OptionButton tool and drag in the dialog (within the Frame) to create an OptionButton control.**

4. **Select the OptionButton, and use the Properties window to change the following properties:**

Property	*Change To*
Name	OptionUpper
Caption	Upper case
Accelerator	U
Value	True

   Note: Setting the Value property to True makes this OptionButton the default option.

5. **Add another OptionButton, and use the Properties window to change the following properties:**

Property	*Change To*
Name	OptionLower
Caption	Lower case
Accelerator	L

6. **Add a third OptionButton and use the Properties window to change the following properties:**

Property	*Change To*
Name	OptionProper
Caption	Proper case
Accelerator	P

7. **Adjust the size and position of the OptionButtons so that your dialog box looks something like Figure 16-5.**

You may wonder why the OptionButtons have accelerator keys but the CommandButtons do not. Generally, OK and Cancel buttons never have accelerator keys because they can be accessed from the keyboard. Pressing Enter is equivalent to clicking OK; pressing Esc is equivalent to clicking Cancel.

Figure 16-5:
The custom dialog box, after adding three OptionButton controls inside a Frame control.

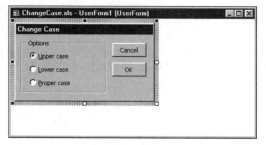

Adding event-handler subroutines

In this section, I describe how to add an event-handler subroutine for the Cancel button and the OK button:

1. **Double-click the Cancel button.**

   VBE activates the Code window for the UserForm and inserts an empty subroutine called:

   ```
   Private Sub CancelButton_Click()
   ```

   The subroutine named CancelButton_Click is executed when the Cancel button is clicked, but only when the dialog box is displayed. In other words, clicking the Cancel button when you're designing the dialog box won't execute the subroutine. Because the Cancel button's Cancel property is set to True, pressing Esc will also trigger the CancelButton_Click subroutine.

2. **Insert the following statement inside the subroutine (before the End Sub statement):**

```
Unload UserForm1
```

This statement simply unloads (closes) the UserForm when the Cancel button is clicked.

3. **Press Shift+F7 to return to the custom dialog box.**

4. **Double-click the OK button.**

   VBE activates the code window for the UserForm and inserts an empty subroutine called

```
Private Sub OKButton_Click()
```

This subroutine is executed when the OK button is clicked. Because this button has its Default property set to True, pressing Enter will also execute the OKButton_Click subroutine.

5. **Enter the following code inside the subroutine:**

```
Private Sub OKButton_Click()
'   Uppercase
    If OptionUpper Then
        For Each cell In Selection
            cell.Value = UCase(cell.Value)
        Next cell
    End If
'   Lowercase
    If OptionLower Then
        For Each cell In Selection
            cell.Value = LCase(cell.Value)
        Next cell
    End If
'   Proper case
    If OptionProper Then
        For Each cell In Selection
            cell.Value = _
                Application.WorksheetFunction.Proper _
                (cell.Value)
        Next cell
    End If
'   Unload the dialog box
    Unload UserForm1
End Sub
```

You may be tempted to use a Select Case construct here. That won't work, however, because the decision is not based on the value of a single variable.

The preceding code is an enhanced version of the original ChangeCase macro that I presented at the beginning of the chapter. The macro consists of three separate blocks of code. Only one block is executed, according to which OptionButton the user selects. The last statement unloads (closes) the dialog box.

Notice that VBA has a UCase function and an LCase function, but not a function to convert text to proper case. Therefore, I use Excel's PROPER worksheet function (preceded by Application.WorksheetFunction) to do the conversion.

Creating a macro to display the dialog box

The only thing missing is a way to display the dialog box. Follow these steps to create the subroutine that will make the dialog box appear:

1. **In the VBE window, choose Insert➪Module.**

   The VBE adds an empty VBA module (named Module1) to the project.

2. **Enter the following subroutine:**

```
Sub ChangeCase()
'    Exit if a range is not selected
     If TypeName(Selection) <> "Range" Then Exit Sub
'    Show the dialog box
     UserForm1.Show
End Sub
```

This subroutine is simple. It checks to make sure that a range is selected. If not, the subroutine ends with no action. If a range is selected, the dialog box is displayed (using the Show method). The user then interacts with the dialog box, and the code stored in the Code pane of the UserForm is executed.

Making the macro available

At this point, everything should be working properly. But you still need an easy way to execute the macro. In this section, you assign a shortcut key (Ctrl+Shift+C) that will execute the ChangeCase macro.

1. **Activate the Excel window (Alt+F11 is the express route).**

2. **Select Tools➪Macro➪Macros (or press Alt+F8).**

3. **In the Macros dialog box, select the ChangeCase macro.**

4. Click the Options button.

Excel displays its Macro Options dialog box.

5. Enter an uppercase *C* for the Shortcut key (see Figure 16-6).

6. Click OK.

7. Click Cancel when you return to the Macro dialog box.

Figure 16-6:
Assigning a
shortcut
key to
execute the
ChangeCase
macro.

After you perform this operation, pressing Ctrl+Shift+C will execute the ChangeCase macro, which displays the custom dialog box if a range is selected.

Testing the macro

Finally, you need to test the macro and dialog box to make sure they work properly:

1. Activate a worksheet (any worksheet in any workbook).

2. Select some cells that contain text.

3. Press Ctrl+Shift+C.

The custom dialog box appears. (Figure 16-7 shows how it should look.)

4. Make your choice and click OK.

If you did everything correctly, the macro makes the specified change to the text in the selected cells.

As long as the workbook is open, you can execute the macro from any other workbook. If you close the workbook that contains your macro, Ctrl+Shift+C will no longer have any function.

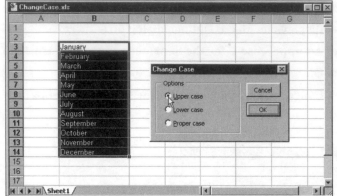

Figure 16-7:
The custom
dialog box
in action.

If the macro doesn't work properly, double-check the preceding steps to try to locate and correct the error. Don't be alarmed. Debugging is a normal part of developing macros.

Chapter 17
Using Dialog Box Controls

In This Chapter

▶ Understanding each type of dialog box control

▶ Changing the properties of each control

▶ Working with dialog box controls

A user responds to a dialog box by using the various controls (buttons, edit boxes, option buttons, and so on) that the dialog box contains. Your VBA code then makes use of these responses to determine which actions to take. You have lots of controls at your disposal, and this chapter tells you about them.

If you worked through the hands-on example in Chapter 16, you already have some experience with custom dialog box controls. This chapter fills in the gaps.

Excel 97 uses an entirely different way of working with dialog boxes. Dialog boxes that you created with a previous version of Excel will still work in Excel 97. Dialog boxes created by using the new methods in Excel 97, however, will *not* work with older versions of Excel.

Getting Started with Dialog Box Controls

In this section, I tell you how to add controls to a dialog box, give them meaningful names, and adjust some of their properties.

Before you can do any of these things, you must have a UserForm, which you get by choosing Insert⇨UserForm in the VBE. When you add a UserForm, make sure that the correct project is selected in the Project window.

Adding controls

Oddly enough, the VBE doesn't have menu commands that let you add controls to a dialog box. To add controls, you must use the toolbox, which I describe in the preceding chapter. Normally, the toolbox pops up automatically when you activate a UserForm in the VBE. If it doesn't, you can display the toolbox by choosing View➪Toolbox.

To add a control to the dialog box, click the toolbox tool that corresponds to the control you want to add. Then click in the dialog box and drag the control into position (an easier task to do than describe). Or you can simply drag a control from the toolbox to the UserForm to create a control with the default dimensions. Figure 17-1 shows a dialog box that contains a few controls.

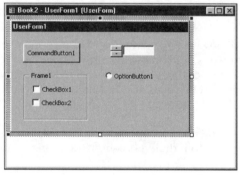

Figure 17-1: A dialog box with a few controls added.

A UserForm may contain vertical and horizontal grid lines. These help you align the controls you add. When you add or move a control, it *snaps* to the grid. If you don't like this feature, you can turn off the grids by choosing Tools➪Options in the VBE. In the Options dialog box, select the General tab and set your desired options in the Form Grid Settings section (see Figure 17-2).

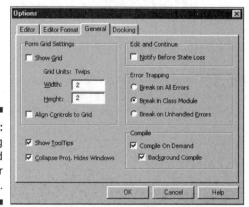

Figure 17-2: Changing the grid settings for UserForms.

Introducing control properties

Every control that you add to a dialox box has a set of properties that determine how the control looks and behaves. You can change a control's properties

- ✔ At design-time — when you're designing the dialog box. You do so manually, using the Properties box.
- ✔ At run-time — while the dialog box is displayed. You do so by writing VBA code.

When you add a control to a dialog box, you will almost always need to make some design-time adjustments to its properties. You make these changes in the Properties window. (To display the Properties window, press F4.) Figure 17-3 shows the Properties window, which displays properties for the object selected in the dialog box.

The only way to change a control's properties at run-time is to use VBA code.

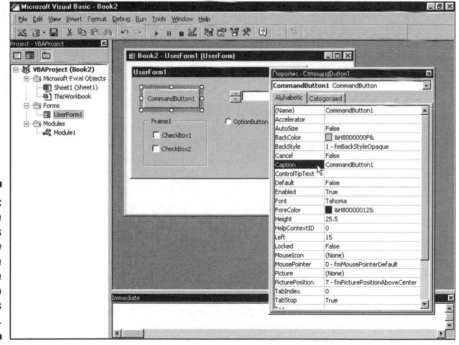

Figure 17-3:
Use the
Properties
window
to make
design-time
changes to
a control's
properties.

Each control has its own set of properties. All controls, however, share some common properties, such as Name, Width, and Value. Table 17-1 lists some common properties available for most controls:

Table 17-1	Common Control Properties
Property	*What It Does*
Accelerator	The letter underlined in the control's caption.
AutoSize	If True, the control resizes itself automatically based on the text in its caption.
BackColor	The background color of the control.
BackStyle	The style of the background (transparent or opaque).
Caption	The text that appears on the control.
Value	The control's value.
Left and Top	Values that determine the control's position.
Width and Height	Values that determine the controls width and height.
Visible	If False, the control is hidden.
Name	The name of the control. By default, a control's name is based on the control type. You can change the name to any valid name, but each control's name must be unique within the dialog box.
Picture	A graphics image to display. The image must be contained in a file — it can't be copied from the Clipboard.

When you select a control, the properties for that control appear in the Properties window. To change a property, just select it in the Properties window and make the change. Some properties give you some help. For example, if you need to change the MousePointer property, you'll find that the Properties window displays a drop-down list that contains all valid property values (see Figure 17-4).

Figure 17-4:
You can
change
some
properties
by selecting
from a
drop-down
list of valid
property
values.

Dialog Box Controls — the Details

In the following sections, I introduce you to each type of control you can use
in your custom dialog boxes, and discuss some of the more useful properties. I don't discuss every property for every control, because that would
take up too much space (and would be very boring).

The online help for controls and properties is thorough. To find complete
details for a particular property, select the property in the Properties
window and press F1. Figure 17-5 shows part of the online help for the
MousePointer property.

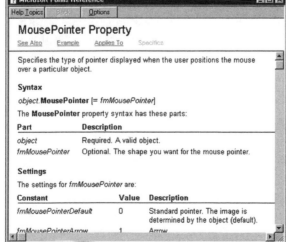

Figure 17-5:
The online
help system
provides
lots of
information
for every
property
and control.

CheckBox control

A CheckBox control is useful for getting a binary choice: yes or no, true or false, on or off, and so on. Figure 17-6 shows some examples of CheckBox controls.

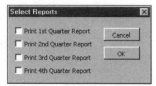

Figure 17-6: CheckBox controls.

The following is a description of the most-useful properties of a CheckBox control:

- ✔ **Accelerator:** A letter that lets the user change the value of the control by using the keyboard. For example, if the accelerator is A, pressing Alt+A changes the value of the CheckBox control.

- ✔ **LinkedCell:** The address of a worksheet cell that's linked to the CheckBox. The cell displays TRUE if the control is checked or FALSE if the control is not checked.

- ✔ **Value:** If True, the CheckBox has a check mark. If False, it does not have a check mark.

ComboBox control

A ComboBox control is similar to a ListBox control. A ComboBox, however, is a drop-down box and displays only one item at a time. Another difference is that the user may be allowed to enter a value that does not appear in the list of items.

Figure 17-7 shows a few ComboBox controls.

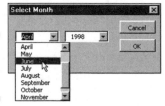

Figure 17-7: ComboBox controls.

The following is a description of the most-useful properties of a ComboBox control:

- ✔ **BoundColumn:** If the list contains multiple columns, this property determines which column contains the returned value.
- ✔ **ColumnCount:** The number of columns in the list.
- ✔ **ListRows:** The number of items to display when the list drops down.
- ✔ **ListStyle:** Determines the appearance of the list items.
- ✔ **Style:** Determines whether the control acts like a drop-down list or a combo box. A drop-down list doesn't allow the user to enter a new value.
- ✔ **Value:** The text displayed in the ComboBox.

CommandButton control

A CommandButton is simply a clickable button. It is of no use unless you provide an event-handler subroutine to execute when the button is clicked. Figure 17-8 shows a dialog box with a few CommandButtons. One of these buttons features a picture.

Figure 17-8:
Command-
Button
controls.

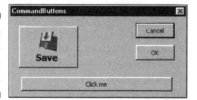

When a CommandButton is clicked, it executes a macro with a name that consists of the CommandButton's name, an underscore, and the word *Click*. For example, if a command button is named MyButton, clicking on it executes the macro named MyButton_Click. This macro is stored in the Code window for the UserForm.

Frame control

A Frame control is used to enclose other controls. You do so either for aesthetic purposes or to logically group a set of controls. A frame is particularly useful when the dialog box contains more than one set of OptionButton controls (see "OptionButton control," later in this chapter).

Image control

An Image control is used to display an image in a file. You may want to use an Image control to display your company's logo in a dialog box. Figure 17-9 shows a dialog box with a few Image controls.

Figure 17-9: Image controls.

The following is a description of the most-useful properties of an Image control:

- ✔ **Picture:** The graphics file that is displayed.
- ✔ **PictureSizeMode:** Determines how the picture is displayed if the control size does not match the image size.

The graphics image is stored in the workbook. That way, if you distribute your workbook to someone else, you don't have to include a copy of the graphics file.

Some graphics files are very large, and using such images can make your workbook increase dramatically in size. For best results, use a file that's as small as possible.

Label control

A Label control simply displays text in your dialog box. Figure 17-10 shows a few Label controls. As you can see, you have a great deal of influence over the formatting of a Label control.

Figure 17-10:
Label
controls.

ListBox control

The ListBox control presents a list of items, and the user can select an item (or multiple items). Figure 17-11 shows a dialog box with several ListBox controls.

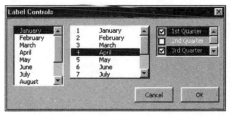

Figure 17-11:
ListBox
controls
on a
worksheet.

ListBox controls are flexible. For example, you can specify a worksheet range that holds the ListBox items, and this range can consist of multiple columns. Or you can fill the ListBox with items by using VBA.

The following is a description of the most-useful properties of a ListBox control:

- **BoundColumn:** If the list contains multiple columns, this property determines which column contains the returned value.
- **ColumnCount:** The number of columns in the list.
- **IntegralHeight:** This is True if the height of the list box adjusts automatically to display full lines of text when the list is scrolled vertically. If False, the list box may display partial lines of text when it is scrolled vertically.
- **LinkedCell:** A worksheet cell that displays the selected item.
- **ListFillRange:** A worksheet range that contains the list items.
- **ListStyle:** Determines the appearance of the list items.

✓ **MultiSelect:** Determines whether the user can select multiple items from the list.

✓ **Value:** The text of the selected item in the ListBox.

If the ListBox has its MultiSelect property set to True, you cannot specify a LinkedCell; you need to write a macro to determine which items are selected. Chapter 18 demonstrates how to do so.

MultiPage control

A MultiPage control lets you create tabbed dialog boxes, like the one that appears when you choose the Tools⇨Options command. Figure 17-12 shows an example of a custom dialog box that uses a MultiPage control. This particular control has three pages, or tabs.

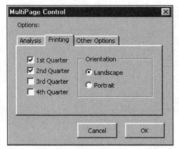

Figure 17-12:
This dialog box uses a MultiPage control.

The following is a description of the most-useful properties of a MultiPage control:

✓ **Style:** Determines the appearance of the control. The tabs can appear normally (on the top), on the left, as buttons, or hidden (no tabs).

✓ **Value:** Determines which page, or tab, is displayed. A Value of 0 displays the first page, a Value of 1 displays the second page, and so on.

By default, a MultiPage control has two pages. To add additional pages, right-click a tab and select New Page from the shortcut menu.

OptionButton control

OptionButtons are useful when the user needs to select from a small number of items. OptionButtons are always used in groups of at least two. Figure 17-13 shows two sets of OptionButtons. One set uses graphics images (set with the Picture property).

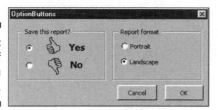

Figure 17-13:
Two sets of
option
buttons.

The following is a description of the most-useful properties of an
OptionButton control:

- ✓ **Accelerator:** A letter that lets the user select the option by using the
  keyboard. For example, if the accelerator for an option button is C, then
  pressing Alt+C selects the control.

- ✓ **GroupName:** A name that identifies an option button as being associated with other option buttons with the same GroupName property.

- ✓ **LinkedCell:** The worksheet cell that's linked to the option button. The
  cell displays TRUE if the control is selected or FALSE if the control is
  not selected.

- ✓ **Value:** If True, the OptionButton is selected. If False, the OptionButton
  is not selected.

If your dialog box contains more than one set of OptionButtons, you *must*
change the GroupName property for all OptionButtons in a particular set.
Otherwise, all OptionButtons become part of the same set. Alternatively,
you can enclose the OptionButtons in a Frame control, which automatically
groups the OptionButtons contained in the frame.

RefEdit control

The RefEdit control is used when you need to let the user select a range in a
worksheet. Figure 17-14 shows a custom dialog box with two RefEdit
controls. Its Value property holds the address of the selected range.

Figure 17-14:
This dialog
box has two
RefEdit
controls.

ScrollBar control

The ScrollBar control is similar to a SpinButton control. The difference is that the user can drag the ScrollBar's button to change the control's value in larger increments.

The following is a description of the most-useful properties of a ScrollBar control:

- ✔ **Value:** The current value of the control.
- ✔ **Min:** The minimum value for the control.
- ✔ **Max:** The maximum value for the control.
- ✔ **LinkedCell:** The worksheet cell that displays the value of the control.
- ✔ **SmallChange:** The amount that the control's value is changed by a click.
- ✔ **LargeChange:** The amount that the control's value is changed by clicking on either side of the button.

The ScrollBar control is most useful for selecting a value that extends across a wide range of possible values.

SpinButton control

The SpinButton control lets the user select a value by clicking the control, which has two arrows (one to increase the value and the other to decrease the value). Figure 17-15 shows a dialog box that uses several SpinButton controls. Each control is linked to the TextBox control to the right (by using VBA subroutines).

Figure 17-15:
SpinButton
controls.

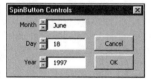

The following is a description of the most-useful properties of a SpinButton control:

- ✔ **Value:** The current value of the control.
- ✔ **Min:** The minimum value of the control.
- ✔ **Max:** The maximum value of the control.

✔ **LinkedCell:** The worksheet cell that displays the value of the control.

✔ **SmallChange:** The amount that the control's value is changed by a click. Usually, this property is set to 1, but you can make it any value.

If you use a linked cell for a SpinButton, you need to understand that the worksheet is recalculated every time the value of the control is changed. Therefore, if the user changes the value from 0 to 12, the worksheet is calculated 12 times. If your worksheet takes a long time to calculate, you may want to avoid using a linked cell to store the value.

TabStrip control

A TabStrip control is similar to a MultiPage control, but it's not as easy to use. In fact, I'm not sure why this control is even included. You can pretty much ignore it and use the MultiPage control instead.

TextBox control

A TextBox control lets the user input text.

The following is a description of the most-useful properties of a TextBox control:

✔ **AutoSize:** Determines whether the control adjusts its size automatically, depending on the amount of text.

✔ **IntegralHeight:** If True, the height of the TextBox adjusts automatically to display full lines of text when the list is scrolled vertically. If False, the list box may display partial lines of text when it is scrolled vertically.

✔ **MaxLength:** The maximum number of characters allowed in the TextBox. If 0, the number of characters is unlimited.

✔ **MultiLine:** If True, the TextBox can display more than one line of text.

✔ **TextAlign:** Determines how the text is aligned in the TextBox.

✔ **WordWrap:** Determines whether the control allows word wrap.

✔ **ScrollBars:** Determines the type of scroll bars for the control: horizontal, vertical, both, or none.

ToggleButton control

A ToggleButton control has two states: on or off. Clicking on the button toggles between these two states, and the button changes its appearance. Its value is either True (pressed) or False (not pressed). You can sometimes use a toggle button in place of a CheckBox control. Figure 17-16 shows a dialog box with some ToggleButton controls.

Figure 17-16:
This dialog box has ToggleButton controls.

Working with Dialog Box Controls

In this section, I discuss how to work with dialog box controls in a UserForm object.

Moving and resizing controls

After you place a control in a dialog box, you can move it and resize it by using standard mouse techniques. Or for precise control, you can use the Properties window to enter a value for the control's Height, Width, Left, or Top property.

You can select multiple controls by Ctrl-clicking the controls. Or you can click and drag to "lasso" a group of controls. When multiple controls are selected, the Properties window displays only the properties common to all selected controls.

A control can hide another control; in other words, you can stack one control on top of another. Usually, doing so is a bad idea. Unless you have a good reason for doing so, make sure that you do not overlap controls.

Aligning and spacing controls

The Format menu in the VBE window provides several commands to help you precisely align and space the controls in a dialog box. Before you use these commands, select the controls you want to work with. These commands work just as you would expect, so I don't explain them here. Figure 17-17 shows a dialog box with several CommandButton controls about to be aligned.

Figure 17-17:
Using the
Format➪
Align
command
to change
the
alignment
of dialog
box
controls.

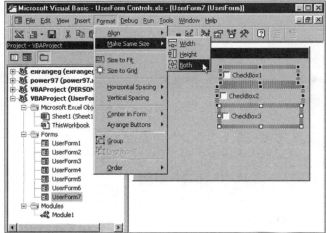

When you select multiple controls, the last control you select appears with white handles rather than the normal black handles. The control with the white handles is used as the basis for aligning or resizing the other selected controls when you use the Format menu.

Accommodating keyboard users

Many users prefer to navigate through a dialog box by using the keyboard: Pressing Tab and Shift+Tab cycles through the controls, while pressing a hot key instantly activates a particular control.

To make sure that your dialog box works properly for keyboard users, you must be mindful of two issues:

- ✔ Tab order
- ✔ Accelerator keys

Changing the tab order

The tab order determines the order in which the controls are activated when the user presses Tab or Shift+Tab. It also determines which control has the initial *focus* — that is, which control is the active control when the dialog box first appears. For example, if a user is entering text into a TextBox, the TextBox has the focus. If the user clicks an OptionButton, the OptionButton has the focus. The first control in the tab order has the focus when Excel displays a dialog box.

To set the tab order of your controls, choose View➪Tab Order. You can also right-click the dialog box and choose Tab Order from the shortcut menu. In either case, Excel displays the Tab Order dialog box shown in Figure 17-18.

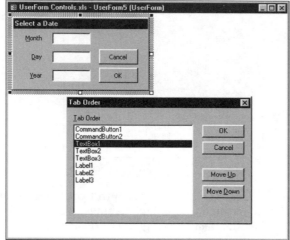

Figure 17-18:
The Tab
Order
dialog box.

The Tab Order dialog box lists all the controls in the dialog box. The tab order in the dialog box corresponds to the order of the items in the list. To move a control, select it and then click the arrow buttons up or down. You can choose more than one control (click while pressing Shift or Ctrl), and move them all at once.

Rather than use the Tab Order dialog box, you can set a control's position in the tab order by using the Properties window. The first control in the tab order has a TabIndex property of 0. If you want to remove a control from the tab order, set its TabStop property to False.

Some controls, such as Frame and MultiPage controls, act as containers for other controls. The controls inside a container control have their own tab order. To set the tab order for a group of OptionButtons inside a Frame control, select the Frame control before you choose the View➪Tab Order command.

Setting hot keys

Normally, you'll want to assign an accelerator key, or hot key, to dialog box controls. You do so by entering a letter for the Accelerator property in the Properties window. If a control doesn't have an Accelerator property (a TextBox, for example), you can still allow direct keyboard access to it by using a Label control. That is, assign an accelerator key to the Label, and put the Label directly before the TextBox in the tab order.

Figure 17-19 shows several TextBoxes. The Labels that describe the TextBoxes have accelerator keys, and each Label precedes its corresponding TextBox in the tab order. Pressing Alt+M, for example, activates the TextBox next to the Month Label.

Figure 17-19:
Using Labels to provide direct access to controls that don't have accelerator keys.

Testing a dialog box

The VBE offers three ways for you to test a dialog box without calling it from a VBA procedure:

✔ Choose the <u>R</u>un➪Run Sub/UserForm command.

✔ Press F5.

✔ Click the Run Sub/UserForm button on the Standard toolbar.

When a dialog box is displayed in this test mode, you can try out the tab order and the accelerator keys.

Dialog Box Aesthetics

Dialog boxes can look good, bad, or somewhere in between. A good looking dialog box is easy on the eye, has nicely sized and aligned controls, and makes its function perfectly clear to the user. Bad looking dialog boxes confuse the user, have misaligned controls, and give the impression that the developer didn't have a plan (or a clue).

A good rule of thumb is to try to make your dialog boxes look like the Excel built-in dialog boxes. As you gain more experience with dialog box construction, you'll be able to duplicate almost all the features of the Excel dialog boxes.

The dialog box controls in previous versions of Excel provided little in the way of formatting options. With Excel 97, you have almost complete control over fonts and colors used in your dialog boxes. My advice? Don't go overboard with colors and fonts. In almost all cases, the default colors and fonts provide the most professional appearance.

Chapter 18

Dialog Box Techniques and Tricks

● ●

In This Chapter

▶ Using a custom dialog box in your application

▶ Creating a dialog box: a hands-on example

▶ More dialog box examples

● ●

The previous chapters show you how to insert a UserForm (which contains a custom dialog box), add controls to the dialog, and adjust some of the control's properties. These skills, however, won't do you much good unless you understand how to make use of custom dialogs in your VBA code. This chapter provides these missing details and presents some useful techniques and tricks in the process.

Using Dialog Boxes

When you use a custom dialog box in your application, you normally write VBA code that will do the following:

✔ Initialize the dialog box controls. This optional step involves clearing edit boxes and setting default options.

✔ Display the dialog box by using the Show method.

✔ Write event-handler subroutines for the various controls.

✔ Validate the information provided by the user (if the user did not cancel the dialog box). This step is optional.

✔ Take some action with the information provided by the user (if the information is valid).

An Example

In Chapter 16, I present a simple hands-on dialog box example. Here's another example that can help you understand how dialog boxes work.

This example demonstrates the five points I describe in the preceding section. You use a dialog box to get two pieces of information: a person's name and sex. The dialog box uses a TextB box control to get the name and three OptionButtons to get the sex (Male, Female, or Unknown). The information collected in the dialog box is then sent to the next blank row in a worksheet.

Creating the dialog box

Figure 18-1 shows the finished custom dialog box for this example. For best results, start with a new workbook with only one worksheet in it. Then follow these steps:

1. **Press Alt+F11 to activate the VBE.**

2. **In the Project window, select the (empty) workbook, and choose Insert➪UserForm.**

   An empty UserForm is added to the dialog box.

3. **Change the UserForm's Caption property to** Get Name and Sex **(if the Properties window isn't visible, press F4).**

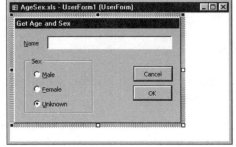

Figure 18-1:
This dialog box asks the user to enter a name and a sex.

This dialog box has eight controls:

✔ **A Label.** I modified the following properties for this control:

Property	Value
Accelerator	N
Caption	Name
TabIndex	0

✔ **A TextBox.** I modified the following properties for this control:

Property	Value
Name	TextName
TabIndex	1

✔ **A Frame object.** I modified the following properties for this control:

Property	Value
Caption	Sex
TabIndex	2

✔ **An OptionButton.** I modified the following properties for this control:

Property	Value
Accelerator	M
Caption	Male
Name	OptionMale
TabIndex	0

✔ **Another OptionButton.** I modified the following properties for this control:

Property	Value
Accelerator	F
Caption	Female
Name	OptionFemale
TabIndex	1

✔ **Another OptionButton.** I modified the following properties for this control:

Property	Value
Accelerator	U
Caption	Unknown
Name	OptionUnknown
TabIndex	2
Value	True

✔ **An OK button.** I modified the following properties for this button:

Property	Value
Caption	OK
Default	True
Name	OKButton
TabIndex	3

✔ **A Cancel button.** I modified the following properties for this button:

Property	Value
Caption	Cancel
Cancel	True
Name	CancelButton
TabIndex	4

If you're following along on your computer (and you should be), take a few minutes to create this dialog box using the preceding information. Make sure that you create the Frame object before adding the OptionButtons to it.

TIP

In some cases, you may find copying an existing control easier than creating a new one. To copy a control, press Ctrl while you drag the control.

Writing code to display the dialog box

Your next step is to develop some VBA code to display this dialog box:

1. In the VBE window, choose Insert⇨Module to insert a VBA module.

2. Enter the following subroutine:

```
Sub GetData()
    UserForm1.Show
End Sub
```

This short subroutine uses the Show method of an object (UserForm1) to display the dialog box.

Making the macro available

The next step makes executing this subroutine an easy task:

1. Activate Excel.

2. Right-click a toolbar, and select Forms from the shortcut menu.

Excel displays its Forms toolbar.

3. Use the Forms toolbar to add a button to the worksheet: Click the Button tool, and then drag in the worksheet to create the button.

The Assign Macro dialog box appears.

4. Assign the GetData macro to the button.

5. Edit the button's caption so that it reads Data Entry.

Trying it out

Click the Data Entry button on the worksheet, and the dialog box appears, as shown in Figure 18-2.

Enter some text into the edit box. Click OK or Cancel. You'll find that nothing happens — which is understandable because you haven't created any subroutines yet.

Click the Close button in the dialog box's title bar to get rid of the dialog box.

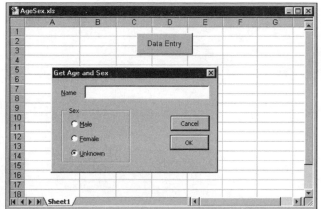

Figure 18-2:
Executing
the GetData
routine
displays the
dialog box.

Adding event-handler subroutines

In this section, I explain how to write the subroutines that will handle the events that occur when the dialog box is displayed:

1. **Press Alt+F11 to activate the VBE.**

2. **Make sure that the dialog box is displayed, and double-click the Cancel button.**

   The VBE activates the Code window for the UserForm and provides an empty subroutine named CancelButton_Click.

3. **Modify the subroutine as follows:**

   ```
   Private Sub CancelButton_Click()
       Unload UserForm1
   End Sub
   ```

   This subroutine, which is executed when the user clicks the Cancel button, simply unloads the dialog box.

4. **Press Shift+F7 to redisplay UserForm1.**

5. **Double-click the OK button and enter the following subroutine:**

   ```
   Private Sub OKButton_Click()
   '    Make sure Sheet1 is active
        Sheets("Sheet1").Activate

   '    Determine the next empty row
   NextRow = _
   ```

(continued)

(continued)

```
        Application.WorksheetFunction.
          CountA(Range("A:A")) + 1
'    Transfer the name
     Cells(NextRow, 1) = TextName.Text

'    Transfer the sex
     If OptionMale Then Cells(NextRow, 2) = "Male"
     If OptionFemale Then Cells(NextRow, 2) = "Female"
     If OptionUnknown Then Cells(NextRow, 2) = "Unknown"

'    Clear the controls for the next entry
     TextName.Text = ""
     OptionUnknown = True
     TextName.SetFocus
End Sub
```

6. Now activate Excel and run the subroutine again.

You'll find that the dialog box works just fine. Figure 18-3 shows how this looks in action.

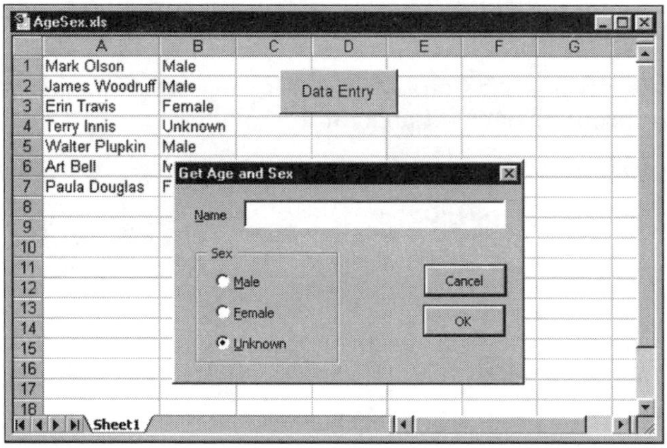

Figure 18-3:
Using the custom dialog box.

Here's how it works. First, the subroutine makes sure that the proper worksheet (Sheet1) is active. It then uses the Excel COUNTA function to determine the next blank cell in Column A. Next, the subroutine transfers the text from the TextBox to Column A. It then uses a series of If statements to determine which OptionButton was selected, and writes the appropriate text (Male, Female, or Unknown) to column B. Finally, the dialog box is reset to make it ready for the next entry. Notice that clicking OK doesn't close the dialog box. To end data entry, click the Cancel button.

Validating the data

Play around with this routine some more, and you'll find that the macro has a small problem: It doesn't ensure that the user actually enters a name into the TextBox. The following code —which is inserted in the OKButton_Click subroutine before the text is transferred to the worksheet— ensures that the user enters a name (well, at least some text) in the TextBox. If the TextBox is empty, a message appears and the routine stops.

```
'    Make sure a name is entered
    If TextName.Text = "" Then
        MsgBox "You must enter a name."
        Exit Sub
    End If
```

Now the dialog box works

After making all these modifications, you'll find that the dialog box works flawlessly. In real life, you'd probably need to collect more information than just name and sex. However, the same basic principles apply. You just have to deal with more dialog box controls.

More Dialog Box Examples

I could probably fill an entire book with interesting and useful tips for working with dialog boxes. Unfortunately, this book has a limited number of pages, so I'll wrap up the topic of custom dialog boxes with a few more examples.

A ListBox example

ListBoxes are useful controls, but working with them can be a bit tricky. Before displaying a dialog box that uses a ListBox, you need to fill the ListBox with items. Then, when the dialog box is closed, you need to determine which item(s) the user selected.

When dealing with list boxes, you need to know about the following properties and methods:

- **AddItem:** You use this method to add an item to a ListBox.
- **ListCount:** This property returns the number of items in the ListBox.

✔ **ListIndex:** This property returns the index number of the selected item or sets the item that's selected (single selections only). The first item has a ListIndex of 0 (not 1).

✔ **MultiSelect:** This property determines whether the user can select more than one item from the ListBox.

✔ **RemoveAllItems:** You use this method to remove all items from a ListBox.

✔ **Selected:** This property returns an array indicating selected items (applicable only when multiple selections are allowed).

✔ **Value:** This property returns the selected item in a ListBox.

Filling a list box

For best results, start with an empty workbook. The example in this section assumes the following:

✔ You've added a UserForm.

✔ The UserForm contains a ListBox control named *ListBox1*.

✔ The UserForm has a CommandButton named *OKButton* that has the following event-handler subroutine:

```
Private Sub OKButton_Click()
    Unload UserForm1
End Sub
```

The following procedure is stored in a VBA module. It uses the AddItem method to fill the ListBox with the names of the months. Then it displays the dialog box:

```
Sub ShowMonthNames()
'   Fill the list box
    With UserForm1.ListBox1
        .AddItem "January"
        .AddItem "February"
        .AddItem "March"
        .AddItem "April"
        .AddItem "May"
        .AddItem "June"
        .AddItem "July"
        .AddItem "August"
        .AddItem "September"
        .AddItem "October"
        .AddItem "November"
        .AddItem "December"
```

```
     End With

'    Select the first item
     UserForm1.ListBox1.ListIndex = 0

'    Show the dialog
     UserForm1.Show
End Sub
```

Determining the selected item

The preceding code merely displays a dialog box with a ListBox filled with month names. What's missing is a procedure to determine which item in the ListBox is selected.

Modify the OKButton_Click subroutine as follows:

```
Private Sub OKButton_Click()
     Msg - "You selected Item # "
     Msg = Msg & ListBox1.ListIndex
     Msg = Msg & vbCrLf
     Msg = Msg & ListBox1.Value
     MsgBox Msg
     Unload UserForm1
End Sub
```

This subroutine displays a message box with the selected item number and the selected item. Figure 18-4 shows how this looks.

The first item in a ListBox has a ListIndex of 0, not 1 (as you may expect). This is always the case, even if you use an Option Base 1 statement to change the default lower bound for arrays.

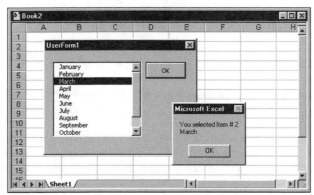

Figure 18-4:
Determining which item is selected.

Determining multiple selections

If your ListBox is set up so that the user can select more than one item, you'll find that the ListIndex and Value properties return only the *last* item selected. To determine all selected items, you need to use the Selected property, which contains an array.

To allow multiple selections in a ListBox, set the MultiSelect property to either 1 or 2. You can do so at design time by using the Properties window or at run time by using a VBA statement such as

```
UserForm1.ListBox1.MultiSelect = 1
```

The following subroutine displays a message box that lists all selected items in a ListBox. Figure 18-5 shows an example.

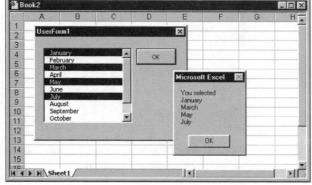

Figure 18-5:
Determining
the
selected
items in a
ListBox that
allows
multiple
selections.

```
Private Sub OKButton_Click()
    Msg = "You selected" & vbCrLf
    For i = 0 To ListBox1.ListCount - 1
        If ListBox1.Selected(i) Then
            Msg = Msg & ListBox1.List(i) & vbCrLf
        End If
    Next i
    MsgBox Msg
    Unload UserForm1
End Sub
```

This routine uses a For-Next loop to cycle though each item in the ListBox. Notice that the loop starts with item 0 (the first item) and ends with the last item (determined by the value of the ListCount property minus 1). If the Selected property for an item is True, it means that the list item was selected.

Selecting a range

In some cases, you may want the user to select a range while a dialog box is displayed. An example of this choice occurs in the second step of the Excel Chart Wizard. The Chart Wizard guesses the range to be charted, but the user is free to change it from the dialog box.

To allow a range selection in your dialog box, add a RefEdit control. The following example displays a dialog box with the current region's range address displayed in a RefEdit control, as shown in Figure 18-6. The current region is the block of nonempty cells that contains the active cell. The user can accept or change this range. When the user closes the dialog box, the subroutine makes the range bold.

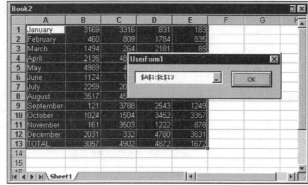

Figure 18-6: This dialog lets the user select a range.

This example assumes the following:

- ✔ You have a UserForm named *UserForm1*.
- ✔ The UserForm contains a RefEdit control named *RefEdit1*.

Here's the code (which is stored in a VBA module) that assigns the current region's address to the RefEdit control and displays the dialog box:

```
Sub BoldCells()
'    Exit if worksheet is not active
    If TypeName(ActiveSheet) <> "Worksheet" Then Exit Sub

'    Select the current region
    ActiveCell.CurrentRegion.Select

'    Initialize RefEdit control
    UserForm1.RefEdit1.Text = Selection.Address
```

(continued)

(continued)

```
'    Show dialog
     UserForm1.Show
End Sub
```

The following subroutine is executed when the OK button is clicked. This subroutine does some simple error checking to make sure that the range specified in the RefEdit control is valid.

```
Private Sub OKButton_Click()
    On Error GoTo BadRange
    Range(RefEdit1.Text).Font.Bold = True
    Unload UserForm1
    Exit Sub
BadRange:
    MsgBox "The specified range is not valid."
End Sub
```

Using multiple sets of OptionButtons

Figure 18-7 shows a custom dialog box with three sets of OptionButtons. If your dialog box contains more than one set of OptionButtons, you need to make sure that each set of OptionButtons works as a set. You can do so in either of two ways:

✔ Enclose each set of OptionButtons in a Frame control. This approach is the best and also makes the dialog box look better. It's easier to add the Frame before you add the OptionButtons. You can, however, also drag existing OptionButtons into a Frame.

✔ Make sure that each set of OptionButtons has a unique GroupName property. If the OptionButtons are in a Frame, you don't have to be concerned with the GroupName property.

Figure 18-7:
This dialog box contains three sets of OptionButton controls.

Using a SpinButton and a TextBox

A SpinButton control and TextBox control form a natural pair. Excel uses them frequently (check out the Print dialog box for a few examples). A SpinButton is useful for letting the user specify a number, which then appears in the companion TextBox. Ideally, the SpinButton and its TextBox should be in sync — that is, if the user clicks the SpinButton, the SpinButton's value should appear in the TextBox. And if the user enters a value directly into the TextBox, the SpinButton should take on that value.

Figure 18-8 shows a custom dialog box with a SpinButton and a TextBox.

Figure 18-8:
A custom
dialog box
with a
SpinButton
and its
companion
TextBox.

This dialog box contains the following controls:

- ✔ A SpinButton named *SpinButton1*, with its Min property set to 0 and its Max property set to 12
- ✔ A TextBox named *TextBox1*
- ✔ A CommandButton that, when clicked, closes the dialog box

The event-handler for the SpinButton follows. To create this subroutine, double-click the SpinButton to activate the Code window for the UserForm. When the SpinButton's value changes (by clicking it), this subroutine assigns the SpinButton's value to the TextBox.

```
Private Sub SpinButton1_Change()
    TextBox1.Text = SpinButton1.Value
End Sub
```

The event-handler for the TextBox, which is listed next, is a bit more complicated. To create this subroutine, double-click the TextBox to activate the Code window for the UserForm. This subroutine is executed whenever the user changes the text in the TextBox. The subroutine checks for three conditions:

✔ The value in the TextBox is greater than or equal to the SpinButton's Min value and less than or equal to the SpinButton's Max value.

✔ The value in the TextBox is less than the SpinButton's Min value; in this case, the Min value is used.

✔ The value in the TextBox is greater than the SpinButton's Max value; in this case, the Max value is used.

The effect is that the text in the TextBox will always display the Value property of the SpinButton.

```
Private Sub TextBox1_Change()
    TextBoxVal = Val(TextBox1.Text)

'   Is user entry within the range?
    If TextBoxVal >= SpinButton1.Min And _
        TextBoxVal <= SpinButton1.Max Then
        SpinButton1.Value = TextBoxVal
    Else
'       Is user entry too small?
        If TextBoxVal < SpinButton1.Min Then
            TextBoxVal = SpinButton1.Min
            TextBox1.Text = SpinButton1.Min
        End If

'       Is user entry too large?
        If TextBoxVal > SpinButton1.Max Then
            TextBoxVal = SpinButton1.Max
            TextBox1.Text = SpinButton1.Max
        End If
    End If
End Sub
```

Using a dialog box as a progress indicator

One of the most common Excel programming questions I hear is, "How can I use a custom dialog box to display the progress of a lengthy macro and then close the dialog when the macro is finished?"

Before Excel 97 became available, the answer was: You can't. But Excel 97, with its new way of handling custom dialog boxes, lets you create an attractive progress indicator, as shown in Figure 18-9. It does, however, require a few tricks — which I'm about to show you.

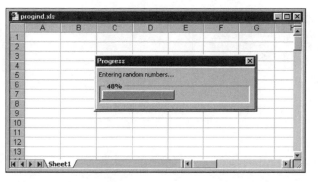

Figure 18-9:
This
dialog box
functions as
a progress
indicator for
a lengthy
macro.

Creating the progress indicator dialog box

The first step is to create your dialog box. In this example, the dialog box displays the progress while a macro inserts random numbers into 25 columns and 100 rows of the active worksheet. To create the dialog box, follow these steps:

1. **Activate the VBE and insert a new UserForm.**

2. **Change the UserForm's caption to** Progress.

3. **Add a Frame object and set the following properties:**

Property	Value
Caption	0%
Name	FrameProgress
SpecialEffect	2 — fmSpecialEffectSunken
Width	204
Height	28

4. **Add a Label object inside the Frame, and set the following properties:**

Property	Value
Name	LabelProgress
BackColor	&H000000FF& (red)
Caption	(no caption)
SpecialEffect	1 — fmSpecialEffectRaised
Width	20
Height	13
Top	5
Left	2

5. **Add another Label above the frame, and change its caption to** Entering random numbers...

The UserForm should resemble Figure 18-10.

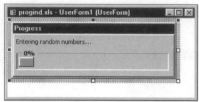

Figure 18-10:
The
progress
indicator
UserForm.

The subroutines

This example uses four subroutines: Start, UserForm_Activate( ), Main, and UpdateProgress.

The Start subroutine (located in a VBA module) is the entry subroutine that is executed to get things going:

```
Sub Start()
'    The UserForm1_Activate sub calls Main
    UserForm1.LabelProgress.Width = 0
    UserForm1.Show
End Sub
```

The UserForm_Activate( ) subroutine, located in the Code window for the UserForm object, is executed when the UserForm is displayed. This subroutine simply calls another subroutine called Main:

```
Private Sub UserForm_Activate()
    Call Main
End Sub
```

The Main subroutine does all the work and is executed when the UserForm is shown. Notice that it calls the UpdateProgress subroutine, which updates the progress indicator in the dialog box:

```
Sub Main()
'    Inserts random numbers on the active worksheet
    Dim Counter As Integer
    Dim RowMax As Integer, ColMax As Integer
    Dim r As Integer, c As Integer
    Dim PctDone As Single

    If TypeName(ActiveSheet) <> "Worksheet" Then Exit Sub
    Cells.Clear
    Application.ScreenUpdating = False
    Counter = 1
    RowMax = 100
```

```
        ColMax = 25
        For r = 1 To RowMax
            For c = 1 To ColMax
                Cells(r, c) = Int(Rnd * 1000)
                Counter = Counter + 1
            Next c
            PctDone = Counter / (RowMax * ColMax)
            Call UpdateProgress(PctDone)
        Next r
        Unload UserForm1
End Sub
```

The UpdateProgress subroutine accepts one argument and updates the progress indicator in the dialog box:

```
Sub UpdateProgress(pct)
    With UserForm1
        .FrameProgress.Caption = Format(pct, "0%")
        .LabelProgress.Width = pct * (.FrameProgress.Width _
            - 10)
    End With
'       The DoEvents statement is responsible for the form
            updating
    DoEvents
End Sub
```

How this example works

When the Start subroutine is executed, It sets the width of the LabelProgress label to 0 and then shows the UserForm — which triggers an Activate event for the UserForm. The UserForm_Activate() subroutine is executed, which in turn executes the Main subroutine.

The Main subroutine checks the active sheet. If it's not a worksheet, the subroutine ends with no action. If the active sheet is a worksheet, the subroutine does the following:

1. **Erases all cells on the active worksheet.**

2. **Turns off screen updating (to speed up the macro).**

3. **Loops through the rows and columns (specified by the RowMax and ColMax variables) and inserts a random number.**

4. **Increments the Counter variable and calculates the percentage completed (which is stored in the PctDone variable).**

5. **Calls the UpdateProgress subroutine, which displays the percentage completed by changing the width of the LabelProgress label.**

6. **Unloads the UserForm.**

If you adapt this technique for you own use, you'll need to figure out how to determine the macro's progress — which will vary, depending on your macro. Then you'll need to call the UpdateProgress subroutine at periodic intervals while your macro is executing.

Creating a tabbed dialog box

Tabbed dialog boxes are useful because they let you present information in small organized chunks. The Excel Options dialog box (which is displayed when you choose Tools➪Options) is a good example. This dialog box uses eight tabs to organize a tremendous number of options.

Creating your own tabbed dialog boxes is relatively easy — thanks to the MultiPage control. Figure 18-11 shows a custom dialog box that uses a MultiPage control with three *pages*, or tabs. When the user clicks a tab, a new page is activated and only the controls on that page are displayed.

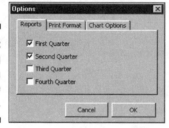

Figure 18-11:
This dialog box uses a MultiPage control.

Keep the following points in mind when you use the MultiPage control to create a tabbed dialog box:

- ✔ Use only one MultiPage control per dialog box.

- ✔ Make sure that you use the MultiPage control, not the TabStrip control. The TabStrip control is more difficult to use.

- ✔ You'll want some controls (such as OK and Cancel buttons) to be visible at all times. Place these controls outside the MultiPage control.

- ✔ Right-click a tab on the MultiPage control to display a shortcut menu that lets you add, remove, rename, or move a tab.

- ✔ At design time, click a tab to activate the page. After it is activated, add other controls to the page using normal procedures.

- ✔ To select the MultiPage control itself (rather than a page on the control), click the border of the MultiPage control. Keep your eye on the Properties window, which displays the name and type of the selected control. You can also select the MultiPage control by selecting its name from the drop-down list in the Properties window.

✔ You can change the look of the MultiPage control by changing the Style and TabOrientation properties.

✔ The Value property of a MultiPage control determines which page is displayed. For example, if you write code to set the Value property to 0, the first page of the MultiPage control will be displayed.

A Dialog Box Checklist

To wrap up this chapter, here's a checklist you can use when creating dialog boxes:

❑ Are the controls aligned with each other?

❑ Are similar controls the same size?

❑ Are controls evenly spaced?

❑ Does the dialog box have an appropriate caption?

❑ Is the dialog box overwhelming? If so, you may want to use a series of dialog boxes.

❑ Can the user access every control with an accelerator key?

❑ Are any accelerator keys duplicated?

❑ Are the controls grouped logically (by function)?

❑ Is the tab order set correctly? The user should be able to tab through the dialog box and access the controls sequentially.

❑ If you plan to store the dialog box in an add-in (which I discuss in Chapter 22), did you test it thoroughly after creating the add-in? Remember that an add-in is never the active workbook.

❑ Will your VBA code take appropriate action if the user cancels the dialog box or presses Esc?

❑ Does the text contain any misspellings? Unfortunately, the Excel spell checker doesn't work with UserForms, so you're on your own when it comes to spelling.

❑ Will your dialog box fit on the screen in 640-by-480 mode? In other words, if you develop your dialog box by using a high-resolution video mode, your dialog box may be too big to fit on a screen in lower resolution.

❑ Do all EditBoxes have the appropriate validation setting?

❑ Do all ScrollBars and SpinButtons allow valid values only?

❑ Do all ListBoxes have their MultiSelect property set properly?

The best way to master custom dialog boxes is by creating dialog boxes — lots of them. Start simply, and experiment with the controls and their properties. And don't forget about the online help; it's your best source for details about every control and property.

Part V
Creating Custom Toolbars and Menus

The 5th Wave   By Rich Tennant

AFTER SPENDING 9 DAYS WITH 12 DIFFERENT VENDORS AND READING
26 BROCHURES, DAVE HAD AN ACUTE ATTACK OF TOXIC OPTION SYNDROME.

In this part . . .

This part consists of only two chapters, both of which deal with customizing the Excel user interface. Chapter 19 focuses on toolbars. In Chapter 20, I discuss the types of modification you can make to the Excel menus.

Chapter 19

Customizing the Excel Toolbars

. . . .

In This Chapter

▶ Using toolbars in Excel

▶ Customizing toolbars in different ways

▶ Creating different images on toolbar buttons

▶ Using VBA to manipulate toolbars

. . . .

*E*xcel is definitely *not* a toolbar-challenged product. It comes with 38 built-in toolbars, and constructing new toolbars is very easy. This chapter shows you how.

Introducing CommandBars

Excel 97 introduced a new way of handling toolbars. A toolbar is technically known as a CommandBar object. In fact, a toolbar is one of the three types of CommandBars:

✔ **Toolbar.** A floating bar with one or more clickable controls. This chapter focuses on this type of CommandBar.

✔ **Menu bar.** The two built-in menu bars are the Worksheet menu bar and the Chart menu bar (see Chapter 20).

✔ **Shortcut menu.** These are the menus that pop up when you right-click an object (see Chapter 20).

What You Can Do with Toolbars

The following list summarizes the ways in which you can customize toolbars. (I discuss these topics in detail later in this chapter.)

✔ **Remove toolbar controls from built-in toolbars.** You can get rid of toolbar controls that you never use — and free up a few pixels of screen space.

✔ **Add toolbar controls to built-in toolbars.** You can add as many toolbar controls as you want to any toolbar. The controls can be custom buttons or buttons copied from other toolbars, or they can come from the stock of toolbar controls that Excel provides for you.

✔ **Create new toolbars.** You can create as many new toolbars as you like, with toolbar controls from any source.

✔ **Change the functionality of built-in toolbar controls.** You do this by attaching your own macro to a built-in toolbar button.

✔ **Change the image that appears on any toolbar button.** Excel includes a rudimentary but functional toolbar button editor. You can also do this by using several other techniques.

Don't be afraid to experiment with toolbars. If you mess up a built-in toolbar, you can easily reset it to its default state. Just choose View⇨Toolbars⇨ Customize, select the toolbar in the list, and click the Reset button.

How Excel handles toolbars

When you start up Excel, it displays the same toolbar configuration that was in effect the last time you used the program. Did you ever wonder how Excel keeps track of this information?

When you exit Excel, it updates a file called EXCEL8.XLB in your Windows folder. This file stores all your custom toolbars, as well as information about the onscreen location of each toolbar and which toolbars are visible.

If you need to restore the toolbars to their previous configuration, choose File⇨Open to open EXCEL8.XLB. This restores your toolbar configuration to the way it was when you started the current session of Excel. You also can make a copy of the EXCEL8.XLB file and give it a different name. Doing so lets you store multiple toolbar configurations that you can load at any time. And if you've made lots of toolbar changes and would like to return to Excel's virgin toolbar state, just delete EXCEL8.XLB and restart Excel.

Working with Toolbars

As you probably know, you can display as many toolbars as you like. A toolbar can be either *docked* or *floating*. A docked toolbar is fixed in place at the top, bottom, left, or right edge of Excel's workspace. Floating toolbars appear in an *always-on-top* window, which means that they are never obscured by other windows. You can change the dimensions of a floating toolbar by dragging a border.

As shown in Figure 19-1, right-clicking any toolbar or toolbar button displays a shortcut menu that lets you hide or display a toolbar. This shortcut menu, however, does not display the names of all toolbars. For a complete list of toolbars, use the Customize dialog box. This dialog box lets you hide or display toolbars (among other things).

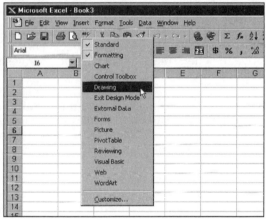

Figure 19-1:
Right-clicking a toolbar or a toolbar button displays this shortcut menu.

You can access the Customize dialog box in two ways:

- ✔ Choose View➪Toolbars➪Customize.
- ✔ Right-click a toolbar and choose Customize from the shortcut menu.

The Toolbars tab

The Toolbars tab of the Customize dialog box, shown in Figure 19-2, lists all the available toolbars, including custom toolbars you have created. This dialog box also lists the two menu bars (Worksheet menu bar and Chart menu bar), which are similar to toolbars.

Figure 19-2:
The
Toolbars
tab of the
Customize
dialog box.

This section describes how to perform various procedures that involve toolbars.

Hiding or displaying a toolbar: The Toolbars tab displays every toolbar (built-in toolbars and custom toolbars). Add a check mark to display a toolbar; remove the check mark to hide it. The changes take effect immediately.

Creating a new toolbar: Click on the New button and then enter a name in the New Toolbar dialog box. Excel creates and displays an empty toolbar. You can then add buttons (or menu commands) to the new toolbar. See "Adding and Removing Toolbar Controls" later in this chapter.

Figure 19-3 shows a custom toolbar that I created. This toolbar, called Custom Formatting, contains the formatting tools that I use most frequently. Notice that this toolbar includes drop-down menus as well as standard toolbar buttons.

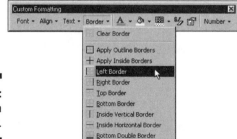

Figure 19-3:
A custom
toolbar.

Renaming a custom toolbar: Select the custom toolbar from the list and click on the Rename button. In the Rename Toolbar dialog box, enter a new name. You can't rename a built-in toolbar.

Deleting a custom toolbar: Select the custom toolbar from the list and click on the Delete button. You can't delete a built-in toolbar.

Deleting a toolbar is one of the few actions that cannot be undone.

Resetting a built-in toolbar: Select a built-in toolbar from the list and click on the Reset button. The toolbar is restored to its default state. If you've added any custom tools to the toolbar, they are removed. If you've removed any default tools, they are restored. The Reset button is not available when a custom toolbar is selected.

Attaching a toolbar to a workbook: If you create a custom toolbar that you'd like to share, you can "attach" it to a workbook. Click on the Attach button and you get a new dialog box that lets you select toolbars to attach to a workbook. You can attach any number of toolbars to a workbook — but remember, attaching toolbars increases the size of your workbook. For more about this, see "Distributing Toolbars" later in this chapter.

The Commands tab

The Commands tab of the Customize dialog box contains a list of every tool that's available. Use this tab when you customize a toolbar. This feature is described later in the chapter (see "Adding and Removing Toolbar Controls").

The Options tab

Figure 19-4 shows the Options tab of the Customize dialog box. Only three options are available.

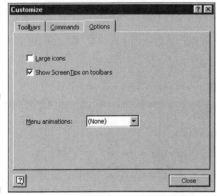

Figure 19-4: The Options tab of the Customize dialog box.

Toolbar autosensing

Normally, Excel displays a particular toolbar automatically when you change contexts; this is called *autosensing*. For example, when you activate a chart, the Chart toolbar appears. When you activate a sheet that contains a pivot table, the PivotTable toolbar appears.

You can easily defeat autosensing by hiding the toolbar (that is, click its Close button). After you do so, Excel no longer displays that toolbar when you switch to its former context.

You can restore this automatic behavior by displaying the appropriate toolbar when you're in the appropriate context. Thereafter, Excel reverts to its normal automatic toolbar display when you switch to that context.

You can simulate this type of behavior by writing VBA code. Refer to "Displaying a toolbar when a worksheet is activated," later in this chapter.

Changing the icon size: To change the size of the icons used in toolbars, select or unselect the Large icons check box. This option affects only the images that are in buttons. Buttons that contain only text (such as buttons in a menu) are not changed. Personally, I think the Large icons look terrible and I don't know why anyone would want to use them.

Toggling the ScreenTips display: ScreenTips are the pop-up messages that display the button names when you pause the mouse pointer over a button. If you find the ScreenTips distracting, remove the check mark from the Show ScreenTips on toolbars check box.

Changing the menu animations: When you select a menu, Excel animates the display of the menu that is dropping down. Choose whichever animation style you prefer.

Adding and Removing Toolbar Controls

When the Customize dialog box is displayed, Excel is in a special customization mode, and you have access to all the commands and options in the Customize dialog box. In addition, you can perform the following actions:

- ✔ Reposition a control on a toolbar
- ✔ Move a control to a different toolbar
- ✔ Copy a control from one toolbar to another
- ✔ Add new controls to a toolbar using the Commands tab of the Customize dialog box
- ✔ Change lots of attributes of toolbar controls

Moving and copying controls

When the Customize dialog box is displayed, you can copy and move toolbar controls freely among any visible toolbars. To move a control, drag it to its new location (the new location can be within the current toolbar or on a different toolbar).

To copy a control, press Ctrl while you drag the control to another toolbar. (You can also copy a toolbar control within the same toolbar, but there is really no reason to have multiple copies of a button on the same toolbar.)

Inserting a new control

To add a new control to a toolbar, you use the Commands tab of the Customize dialog box (refer to Figure 19-5).

Figure 19-5: The Commands tab contains a list of every available control.

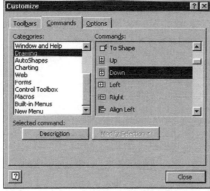

The controls are arranged in 17 categories. When you select a category, the controls in that category appear to the right. To find out what a control does, select it and click on the Description button.

To add a control to a toolbar, locate it in the Commands tab, click on it, and drag it to the toolbar.

Other toolbar button operations

When Excel is in customization mode (that is, when the Customize dialog box is displayed), you can right-click on a toolbar control to display a shortcut menu of additional actions for the tool. Figure 19-6 shows the shortcut menu that appears when you right-click on a button in customization mode.

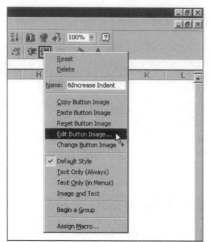

Figure 19-6:
In customiz-
ation mode,
right-
clicking on
a button
displays
this
shortcut
menu.

These commands are described in the following list. (Note that some of these commands are not available for certain toolbar controls.)

✔ **Reset:** Resets the control to its original state.

✔ **Delete:** Deletes the control.

✔ **Name:** Lets you change the name of the control.

✔ **Copy Button Image:** Makes a copy of the control's image and places it on the Clipboard.

✔ **Paste Button Image:** Pastes the image from the Clipboard to the control.

✔ **Reset Button Image:** Restores the control's original image.

✔ **Edit Button Image:** Lets you edit the control's image using the Excel button editor.

✔ **Change Button Image:** Lets you change the image by selecting from a list of 42 button images.

✔ **Default Style:** Displays the control using its default style (text only or image and text).

✔ **Text Only (Always):** Always displays text (no image) for the control.

✔ **Text Only (In Menus):** Displays text (no image) if the control is in a menu bar.

✔ **Image and Text:** Displays the control's image and text.

✔ **Begin a Group:** Inserts a divider in the toolbar. In a drop-down menu, a separator bar appears as a horizontal line between commands. In a toolbar, a separator bar appears as a vertical line.

✔ **Assign a Macro:** Lets you assign a macro that is executed when the control is clicked.

Distributing Toolbars

If you want to distribute a custom toolbar to other users, you can store it in a workbook. To store a toolbar in a workbook file, follow these steps:

1. **Create the custom toolbar and then test it to make sure it works correctly.**

2. **Activate the workbook that will store the new toolbar.**

3. **Choose View⇨Toolbars⇨Customize.**

4. **In the Customize dialog box, click the Toolbars tab.**

5. **Click the Attach button.**

   Excel displays the Attach Toolbars dialog box, shown in Figure 19-7. This dialog box lists all custom toolbars stored on your system.

6. **To attach a toolbar, select it and then click the Copy button.**

   When a toolbar in the Toolbars in workbook list box is selected, the Copy button says Delete; you can click the Delete button to remove the selected toolbar from the workbook.

Figure 19-7:
The Attach
Toolbars
dialog box
lets you
attach one
or more
toolbars to
a workbook.

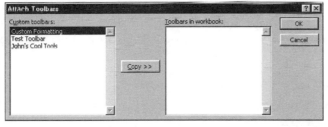

 A toolbar that's attached to a workbook appears automatically when the workbook is opened, and that toolbar is then saved in the user's EXCEL8.XLB file when Excel closes down. If the user's workspace already has a toolbar by the same name, however, the toolbar attached to the workbook does *not* replace the existing one.

 The toolbar that's stored in the workbook is an exact copy of the toolbar at the time that you attach it. If you modify the toolbar after attaching it, the changed version is not stored in the workbook automatically. You must manually remove the old toolbar and then attach the new one.

Using VBA to Manipulate Toolbars

As you may expect, you can write VBA code to do things with toolbars. In this section, I provide some background information that you simply must know before you start mucking around with toolbars (or menus).

The CommandBars collection

You manipulate Excel toolbars (and menus, for that matter) by using objects located in the CommandBars collection. The CommandBars collection consists of

- All Excel built-in toolbars
- Any other custom toolbars that you create
- A built-in menu bar named Worksheet menu bar, which apears when a worksheet is active
- A built-in menu bar named Chart menu bar, which appears when a chart sheet is active
- Any other custom menu bars that you create
- All built-in shortcut menus

As I mention at the beginning of this chapter, there are actually three types of CommandBars, differentiated by their Type properties. The Type property can be

- msoBarTypeNormal: A toolbar (Type = 0)
- msoBarTypeMenuBar: A menu bar (Type = 1)
- msoBarTypePopUp: A shortcut menu (Type = 2)

Listing all CommandBar objects

If you're curious about the objects in the CommandBars collection, enter the following subroutine and execute it. The result is a list of all CommandBar objects in the CommandBars collection, plus any custom menu bars or toolbars. For each CommandBar, the subroutine lists its Index, its Name, and its Type (either 0, 1, or 2).

```
Sub ShowCommandBarNames()
    Row = 1
    For Each cbar In Application.CommandBars
```

```
        Cells(Row, 1) = cbar.Index
        Cells(Row, 2) = cbar.Name
        Cells(Row, 3) = cbar.Type
        Row = Row + 1
    Next cbar
End Sub
```

Figure 19-8 shows a portion of the result of running this subroutine. It shows that the CommandBars collection consists of 38 built-in toolbars, two menu bars, and 43 shortcut menus.

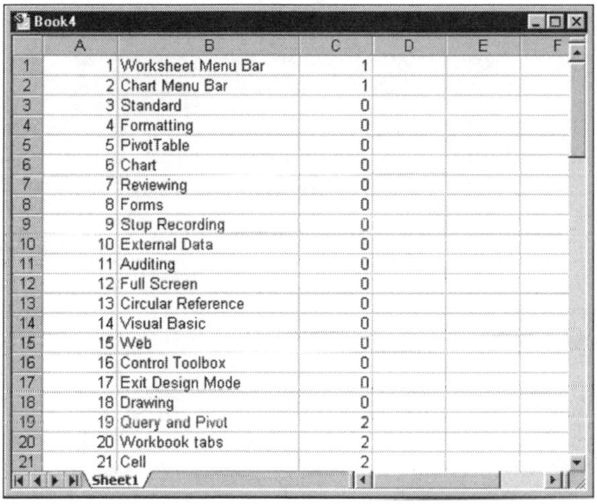

	A	B	C	D	E	F
1	1	Worksheet Menu Bar	1			
2	2	Chart Menu Bar	1			
3	3	Standard	0			
4	4	Formatting	0			
5	5	PivotTable	0			
6	6	Chart	0			
7	7	Reviewing	0			
8	8	Forms	0			
9	9	Stop Recording	0			
10	10	External Data	0			
11	11	Auditing	0			
12	12	Full Screen	0			
13	13	Circular Reference	0			
14	14	Visual Basic	0			
15	15	Web	0			
16	16	Control Toolbox	0			
17	17	Exit Design Mode	0			
18	18	Drawing	0			
19	19	Query and Pivot	2			
20	20	Workbook tabs	2			
21	21	Cell	2			

Figure 19-8: VBA code produced this list of all CommandBar objects.

Referring to CommandBars

You can refer to a particular CommandBar by its Index or by its Name. For example, the Standard toolbar has an Index of 3, so you can refer to the toolbar like this:

```
Application.CommandBars(3)
```

or like this:

```
Application.CommandBars("Standard")
```

Referring to controls in a CommandBar

A CommandBar object contains Control objects, which are buttons, menus, or menu items. The following subroutine displays the Caption property for the first Control in the Standard toolbar (which has an Index of 3).

```
Sub Test()
    MsgBox Application.CommandBars(3).Controls(1).Caption
End Sub
```

When you execute this subroutine, you'll see the message box shown in Figure 19-9.

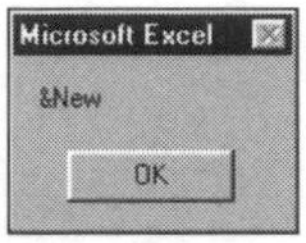

Figure 19-9:
Displaying
the Caption
property for
a control.

Rather than use index numbers, you can also use the captions. The following subroutine has the same result as the preceding subroutine:

```
Sub Test2()
    MsgBox Application.CommandBars("Standard"). _
        Controls("New").Caption
End Sub
```

In some cases, these Control objects can contain other Control objects. For example, the first control on the Drawing toolbar contains other controls. (This also demonstrates that you can include menu items on a toolbar.) The concept of Controls within Controls becomes clearer in Chapter 20, when I discuss menus.

Properties of CommandBar controls

Command bar controls have a number of properties that determine how they look and work. Here's a list of a few of the more useful properties for CommandBar controls:

- ✔ **Caption:** The text displayed for the control. If the control shows only an image, the Caption appears when you move the mouse over the control.

- ✔ **FaceID:** A number that represents a graphics image displayed next to the control's text.

- ✔ **BeginGroup:** True if a separator bar appears before the control.

- ✔ **OnAction:** The name of a VBA macro that executes when the user clicks the control.

> ✔ **BuiltIn:** True if the control is an Excel built-in control.
>
> ✔ **Enabled:** True if the control can be clicked.
>
> ✔ **ToolTipText:** Text that appears when the user moves the mouse pointer over the control.

More object stuff

When you work with toolbars, you can turn on the macro recorder to see what's happening in terms of VBA code. Unless you're editing button images, the steps you take while customizing toolbars generate VBA code. By examining this code, you can discover how Excel arranges the object model for toolbars. The model is pretty simple.

The CommandBars collection — which is contained in the Application object — is a collection of all Toolbar objects, and each Toolbar object has a collection of ToolbarButtons. These objects have properties and methods that allow you to control toolbars using VBA procedures.

VBA Examples

This section contains a few examples of using VBA to manipulate the Excel toolbars.

Resetting all built-in toolbars

The following procedure resets all built-in toolbars to their virgin state:

```
Sub ResetAll()
    For Each Bar In Application.CommandBars
                If Bar.Type = msoBarTypeNormal Then
                    Bar.Reset
                End If
    Next Bar
End Sub
```

Using the Reset method on a custom toolbar has no effect (and does not generate an error).

Be careful with the preceding routine. Calling it erases all customizations to all built-in toolbars. The toolbars will be just as they were when you first installed Excel.

Toggling the display of all toolbars

The following example isn't all that useful, but it causes lots of onscreen action (try it!). This subroutine loops through all CommandBar objects. If the CommandBar is a toolbar, it toggles the Visible property (that is, hidden toolbars are displayed, and visible toolbars are hidden).

```
Sub ToggleAllToolbars()
    For Each cbar In Application.CommandBars
        If cbar.Type = msoBarTypeNormal Then
            cbar.Visible = Not cbar.Visible
        End If
    Next cbar
End Sub
```

Figure 19-10 shows how my system looked after I executed this subroutine. To get things back to normal, just execute the subroutine a second time.

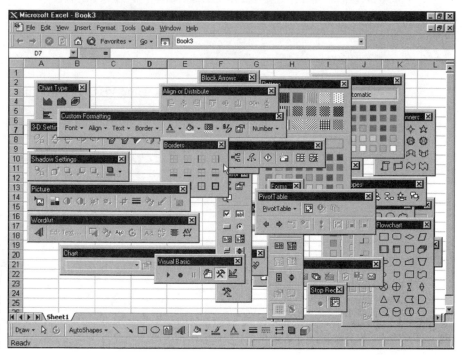

Figure 19-10:
Toolbar
overload!

Displaying a toolbar when a worksheet is activated

Assume that you have a workbook that holds your budget information (stored in a worksheet named Budget). In addition, assume that you've developed a custom toolbar (named Budget Tools) that you use with this workbook. The toolbar should be visible when you work on the Budget sheet; otherwise, it should remain hidden and out of the way.

The following subroutines, which are stored in the code window for the ThisWorkbook object, display the Budget Tools toolbar when the Budget workbook is active and hide the toolbar when the Budget workbook is deactivated.

```
Private Sub Workbook_WindowActivate(ByVal Wn As _
        Excel.Window)
    Application.CommandBars("Budget Tools").Visible = True
End Sub

Private Sub Workbook_WindowDeactivate(ByVal Wn As _
        Excel.Window)
    Application.CommandBars("Budget Tools").Visible = False
End Sub
```

For more information about using automatic procedures, refer to Chapter 11.

Ensuring that an attached toolbar is displayed

As I explained earlier in this chapter, you can attach any number of toolbars to a workbook. But I also noted that the attached toolbar won't replace an existing toolbar that has the same name.

In some cases, the failure to display a toolbar can present a problem. For example, assume that you distribute a workbook to your coworkers, and this workbook has an attached toolbar that executes your macros. Later, you update the workbook and add some new controls to your attached toolbar. When you distribute this new workbook, the updated toolbar will not be displayed because the old toolbar already exists!

One solution is to simply use a new toolbar name for the updated application. Perhaps a better solution is to write VBA code to delete the toolbar when the workbook closes. That way, the toolbar will not be stored on the user's system and you can be assured that the latest copy of your toolbar will always be displayed when the workbook is opened.

The following subroutine, which is stored in the code window for the ThisWorkbook object, displays the toolbar named Budget Tools when the workbook is opened. The Budget Tools toolbar is attached to the workbook.

```
Private Sub Workbook_Open()
    Application.CommandBars("Budget Tools").Visible = True
End Sub
```

The next subroutine, which is also stored in the code window for the ThisWorkbook object, deletes the toolbar named Budget Tools when the workbook is closed:

```
Private Sub Workbook_BeforeClose(Cancel As Boolean)
    Application.CommandBars("Budget Tools").Delete
End Sub
```

Hiding and restoring toolbars

In some cases, you may want to remove all the toolbars when a workbook is opened. It's only polite, however, to restore the toolbars when your application closes. In this section, I present two subroutines, both stored in the code window of the ThisWorkbook object.

The Workbook_Open subroutine is executed when the workbook is opened. This subroutine saves the names of all visible toolbars in column A of Sheet1, and then hides all the toolbars:

```
Private Sub Workbook_Open()
    Sheets("Sheet1").Range("A:A").ClearContents
    TBarCount = 0
    For Each cbar In Application.CommandBars
        If cbar.Type = msoBarTypeNormal Then
            If cbar.Visible Then
                TBarCount = TBarCount + 1
                Sheets("Sheet1").Cells(TBarCount, 1) = _
                    cbar.Name
                cbar.Visible = False
            End If
        End If
    Next cbar
End Sub
```

The following subroutine is executed before the workbook is closed. This routine loops through the toolbar names stored on Sheet1 and changes their Visible property to True:

```
Private Sub Workbook_BeforeClose(Cancel As Boolean)
    Row = 1
    TBar = Sheets("Sheet1").Cells(Row, 1)
    Do While TBar <> ""
        Application.CommandBars(TBar).Visible = True
        Row = Row + 1
        TBar = Sheets("Sheet1").Cells(Row, 1)
    Loop
End Sub
```

Notice that the Workbook_Open routine saves the toolbar names in a worksheet range rather than in an array, ensuring that the toolbar names are still available when the Workbook_BeforeClose routine is executed. Values stored in an array may be lost between the time the Workbook_Open subroutine is executed and the Workbook_BeforeClose subroutine is executed.

Chapter 20

When Excel's Normal Menus Aren't Good Enough

• •

In This Chapter

▶ Your official guide to menu terminology

▶ Types of menu modifications you can make

▶ What you need to know about the object model

▶ Modifying menus by using VBA

• •

You may not realize it, but you can change almost every aspect of Excel's menus. Typical Excel users get by just fine with the standard menus. Because you're reading this book, however, you're probably not the typical Excel user. You might modify menus to make life easier for you and for your applications' users. In this chapter, I describe how to make changes to the Excel menu system.

Why Bother?

Most of the Excel applications you develop will get along just fine with the standard menu system. In some cases, however, you might want to add a new menu to make it easier to run your VBA macros. In other cases, you might want to remove some menu items to prevent users from accessing certain features. If these sorts of changes seem useful, you should read this chapter. Otherwise, you can safely skip it until the need arises.

Menu Terminology

Before I get too far into this, I need to discuss terminology. At first, menu terminology confuses people because many of the terms are similar. The following list describes official Excel menu terminology, which I use through-out this book:

- ✔ **Menu bar:** The row of words that appears directly below the application's title bar. Excel has nine menu bars that appear automatically, depending on the context. For example, the menu bar displayed when a worksheet is active differs from the menu bar displayed when a chart sheet is active.

- ✔ **Menu:** A single, top-level element of a menu bar. For example, each of Excel's menu bars has a menu called File.

- ✔ **Menu item:** An element that appears in the drop-down list when you select a menu. For example, the first menu item under the File menu is New. Menu items also appear in submenus and shortcut menus.

- ✔ **Separator bar:** A horizontal line that appears between two menu items. The separator bar is used to group similar menu items.

- ✔ **Submenu:** A second-level menu that is under some menus. For example, the Edit menu has a submenu called Clear.

- ✔ **Submenu item:** A menu item that appears in the list when you select a submenu. For example, the Edit⇨Clear submenu contains the following submenu items: All, Formats, Contents, and Notes.

- ✔ **Shortcut menu:** The floating list of menu items that appears when you right-click a selection or an object. Excel has 25 shortcut menus.

- ✔ **Enabled:** A menu item that can be used. If a menu item isn't enabled, its text appears grayed and it can't be used.

- ✔ **Checked:** A menu item can display a graphical box that is checked or unchecked. The View⇨Status Bar menu item is an example.

How Excel Handles Menus

Excel provides you with two ways to change the menu system:

- ✔ Use the View⇨Toolbars⇨Customize command. This displays the Customize dialog box, which lets you change menus (and toolbars).

- ✔ Write VBA code to modify the menu system.

When you close Excel, it saves any changes that you've made to the menu system, and these changes appear the next time you open Excel. The information about menu modifications is stored in a file called excel8.xlb. In most cases, *you won't want your menu modifications to be saved between sessions.* Generally, you'll need to write VBA code to change the menus while a particular workbook is open, and then change them back when the workbook closes.

This stuff is all new!

Excel 97 has lots of similarities with Excel 5 and Excel 95. But the topic of menus is one area that is completely different. And I mean *completely* different. If you've customized menus using previous versions of Excel, you can forget everything you ever learned.

What's different?

✔ A menu bar is actually a toolbar in disguise. If you don't believe me, grab the vertical bars at the very left of the menu bar and drag the bar away. As the figure shows, you can make the menu bar a floating toolbar! The offical (VBA) term for both menus and toolbars is *CommandBar*.

✔ The Excel 5/95 Menu Editor is gone. To edit a menu manually, you need to use the View➪ Toolbars➪Customize command. Understand, however, that Excel 5/95 workbooks that contain menus customized using the old Menu Editor will still work in Excel 97.

✔ Menu items can now have images (as you've undoubtedly noticed).

✔ There is no easy way to assign a VBA macro to a new menu item on the Tools menu. This was a piece of cake with Excel 5/95. However, later in this chapter, I provide VBA code that you can use to add a new menu item to the Tools menu.

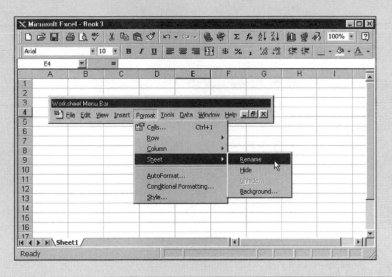

Customizing Menus Directly

Because a menu bar is actually a toolbar in disguise, you can modify a menu bar using the View➪Toolbars➪Customize command. To demonstrate how easy it is to change the Excel menu, try this:

1. Choose <u>V</u>iew⇨<u>T</u>oolbars⇨<u>C</u>ustomize.

2. Click the Help menu (in the menu bar) and drag it away.

3. Click Close to close the Customize dialog box.

You've just wiped out your Help menu (see Figure 20-1). Exit Excel and then restart it. Although you may expect the menu bar to be restored when you restart Excel, it's not! The Help menu is still missing. To get things back to normal:

1. Choose <u>V</u>iew⇨<u>T</u>oolbars⇨<u>C</u>ustomize.

   The Customize dialog box appears.

2. Select the Worksheet Menu Bar item.

3. Click Reset to restore the Worksheet menu bar to its default state.

I think Microsoft made it far too easy to mess up your menus. My advice? Don't use the <u>V</u>iew⇨<u>T</u>oolbars⇨<u>C</u>ustomize command to change menus. In almost every case, you want your menu modifications to be in effect only when a particular workbook is open. To do that, you need to use VBA to make your menu changes — which is the topic of this chapter.

Refer to Chapter 19 for details regarding the Customize dialog box. The procedures that I describe for toolbars also works for menu bars.

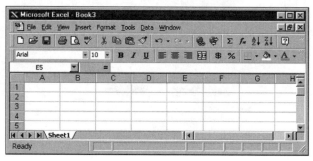

Figure 20-1:
The
Worksheet
menu bar,
after
zapping the
Help menu.

A Real Example

My Power Utility Pak is a collection of Excel add-ins. When the main add-in is opened, VBA code creates a new Utilities menu, with submenus. Figure 20-2 shows how this looks.

The Power Utility Pak normally sells for $39.95. But because you bought this book, you can get a free copy (shipping and handling fee only). Use the coupon in the back of the book to order your copy.

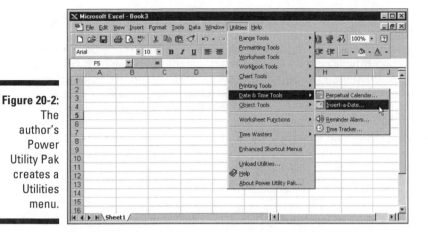

Figure 20-2:
The
author's
Power
Utility Pak
creates a
Utilities
menu.

The information used to create the menu is stored in a worksheet. The VBA routine reads the worksheet cells and creates the menu using that information. On a moderately fast system, the entire menu takes about 3–4 seconds to build and display. When the add-in is uninstalled, VBA code deletes the Utilities menu.

The CommandBar Object

For an introduction to the CommandBar object, refer to Chapter 19. In that chapter, I explain that a menu bar is one of three types of CommandBars.

Referring to CommandBars

Because this chapter deals with menus, you're interested in the two CommandBar objects that are built-in menu bars. The Worksheet Menu Bar is the first object in the CommandBars collection, so you can refer to it as

```
CommandBars(1)
```

or as

```
CommandBars("Worksheet Menu Bar")
```

Similarly, you can refer to the Chart Menu Bar object using either

```
CommandBars(2)
```

or

```
CommandBars("Chart Menu Bar")
```

Referring to Controls in a CommandBar

A CommandBar object contains Control objects, and these Control objects can contain other Control objects. When you choose the File⇨Open command, you're actually manipulating a Control (a menu with a Caption of *Open*) that's contained in another Control (a menu item with a Caption of *File*) that's contained in a CommandBar (the Worksheet menu bar).

Confused? Here's an example that may help clear things up. The following subroutine displays the Caption property for the first Control contained in the first Control of the first CommandBar object. When you execute this subroutine, you see the message box shown in Figure 20-3.

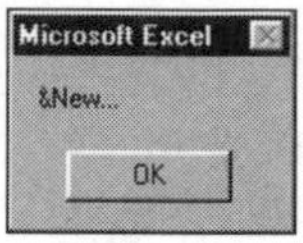

Figure 20-3:
Displaying
the Caption
property for
a control.

```
Sub Test()
    MsgBox CommandBars(1).Controls(1).Controls(1).Caption
End Sub
```

Rather than use index numbers, you can also use the captions. The next subroutine has the same result as the preceding subroutine:

```
Sub Test2()
    MsgBox CommandBars("Worksheet Menu Bar"). _
        Controls("File").Controls("New...").Caption
End Sub
```

If you refer to a control by using its caption, the caption must match exactly. In the preceding subroutine, I had to use an ellipsis (three dots) after the word *New* because that's how it appears in the menu. You can mix and match index numbers with captions, if you like.

You might find the next subroutine instructive. It loops through all the Controls (menus) in the Worksheet menu bar. For each of these menus, it then loops through the Controls (menu items) within the menu. For each of these menu items, it loops through the Controls (submenu items). The result is a listing of all menus, menu items, and submenu items in the Worksheet menu bar.

```
Sub ListMenuStuff()
    Row = 1
    On Error Resume Next
    For Each Menu In CommandBars(1).Controls
        For Each MenuItem In Menu.Controls
            For Each SubMenuItem In MenuItem.Controls
                Cells(Row, 1) = Menu.Caption
                Cells(Row, 2) = MenuItem.Caption
                Cells(Row, 3) = SubMenuItem.Caption
                Row = Row + 1
            Next SubMenuItem
        Next MenuItem
    Next Menu
End Sub
```

Figure 20-4 shows part of the output from this subroutine. Notice that I use On Error Resume Next to ignore the error that occurs if a menu item doesn't have any submenu items.

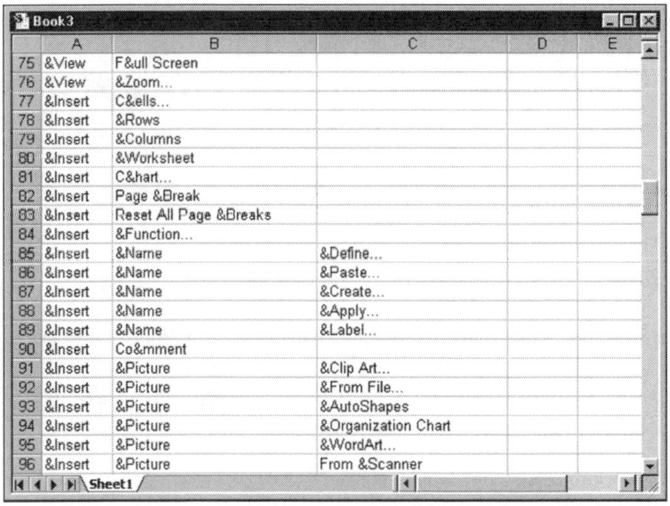

Book3

	A	B	C	D	E
75	&View	F&ull Screen			
76	&View	&Zoom...			
77	&Insert	C&ells...			
78	&Insert	&Rows			
79	&Insert	&Columns			
80	&Insert	&Worksheet			
81	&Insert	C&hart...			
82	&Insert	Page &Break			
83	&Insert	Reset All Page &Breaks			
84	&Insert	&Function...			
85	&Insert	&Name	&Define...		
86	&Insert	&Name	&Paste...		
87	&Insert	&Name	&Create...		
88	&Insert	&Name	&Apply...		
89	&Insert	&Name	&Label...		
90	&Insert	Co&mment			
91	&Insert	&Picture	&Clip Art...		
92	&Insert	&Picture	&From File...		
93	&Insert	&Picture	&AutoShapes		
94	&Insert	&Picture	&Organization Chart		
95	&Insert	&Picture	&WordArt...		
96	&Insert	&Picture	From &Scanner		

Sheet1

Figure 20-4: A listing of all menus, menu items, and submenu items in the Worksheet menu bar.

Properties of CommandBar Controls

CommandBar controls have a number of properties that determine how they look and work. Here's a list of a few of the more useful properties for CommandBar controls:

- ✔ **Caption:** The text displayed for the control.
- ✔ **FaceID:** A number that represents a graphics image displayed next to the control's text.
- ✔ **BeginGroup:** True if a separator bar appears before the control.
- ✔ **OnAction:** The name of a VBA macro to execute when the user clicks the control. If the control is a menu (rather than a menu item or submenu item), the macro is executed when the mouse is moved over the control.
- ✔ **BuiltIn:** True if the control is an Excel built-in control.
- ✔ **Enabled:** True if the control can be clicked.
- ✔ **ToolTipText:** Text that appears when the user moves the mouse pointer over the control.

Where to put your menu code

Most of the time, you'll want the menu changes that you make to be in effect only when a particular workbook is open. Therefore, you'll need VBA code to modify the menu when the workbook is opened, and more VBA code to return the menus to normal when the workbook is closed. A good place for your menu-manipulating code is in the code window for the ThisWorkbook object. More specifically, you'll use the following two subroutines:

- ✔ Sub Workbook_Open( )
- ✔ Sub Workbook_BeforeClose(Cancel As Boolean)

See Chapter 11 for specifics on these subroutines.

If you would like to set things up so that a particular menu modification appears only when a particular workbook is active, you can store your menu manipulation subroutines in the Workbook_BeforeActivate and Workbook_BeforeDeactivate subroutines.

Some Menu Examples

In this section, I present some practical examples of VBA code that manipulates Excel's menus. You'll need to adapt these examples for your own use.

So you messed up your menus, eh?

As you work your way through this chapter, I hope you try out various examples and write your own code to change the Excel menus. In the process, your menus might get messed up. (Mine did as I was writing this chapter.)

Don't fret. It's easy to restore the menu bar to its default state:

1. **Activate a worksheet.**

2. **Choose View⇨Toolbars⇨Customize.**

The Customize dialog box appears.

3. **Select the Worksheet Menu Bar item (or the Chart Menu Bar item if you've messed up that menu).**

4. **Click Reset.**

The menu bar is restored to its default state.

Creating a menu

When you create a menu, you add a new "word" to a menu bar. The control that you add will be of the PopUp type because the menu will always contain menu items.

The following subroutine adds a new menu (Budgeting) between the Window menu and the Help menu on the Worksheet menu bar:

```
Sub AddNewMenu()
'    Get Index of Help menu
     HelpIndex = CommandBars(1).Controls("Help").Index

'    Create the control
     Set NewMenu = CommandBars(1). _
        Controls.Add(Type:=msoControlPopup, _
        Before:=HelpIndex, Temporary:=True)
'    Add a caption
     NewMenu.Caption = "&Budgeting"
End Sub
```

Notice that this subroutine creates an essentially worthless menu — it has no menu items. See the next section, "Adding a menu item," for an example of adding a menu item to a menu.

Figure 20-5 shows the Worksheet menu bar after executing this subroutine.

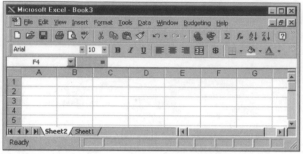

Figure 20-5:
A new
menu was
added
to this
menu bar.

Adding the menu is a two-step process:

1. Create an object variable that refers to the new Control.

In this case, the object variable is named NewMenu.

2. Adjust the properties of the new Control.

In this case, I changed only one property (Caption).

The preceding subroutine uses arguments for the Add method. Specifically, the arguments

🖙 Identify the type of control (msoControlPopup is a built-in constant).

🖙 Identify the position on the menu bar. I determined the position of the Help menu and assigned it to the variable HelpIndex.

🖙 Are temporary. The menu change will not be permanent. In other words, when you restart Excel, the Budgeting menu will not appear.

Adding a menu item

The example in the preceding section demonstrates how to add a menu item to a built-in menu or to a custom menu that you created. The following example adds a menu item to the Excel Format menu. This menu item, when clicked, executes a macro named ToggleWordWrap. The ToggleWordWrap subroutine changes the WrapText property of the selected cells.

After creating the menu item, I change the Caption, OnAction, and BeginGroup properties. Setting BeginGroup to True displays a separator bar before the new menu item. Figure 20-6 shows the modified Format menu.

Figure 20-6:
The Format
menu has a
new item,
Toggle
Word Wrap.

```
Sub AddMenuItem()
   Set Item = CommandBars(1).Controls("Format").Controls.Add
   Item.Caption = "&Toggle Word Wrap"
   Item.OnAction = "ToggleWordWrap"
   Item.BeginGroup = True
End Sub
```

The ToggleWordWrap subroutine is shown next:

```
Sub ToggleWordWrap()
    If TypeName(Selection) = "Range" Then
        Selection.WrapText = Not ActiveCell.WrapText
End If
End Sub
```

Deleting a menu

In some cases, you may want to delete one or more Excel built-in menus while a particular workbook is open. Or you may want to delete a custom menu that you added.

The following statements delete the Help menu for the Worksheet menu bar and the Chart menu bar:

```
Application.CommandBars(1).Controls("Help").Delete
Application.CommandBars(2).Controls("Help").Delete
```

You get an error message if the Help menu does not exist. Therefore, you might want to precede the statements with the following statement, which causes Excel to ignore any errors:

```
On Error Resume Next
```

You can restore built-in menu items that you've deleted in two ways:

✓ Reset the entire menu bar.

✓ Use the Add method to add the built-in menu and then add all the menu items. You may want to record your actions while you use the Customize dialog box to restore a menu.

The following statements reset the Worksheet menu bar and the Chart menu bar:

```
Application.CommandBars(1).Reset
Application.CommandBars(2).Reset
```

Resetting a menu bar destroys any customization you may have performed. For example, if you added a new menu item to the Tools menu, that menu item is removed when the menu bar is reset.

Deleting a menu item

Use the Delete method to delete custom or built-in menu items. The following statement deletes the Exit menu item from the File menu on the Worksheet menu bar:

```
CommandBars(1).Controls("File").Controls("Exit").Delete
```

To get this menu item back, use the Add method. For example:

```
CommandBars(1).Controls("File").Controls.Add _
    Type:=msoControlButton, Id:=752
```

Notice that I have to supply the Id for the Control that I add. The Id for the Exit menu item is 752. How did I figure that out? I entered the following statement in the Immediate window of the VBE:

```
? CommandBars(1).Controls("File").Controls("Exit").Id
```

Changing menu captions

You can change the text displayed (that is, the Caption) for both custom and built-in menus and menu items. You do so by changing the Caption property. This example changes the Help menu in the Worksheet menu bar so that it displays *Assistance:*

```
Sub ChangeHelp()
    CommandBars(1).Controls("Help"). _
      Caption = "&Assistance"
End Sub
```

The following example changes the text of all the menus, menu items, and submenu items to uppercase — probably not something you'd want to do, but it *does* give Excel a new look:

```
Sub UpperCaseMenus()
    On Error Resume Next
    For Each Menu In CommandBars(1).Controls
        Menu.Caption = UCase(Menu.Caption)
        For Each MenuItem In Menu.Controls
            MenuItem.Caption = UCase(MenuItem.Caption)
            For Each SubMenu In MenuItem.Controls
                SubMenu.Caption = UCase(SubMenu.Caption)
            Next SubMenu
        Next MenuItem
    Next Menu
End Sub
```

Figure 20-7 shows how the menus look after you execute this routine. To return things to normal, see the "So you messed up your menus, eh?" sidebar.

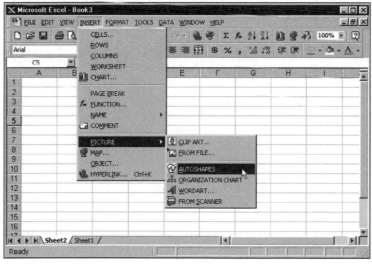

Figure 20-7:
Excel's menus, after being converted to uppercase.

Menu-making conventions

You may have noticed that menus in Windows programs typically adhere to some established conventions. No one knows where these conventions came from, but you should follow them if you want to give the impression that you know what you're doing. When you modify menus, keep the following points in mind:

- The File menu is always first, and the Help menu is always last. It's traditional.

- Menu item text is always proper case — the first letter of each word is uppercase, except for minor words such as *the*, *a*, and *and*.

- Menu items are usually limited to three or fewer words.

- Every menu item should have a hot key

(underlined letter) that's unique to the menu.

- Menu items that display a dialog box are followed by ellipses (...).

- Avoid having a long list of menu items. Sometimes, submenus provide a good alternative. If you must have a lengthy list of menu items, use a separator bar to group items into logical groups.

- Menu items that are not appropriate in the current context appear *grayed*. In VBA terminology, the menu item's Enabled property is set to False.

- Some menu items serve as a toggle. When the option is on, the menu item is preceded by a check mark.

Adding a menu item to the Tools menu

With Excel 5 and Excel 95, it was very easy to assign a macro to a new menu item on the Tools menu. For some reason, this feature was removed from Excel 97 (although you *can* still assign a shortcut key combination by using the Tools⇨Macro⇨Macros command).

With Excel 97, if you want to assign a macro to a menu item on the Tools menu (or any other menu, for that matter), you must write VBA code to do so. Or you can simply use the code that follows. No charge. The two macros are stored in the code window for the ThisWorkbook object. The subroutines are event-handlers that respond to the Workbook Open event and the Workbook BeforeClose event. They include some simple error-handling code to handle the case in which there is no Tools menu.

```
Const MenuItemName = "Run Budget Macro"
Const MenuItemMacro = "UpdateBudget"

Private Sub Workbook_Open()
'    Add a menu item to the Tools menu
'    Delete existing item just in case
     On Error Resume Next
```

```
      Application.CommandBars(1). _
         Controls("Tools").Controls(MenuItemName).Delete

'    Set up error trapping
     On Error GoTo NoCanDo

'    Create the new menu item
     Set NewItem = Application.CommandBars(1). _
        Controls("Tools").Controls.Add

'    Specify the Caption and OnAction properties
     NewItem.Caption = MenuItemName
     NewItem.OnAction = MenuItemMacro

'    Add a separator bar before the menu item
     NewItem.BeginGroup = True
     Exit Sub

'    Error handler
NoCanDo:
     Msg = "An error occurred." & vbCrLf
     Msg = Msg & MenuItemName & _
            " was added to the Tools menu."
     MsgBox Msg, vbCritical
End Sub

Private Sub Workbook_BeforeClose(Cancel As Boolean)
'    Delete existing item just in case
     On Error Resume Next
     Application.CommandBars(1). _
     Controls("Tools").Controls(MenuItemName).Delete
End Sub
```

The example adds a new menu item (Run Budget Macro) to the Tools menu when the workbook is opened. When the workbook is closed, the menu item is removed from the Tools menu.

To use this code in your own application, enter the code into the code window for the ThisWorkbook object. Then change the values for the two constants (MenuItemName and MenuItemMacro).

Working with Shortcut Menus

You can't use the Customize dialog box to remove or modify shortcut menus. The only way to customize shortcut menus is to use VBA.

A shortcut menu appears when you right-click an object. Excel has lots of shortcut menus — 43 to be exact. To work with a shortcut menu, you need to know the Caption or the Index of the shortcut menu. This information isn't available anywhere, but you can use the following subroutine to generate a list of all shortcut menus and the Index and Caption for each:

```
Sub ListShortCutMenus()
    Row = 1
    For Each cbar In CommandBars
        If cbar.Type = msoBarTypePopup Then
            Cells(Row, 1) = cbar.Index
            Cells(Row, 2) = cbar.Name
            For col = 1 To cbar.Controls.Count
                Cells(Row, col + 2) = _
                cbar.Controls(col).Caption
            Next col
            Row = Row + 1
        End If
    Next cbar
End Sub
```

Figure 20-8 shows a portion of the output. The shortcut menus have indexes that range from 19–47 and 70–83.

Be careful when you modify shortcut menus. Like normal menus, changes to shortcut menus are saved between sessions. Therefore, you'll probably want to reset the shortcut menus when your application ends.

Adding menu items to a shortcut menu

Adding a menu item to a shortcut menu works just like adding a menu item to a regular menu. You need to know the Index or the Caption for the shortcut menu. See the preceding section to find out how to get a list of all shortcut menus.

The following example demonstrates how to add a menu item to the shortcut menu that appears when you right-click a cell. This shortcut menu has an Index of 21. This menu item is added to the end of the shortcut menu.

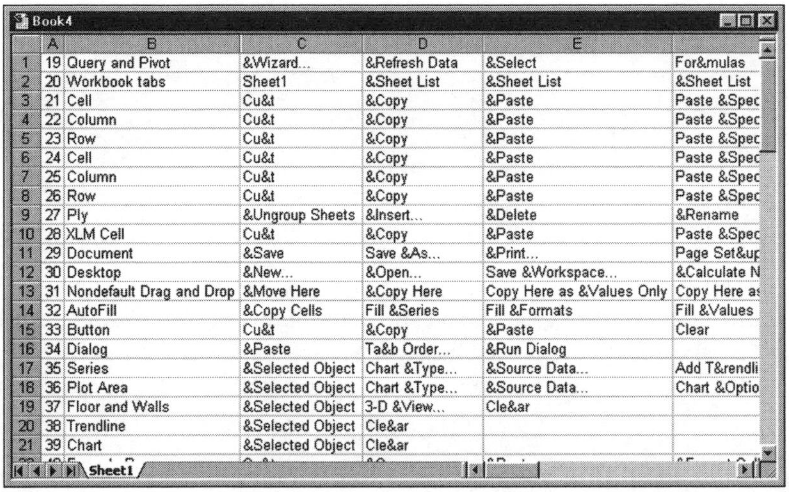

	A	B	C	D	E	
1	19	Query and Pivot	&Wizard...	&Refresh Data	&Select	For&mulas
2	20	Workbook tabs	Sheet1	&Sheet List	&Sheet List	&Sheet List
3	21	Cell	Cu&t	&Copy	&Paste	Paste &Spec
4	22	Column	Cu&t	&Copy	&Paste	Paste &Spec
5	23	Row	Cu&t	&Copy	&Paste	Paste &Spec
6	24	Cell	Cu&t	&Copy	&Paste	Paste &Spec
7	25	Column	Cu&t	&Copy	&Paste	Paste &Spec
8	26	Row	Cu&t	&Copy	&Paste	Paste &Spec
9	27	Ply	&Ungroup Sheets	&Insert...	&Delete	&Rename
10	28	XLM Cell	Cu&t	&Copy	&Paste	Paste &Spec
11	29	Document	&Save	Save &As...	&Print...	Page Set&up
12	30	Desktop	&New...	&Open...	Save &Workspace...	&Calculate N
13	31	Nondefault Drag and Drop	&Move Here	&Copy Here	Copy Here as &Values Only	Copy Here a
14	32	AutoFill	&Copy Cells	Fill &Series	Fill &Formats	Fill &Values
15	33	Button	Cu&t	&Copy	&Paste	Clear
16	34	Dialog	&Paste	Ta&b Order...	&Run Dialog	
17	35	Series	&Selected Object	Chart &Type...	&Source Data...	Add T&rendli
18	36	Plot Area	&Selected Object	Chart &Type...	&Source Data...	Chart &Optio
19	37	Floor and Walls	&Selected Object	3-D &View...	Cle&ar	
20	38	Trendline	&Selected Object	Cle&ar		
21	39	Chart	&Selected Object	Cle&ar		

Figure 20-8:
A listing of all shortcut menus, plus the menu items in each.

```
Sub AddItemToShortcut()
    Set NewItem = CommandBars(21).Controls.Add
    NewItem.Caption = "Toggle Word Wrap"
    NewItem.OnAction = "ToggleWordWrap"
    NewItem.BeginGroup = True
End Sub
```

Selecting the new menu item executes the ToggleWordWrap subroutine.

Deleting menu items from a shortcut menu

The following routine removes the Hide menu item from two shortcut menus: the menus that appear when you right-click a row header (shortcut menu 23) or a column header (shortcut menu 22).

```
Sub RemoveHideMenuItem()
    CommandBars(22).Controls("Hide").Delete
    CommandBars(23).Controls("Hide").Delete
End Sub
```

Disabling shortcut menus

You may want to disable one or more shortcut menus while your application is running. For example, you may not want the user to access the commands by right-clicking a cell. If you want to disable all shortcut menus, use the following subroutine:

```
Sub DisableShortcuts()
    For i = 19 To 47
    CommandBars(i).Enabled = False
    Next i
For i = 70 To 84
    CommandBars(i).Enabled = False
    Next i
End Sub
```

Disabling the shortcut menus "sticks" between sessions. Therefore, you'll probably want to restore the shortcut menus before closing Excel. To restore the shortcut menus, modify the preceding subroutine to set the Enabled property to True.

Finding Out More

This chapter introduces the concept of menu modifications made with VBA and presents several examples that you can adapt to your own needs. A good way to find out more about using VBA to modify menus is to record your actions while you make menu changes using the View⇨Toolbars⇨ Customize command. And, of course, the online help system contains all the details you need.

Part VI
Putting It All Together

The 5th Wave   By Rich Tennant

"...AND FOR THE HI-TECH MAN IN YOUR LIFE, WE HAVE THIS LOVELY PC-ON-A-ROPE."

In this part . . .

The preceding 20 chapters cover quite a bit of material. At this point, you may still feel a bit disjointed about all this VBA stuff. The four chapters in this part fill in the gaps and tie everything together. I discuss custom worksheet functions (a very useful feature), describe add-ins, provide more programming examples, and wrap up with a discussion of user-oriented applications.

Chapter 21

Creating Worksheet Functions — and Living to Tell about It

In This Chapter

▶ Why custom worksheet functions are so useful

▶ Examples of functions that use various types of arguments

▶ What you need to know about the Paste Function dialog box

*F*or many people, the main attraction of VBA is the capability to create custom worksheet functions — functions that look, work, and feel just like those that Microsoft built into Excel. A custom function offers the added advantage of working exactly how you want it to. I introduce custom functions in Chapter 5. In this chapter, I get down to the nitty-gritty and describe some tricks of the trade.

Why Create Custom Functions?

You are undoubtedly familiar with Excel's worksheet functions — even Excel novices know how to use common worksheet functions such as SUM, AVERAGE, and IF. By my count, Excel contains more than 300 predefined worksheet functions. And if that's not enough, you can create custom functions by using VBA.

With all the functions available in Excel and VBA, you may wonder why you would ever need to create functions. The answer: to simplify your work. With a bit of planning, custom functions are very useful in worksheet formulas and VBA procedures. Often, for example, you can significantly shorten a formula by creating a custom function. After all, shorter formulas are more readable and easier to work with.

What custom worksheet functions can't do

As you develop custom functions for use in your worksheet formulas, it's important that you understand a key point. VBA worksheet function procedures are essentially *passive*. For example, code within a function procedure cannot manipulate ranges, change formatting, or perform many of the other actions that a subroutine can perform. An example may help you understand this important point.

You might try to write a custom function that changes the formatting of a cell. For example, it might be useful to create a function that changes the color of text in a cell, based on the cell's value. Try as you might, however, you can't write such a function. Just remember this: A function returns a value — it does not perform actions with objects.

Function Basics

A VBA function is a procedure that's stored in a VBA module. These functions can be

✔ Used in other VBA procedures

✔ Used in your worksheet formulas

Functions are stored in a VBA module, and a module can contain any number of functions. You can use a custom function in a formula just as if it were a built-in function. If the function is defined in a different workbook, however, you must precede the function name with the workbook name. For example, assume that you've developed a function called DiscountPrice (which takes one argument), and the function is stored in a workbook named PRICING.XLS.

To use this function in the same workbook, enter a formula such as

```
=DiscountPrice(A1)
```

If you want to use this function in a *different* workbook, enter a formula, such as

```
=pricing.xls!discountprice(A1)
```

If the custom function is stored in an add-in, you don't need to precede the function name with the workbook name. I discuss add-ins in Chapter 22.

Custom functions appear in the Paste Function dialog box, in the User Defined category. The easiest way to enter a custom function into a formula is to use the Insert⇨Function command or click the Insert Function button on the Standard toolbar. Both of these methods display the Paste Function dialog box.

Writing Functions

Remember that a function's name acts like a variable. The final value of this variable is the value returned by the function. To demonstrate, examine the following function, which returns the first name of the user:

```
Function FirstName()
    FullName = Application.UserName
    FirstSpace = InStr(FullName, " ")
    If FirstSpace = 0 Then
        FirstName = FullName
    Else
        FirstName = Left(FullName, FirstSpace - 1)
    End If
End Function
```

This function starts by assigning the UserName property of the Application object to a variable named FullName. Next, it uses the VBA InStr function to locate the first space in the name. If there is no space, FirstSpace is equal to 0 and FirstName is equal to the entire name. If FullName *does* have a space, the Left function extracts the text to the left of the space and assigns it to FirstName.

Notice that FirstName is the name of the function and is also used as a variable name in the function. The final value of FirstName is the value that's returned by the function. Several intermediate calculations may be going on in the function, but the function always returns the last value assigned to the variable that represents the function's name.

Function Arguments

To work with functions, you need to understand how to work with arguments. The following points apply to the arguments for Excel worksheet functions and custom VBA functions:

- ✔ Arguments can be variables (including arrays), constants, literals, or expressions.
- ✔ Some functions have no arguments.

✔ Some functions have a fixed number of required arguments (from 1 to 60).

✔ Some functions have a combination of required and optional arguments.

Function Examples

The examples in this section demonstrate how to work with various types of arguments.

A function with no argument

Like subroutines, functions need not have arguments. For example, Excel has a few built-in worksheet functions that don't use arguments, including RAND, TODAY, and NOW.

Here's a simple example of a function with no arguments. The following function returns the UserName property of the Application object. This name appears in the Options dialog box (General tab). This simple but useful example shows the only way you can get the user's name to appear in a worksheet formula:

```
Function User()
'   Returns the name of the current user
    User = Application.UserName
End Function
```

When you enter the following formula into a worksheet cell, the cell displays the name of the current user:

```
=User()
```

As with the Excel built-in functions, when you use a function with no arguments, you must include a set of empty parentheses.

A function with one argument

This section describes a function designed for sales managers who need to calculate the commissions earned by their salespeople. The commission rate depends on the monthly sales volume — those who sell more earn a higher commission rate. The function returns the commission amount, based on the monthly sales (which is the function's only argument — a required argument). The calculations in this example are based on the following table:

Monthly Sales	Commission Rate
0 – $9,999	8.0%
$10,000 – $19,999	10.5%
$20,000 – $39,999	12.0%
$40,000+	14.0%

You can use several approaches to calculate commissions for various sales amounts entered into a worksheet. You *could* write a formula such as this:

```
=IF(AND(A1>=0,A1<=9999.99),A1*0.08,IF(AND(A1>=10000,A1<=199
        99.99),A1*0.105,IF(AND(A1>=20000,A1<=39999.99),A1*0.12,IF(A1
        >=40000,A1*0.14,0))))
```

This is a bad approach for a couple reasons. First, the formula is overly complex. Second, the values are hard-coded into the formula, making the formula difficult to modify if the commission structure changes.

A better approach is to create a table of commission values and then use a lookup table function to compute the commissions, as shown in the following example:

```
=VLOOKUP(A1,Table,2)*A1
```

Yet another approach, which doesn't require a table of commissions, is to create a custom function such as the following:

```
Function Commission(Sales)
'    Calculates sales commissions
    Tier1 = 0.08
    Tier2 = 0.105
    Tier3 = 0.12
    Tier4 = 0.14
    Select Case Sales
        Case 0 To 9999.99: Commission = Sales * Tier1
        Case 10000 To 19999.99: Commission = Sales * Tier2
        Case 20000 To 39999.99: Commission = Sales * Tier3
        Case Is >= 40000: Commission = Sales * Tier4
    End Select
End Function
```

After you define this function in a VBA module, you can use it in a worksheet formula. Entering the following formula into a cell produces a result of 3,000 (the amount, 25,000, qualifies for a commission rate of 12 percent):

```
=Commission(25000)
```

Figure 21-1 shows a worksheet that uses this new function.

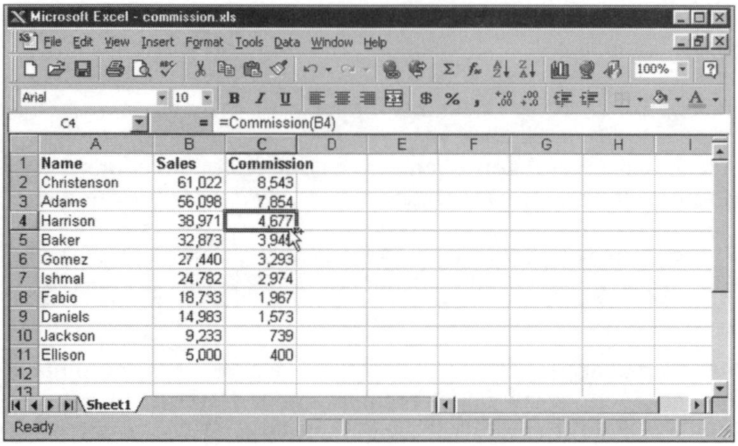

Figure 21-1:
Using the
Commission
function
in a
worksheet.

A function with two arguments

The next example builds on the preceding one. Imagine that the sales manager implements a new policy: The total commission paid increases by 1 percent for every year the salesperson has been with the company.

I modified the custom Commission function (defined in the preceding section) so that it takes two arguments — both of which are required arguments. Call this new function *Commission2*:

```
Function Commission2(Sales, Years)
'    Calculates sales commissions based on years in service
     Tier1 = 0.08
     Tier2 = 0.105
     Tier3 = 0.12
     Tier4 = 0.14
     Select Case Sales
         Case 0 To 9999.99: Commission2 = Sales * Tier1
         Case 10000 To 19999.99: Commission2 = Sales * _
           Tier2
         Case 20000 To 39999.99: Commission2 = Sales * _
```

```
              Tier3
          Case Is >= 40000: Commission2 = Sales * Tier4
      End Select
      Commission2 = Commission2 + (Commission2 * Years / _
          100)
End Function
```

I simply added the second argument (Years) to the Function statement and included an additional computation that adjusts the commission before exiting the function.

Here's an example of how you can write a formula by using this function. (It assumes that the sales amount is in cell A1; cell B1 specifies the number of years the salesperson has worked.)

```
=Commission2(A1,B1)
```

A function with a range argument

The following example demonstrates how to use a worksheet range as an argument. Actually, it's not at all tricky; Excel takes care of the behind-the-scenes details.

Assume that you want to calculate the average of the five largest values in a range named Data. Excel doesn't have a function that can do this, so you would probably write a formula such as

```
=(LARGE(Data,1)+LARGE(Data,2)+LARGE(Data,3)+LARGE(Data,4)+ _
          LARGE(Data,5))/5
```

This formula uses Excel's LARGE function, which returns the nth largest value in a range. The formula adds the five largest values in the range named Data and then divides the result by 5. The formula works fine, but it's rather unwieldy. And what if you decide that you need to compute the average of the top *six* values? You would need to rewrite the formula — and make sure that you update all copies of the formula.

Wouldn't this be easier if Excel had a function named TopAvg? Then you could compute the average by using the following (nonexistent) function:

```
=TopAvg(Data,5)
```

This example shows a case in which a custom function can make things much easier for you. The following custom VBA function, named *TopAvg*, returns the average of the N largest values in a range:

```
Function TopAvg(InRange, N)
'    Returns the average of the highest N values in InRange
     Sum = 0
     For i = 1 To N
         Sum = Sum + _
             Application.WorksheetFunction.LARGE(InRange, i)
     Next i
     TopAvg = Sum / N
End Function
```

This function takes two arguments: InRange (which is a worksheet range) and N (the number of values to average). It starts by initializing the Sum variable to 0. It then uses a For-Next loop to calculate the sum of the *N* largest values in the range. Note that I use the Excel LARGE function within the loop. Finally, TopAvg is assigned the value of Sum divided by N.

You can use all Excel worksheet functions in your VBA procedures *except* those that have equivalents in VBA. For example, VBA has a Rand function that returns a random number. Therefore, you can't use the Excel RND function in a VBA procedure.

A function with an optional argument

Many Excel built-in worksheet functions use optional arguments. An example is the LEFT function, which returns characters from the left side of a string; its official syntax is

```
LEFT(text[,num_chars])
```

The first argument is required, but the second is optional. If you omit the optional argument, Excel assumes a value of 1. Therefore, the following formulas return the same result:

```
=LEFT(A1,1)
=LEFT(A1)
```

The custom functions you develop in VBA also can have optional arguments. You specify an optional argument by preceding the argument's name with the keyword *Optional*. Your function then needs to test for the existence of the optional argument. If it's missing, the code must assign a default value for the optional argument.

The following example shows a custom function that uses an optional argument. This function randomly chooses one cell from an input range. The range passed as an argument is actually an array, and the function selects one item from the array at random. If the second argument is 1, the selected value changes whenever the worksheet is recalculated (the function is made *volatile*). If the second argument is 0 (or omitted), the function is not recalculated unless one of the cells in the input range is modified. I used the VBA IsMissing function to determine whether the second argument was supplied.

```
Function DrawOne(InputRange, Optional Recalc)
'    Chooses one cell at random from a range

'    Assign default value (0) if 2nd argument is missing
     If IsMissing(Recalc) Then Recalc = 0

'    Make function volatile if Recalc is 1
     If Recalc = 1 Then Application.Volatile True

'    Determine a random cell
     DrawOne = InputRange(Int((InputRange.Count) * Rnd + _
          1))
End Function
```

You may use this function for choosing lottery numbers, selecting a winner from a list of names, and so on.

Keep the following points in mind when you create a function with optional arguments:

- ✔ Optional arguments are always of the variant data type.
- ✔ If you specify an optional argument, all subsequent arguments in the argument list must also be optional and declared with the optional keyword.
- ✔ Each optional argument must be tested in the function to determine its existence and assigned a default value if it's not supplied.

A function with an indefinite number of arguments

Some Excel worksheet functions take an indefinite number of arguments. A familiar example is the SUM function, which has the following syntax:

```
SUM(number1,number2...)
```

Debugging custom functions

Debugging a function procedure can be a bit more challenging than debugging a subroutine procedure. If you develop a function for use in worksheet formulas, you'll find that an error in the function procedure simply results in an error display in the formula cell (usually #VALUE!). In other words, you don't receive the normal run-time error message that helps you locate the offending statement.

Here are three methods you can use for debugging custom functions:

✔ **Place MsgBox functions at strategic locations to monitor the value of specific variables.** Fortunately, message boxes in function procedures do pop up when you execute the procedure. Make sure that only one formula in the worksheet uses your function, or the message boxes will appear for each formula that's evaluated — which could get very annoying.

✔ **Test the procedure by calling it from a subroutine procedure.** Run-time errors appear normally in a pop-up window, and you can either correct the problem (if you know it) or jump right into the debugger.

✔ **Set a breakpoint in the function and then use the Excel debugger to step through the function.** You can then access all the usual debugging tools. Refer to Chapter 13 to learn about the debugger.

The first argument is required, but you can have as many as 29 additional arguments. Here's an example of a SUM function with four range arguments:

```
=SUM(A1:A5,C1:C5,E1:E5,G1:G5)
```

Here's a function that can have any number of single-value arguments (it doesn't work with multicell range arguments):

```
Function Concat(string1, ParamArray string2())
'    Demonstrates indefinite number of function arguments

'    Process the first argument
    Concat = string1

'    Process additional arguments (if any)
    If UBound(string2) <> -1 Then
        For args = LBound(string2) To UBound(string2)
            Concat = Concat & " " & string2(args)
        Next args
    End If
End Function
```

This function is similar to the Excel CONCATENATE function, which combines text arguments into a single string. The difference is that this custom function inserts a space between each pair of concatenated strings.

The second argument, string2( ), is an array preceded by the ParamArray keyword. If the second argument is empty, the UBound function returns –1 and the function ends. If the second argument is not empty, the procedure loops through the elements of the string2 array and processes each additional argument. The LBound and UBound functions determine the beginning and ending elements of the array, and the beginning element is normally 0 unless you declare it as something else or use an Option Base 1 statement at the beginning of your module.

ParamArray can apply to only the *last* argument in the procedure. It is always a variant data type, and it is always an optional argument (although you don't use the Optional keyword).

Figure 21-2 shows this function in use. It also shows how the results differ from those produced by the Excel CONCATENATE function, which doesn't insert a space between the concatenated items.

Figure 21-2:
Using the
Concat
function
and the
Excel
CONCA-
TENATE
function.

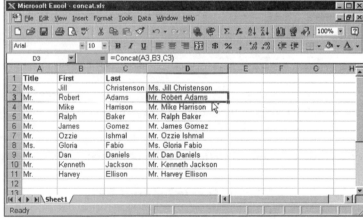

The Paste Function Dialog Box

The Excel Paste Function dialog box is a handy tool that lets you choose a worksheet function from a list and prompts you for the function's arguments. And, as I note earlier in this chapter, your custom worksheet functions also appear in the Paste Function dialog box. Custom functions appear in the User Defined category.

Function procedures defined with the Private keyword do not appear in the Function Wizard.

Displaying the function's description

The Paste Function dialog box displays a description of each built-in function. But, as you can see in Figure 21-3, a custom function displays the following text as its description: *Choose the Help button for help on this function and its arguments.* This description isn't very descriptive; in fact, it's downright wrong — clicking the Help button *won't* give you any help regarding the function.

Figure 21-3:
By default,
a custom
function
displays a
generic
description
in the Paste
Function
dialog box.

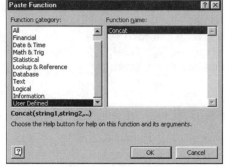

To display a meaningful description of your custom function in the Paste Function dialog box, you need to perform a few additional (nonintuitive) steps:

1. **Activate a worksheet in the workbook that contains the custom function.**

2. **Choose Tools⇨Macro⇨Macros (or press Alt+F8).**

   The Macro dialog box appears.

3. **In the Macro Name field, type the function's name.**

4. **Click the Options button.**

   The Macro Options dialog box appears.

5. **In the Description field, type a description for the function.**

6. **Click OK.**

7. **Click Cancel.**

After performing these steps, the Paste Function dialog box will display the description for your function (see Figure 21-4).

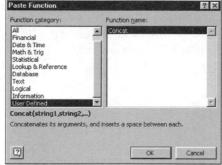

Figure 21-4:
The custom
function
now
displays a
description.

Function categories

Custom functions are always listed under the User Defined category; there is
no straightforward, reliable way to create a new function category for your
custom functions.

Argument descriptions

When you access a built-in function from the Paste Function dialog box, the
Formula Palette displays a description of each argument. (See Figure 21-5.)
Unfortunately, you can't provide such descriptions for custom functions.
You can, however, make your argument names descriptive — which is a
good idea.

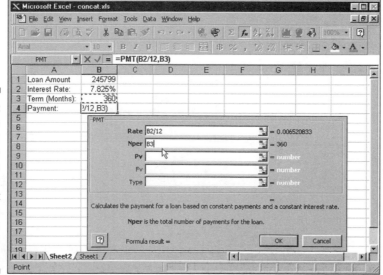

Figure 21-5:
The
Formula
Palette
displays
function
argument
descriptions
for built-in
functions
only.

This chapter provides lots of information about creating custom worksheet functions. Use these examples as models when you create functions for your own work. As usual, the online help provides additional details. See the next chapter if you want to find out how to make your custom functions more accessible by storing them in an add-in.

Chapter 22
Creating Excel Add-Ins

● ●

In This Chapter

▶ Add-ins: What a concept!

▶ Why you might want to create your own add-ins

▶ Creating custom add-ins

● ●

*O*ne of the slickest features of Excel — at least in *my* mind — is the capability to create add-ins. In this chapter, I explain why this feature is so slick, and I show you how to create your own add-ins by using only the tools built into Excel.

Okay . . . So What Is an Add-In?

What's an add-in? Glad you asked. A spreadsheet add-in is something you add to enhance a spreadsheet's functionality. Some add-ins provide new worksheet functions you can use in formulas; other add-ins provide new commands or utilities. The new features usually blend in well with the original interface, so they appear to be part of the program.

Excel ships with several add-ins you can use. Some of the more popular add-ins include the Analysis ToolPak, Internet Assistant Wizard, and Solver. You can also get Excel add-ins from third-party suppliers or as shareware (my Power Utility Pak is an example).

Any knowledgeable user can create Excel add-ins. (No special C++ programming skills are required.) An Excel add-in is basically a different form of an XLS workbook file. More specifically, an add-in is a normal XLS workbook with the following differences:

  ✔ The IsAddin property of the Workbook is True.

  ✔ The workbook window is hidden, and can't be unhidden using the Window➪Unhide command.

  ✔ The workbook is not a member of the Workbooks collection.

You can convert any XLS file into an add-in. Because add-ins are always hidden, you can't display worksheets or chart sheets that an add-in contains. But you can access an add-in's VBA subroutines and functions, and display dialog boxes contained on UserForms.

Why Create Add-Ins?

You might decide to convert your XLS application into an add-in for any of the following reasons:

- ✔ **Prevent access to your code.** When you distribute an application as an add-in (and you protect it), users can't view the sheets in the workbook. If you use proprietary techniques in your VBA code, you can prevent anyone from copying the code.

- ✔ **Avoid confusion.** If a user loads your application as an add-in, the file is not visible and is therefore less likely to confuse novice users or get in the way. Unlike a hidden XLS workbook, an add-in can't be unhidden.

- ✔ **Simplify access to worksheet functions.** Custom worksheet functions that you store in an add-in don't require the workbook name qualifier. For example, if you store a custom function named MOVAVG in a workbook named NEWFUNC.XLS, you must use syntax like the following to use this function in a different workbook:

```
=NEWFUNC.XLS!MOVAVG(A1:A50)
```

But if this function is stored in an add-in file that's open, you can use much simpler syntax because you don't need to include the file reference:

```
=MOVAVG(A1:A50)
```

- ✔ **Provide easier access for users.** After you identify the location of your add-in, it appears in the Add-Ins dialog box, with a friendly name and a description of what it does.

- ✔ **Gain better control over loading.** Add-ins can be opened automatically when Excel starts, regardless of the directory in which they are stored.

- ✔ **Avoid displaying prompts when unloading.** When an add-in is closed, the user never sees the "Save change in...?" prompt.

Working with Add-Ins

The most efficient way to load and unload add-ins is by using the Excel Add-Ins dialog box, which you access by choosing Tools⇨Add-Ins. This command displays the dialog box shown in Figure 22-1. The list box contains the names of all add-ins that Excel knows about. In this list, check marks identify any currently open add-ins. You can open and close add-ins from this dialog box by checking or unchecking the check boxes.

Figure 22-1:
The Add-Ins
dialog box
lists all add-
ins known
to Excel.

You can open most add-in files also by choosing the File⇨Open command. However, you can't close an open add-in by choosing File⇨Close. You can remove the add-in only by exiting and restarting Excel or by writing a macro to close the add-in.

When you open an add-in, you may or may not notice anything different. In almost every case, however, the menu changes in some way — Excel displays either a new menu or one or more new menu items on an existing menu. For example, when you open the Analysis ToolPak add-in, this add-in gives you a new menu item on the Tools menu: Data Analysis. When you open my Power Utility Pak add-in, you get a new Utilities menu, located between the Data menu and the Window menu. If the add-in contains only custom worksheet functions, the new functions will appear in the Paste Function dialog box.

Add-In Basics

Although you can convert any workbook to an add-in, not all workbooks benefit from this change. Workbooks that consist only of worksheets will become unusable because add-ins are hidden and you can't access the worksheets.

In fact, the only types of workbooks that benefit from being converted to an add-in are those with macros. For example, a workbook that consists of general-purpose macros (subroutines and functions) makes an ideal add-in.

Creating an add-in is simple. These steps describe how to create an add-in from a normal workbook file:

1. **Develop your application, and make sure that everything works properly.**

   Don't forget to include a method for executing the macro or macros. You might want to add a new menu item to the Tools menu, or create a custom toolbar. See Chapter 20 for details on customizing the menus, and Chapter 19 for a discussion of custom toolbars.

2. **Test the application by executing it when a *different* workbook is active.**

   This simulates the application's behavior when it's used as an add-in because an add-in is never the active workbook.

3. **Activate the VBE and select the workbook in the Project window. Choose Tools⇨*xxx* Properties and click the Protection tab. Select the Lock project for viewing check box and enter a password (twice). Click OK.**

   This step is necessary only if you want to prevent others from viewing or modifying your macros or custom dialog boxes.

4. **In Excel, choose File⇨Properties, click the Summary tab, and enter a brief descriptive title in the Title field and a longer description in the Comments field.**

   This step is not required, but it makes the add-in easier to use.

5. **Choose Excel's File⇨Save As.**

6. **In the Save As dialog box, select Microsoft Excel add-in (*.xla) from the Save as type drop-down list.**

7. **Click Save.**

You've just created an add-in! The file is saved with an XLA extension, and the original workbook remains open.

With previous versions of Excel, if you needed to make a change to an add-in, you had to use the original XLS, make the change, and then re-create the add-in. With Excel 97, this is no longer necessary. As long as the add-in is not protected, you can make changes to the add-in in the VBE and then save your changes. If the add-in is protected, you need to enter the password to unprotect it.

An Add-In Example

In this section, I discuss the basic steps involved in creating a useful add-in. The example uses the ChangeCase text conversion utility that I describe in Chapter 16.

Setting up the workbook

The workbook consists of one (blank) worksheet, a VBA module, and a UserForm. In addition, I added code to the ThisWorkbook object that creates a new menu item on the Tools menu.

The ThisWorkbook object

The following code, located in the Code window for the ThisWorkbook object, is executed when the workbook (soon to be an add-in) is opened. This subroutine creates a new menu item (Change Case of Text) on the Tools menu. This menu item executes the ChangeCase subroutine (which is listed in the next section).

See Chapter 20 for details on working with menus.

```
Const MenuItemName = "Change Case of Te&xt..."
Const MenuItemMacro = "ChangeCase"

Private Sub Workbook_Open()
'   Adds a menu item to the Tools menu
'   Delete existing item just in case
    On Error Resume Next
    Application.CommandBars(1). _
        Controls("Tools").Controls(MenuItemName).Delete

'   Set up error trapping
    On Error GoTo NoCanDo

'   Create the new menu item
    Set NewItem = Application.CommandBars(1). _
        Controls("Tools").Controls.Add

'   Specify the Caption and OnAction properties
    NewItem.Caption = MenuItemName
    NewItem.OnAction = MenuItemMacro
```

(continued)

(continued)

```
'    Add a separator bar before the menu item
     NewItem.BeginGroup = True
     Exit Sub

'    Error handler
NoCanDo:
     Msg = "An error occurred." & vbCrLf
     Msg = Msg & MenuItemName & " was added to the Tools _
           menu."
     MsgBox Msg, vbCritical
End Sub
```

The following subroutine is executed before the workbook is closed. This subroutine removes the menu item from the Tools menu.

```
Private Sub Workbook_BeforeClose(Cancel As Boolean)
'    Delete existing item just in case
     On Error Resume Next
     Application.CommandBars(1). _
     Controls("Tools").Controls(MenuItemName).Delete
End Sub
```

The Module 1 module

The VBA module contains a short subroutine that serves as the "entry point" — it makes sure that a range is selected. If so, the dialog box is displayed.

```
Sub ChangeCase()
'    Exit if a range is not selected
     If TypeName(Selection) <> "Range" Then Exit Sub
'    Display the dialog box
     UserForm1.Show
End Sub
```

The UserForm

Figure 22-2 shows UserForm1. It consists of three OptionButtons, named OptionUpper, OptionLower, and OptionProper. In addition, it has a Cancel button (named CancelButton) and an OK button (named OKButton).

The code executed when the Cancel button is clicked is listed next. This subroutine simply unloads the UserForm with no action.

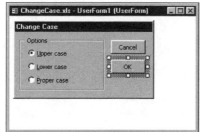

Figure 22-2:
UserForm1.

```
Private Sub CancelButton_Click()
    Unload UserForm1
End Sub
```

The code executed when the OK button is clicked follows. This is the code that does all the work.

```
Private Sub OKButton_Click()
'   Create an object with just text constants
    On Error Resume Next
    Set TextCells = Selection.SpecialCells(xlConstants, _
        xlTextValues)

'   Turn off screen updating
    Application.ScreenUpdating = False

'   Uppercase
    If OptionUpper Then
        For Each cell In TextCells
            cell.Value = UCase(cell.Value)
        Next cell
    End If
'   Lowercase
    If OptionLower Then
        For Each cell In TextCells
            cell.Value = LCase(cell.Value)
        Next cell
    End If
'   Proper case
    If OptionProper Then
        For Each cell In TextCells
            cell.Value = _
```

(continued)

(continued)

```
            Application.WorksheetFunction.Proper(cell.Value)
        Next cell
    End If

'   Unload the dialog box
    Unload UserForm1
End Sub
```

This version of ChangeCase differs from the version in Chapter 16. For this example, I use the SpecialCells Method to create an object variable that consists of only those cells in the selection that contain constants (not formulas) or text. This makes the routine run much faster. See Chapter 14 for more information on this technique.

Testing the workbook

Before converting this workbook to an add-in, you need to test it. To simulate what happens when the workbook is an add-in, you should test the workbook when a different workbook is active. Remember, an add-in is never the active sheet. Because this workbook has a Workbook_Open subroutine (to add a menu item), you should close the workbook and then reopen it to ensure that this subroutine is working correctly.

Open a new workbook, and enter information into some cells. For testing purposes, enter various types of information, including text, values, and formulas. Or just open an existing workbook and use it for your tests. Select one or more cells (or entire rows and columns), and execute the ChangeCase macro by choosing the new Tools➪Change Case of Text command. I think you'll find that it works just fine.

Adding descriptive information

I recommend entering a description of your add-in, but this step is not required. Choose the File➪Properties command, which opens the Properties dialog box. Then click the Summary tab, as shown in Figure 22-3.

Enter a title for the add-in in the Title field. This text appears in the Add-Ins dialog box. In the Comments field, enter a description. This information appears at the bottom of the Add-Ins dialog box when the add-in is selected.

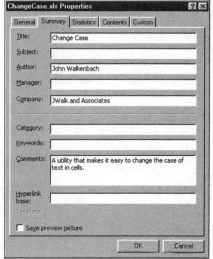

Figure 22-3:
Use the
Properties
dialog box
to enter
descriptive
information
about your
add-in.

Creating the add-in

To create the add-in:

1. **Activate the VBE and select the workbook in the Project window.**

2. **Choose Tools⇨*xxx* Properties, and click the Protection tab.**

3. **Select the Lock project for viewing check box and enter a password (twice). Click OK.**

4. **Save the workbook.**

5. **Activate the worksheet and choose File⇨Save As.**

   Excel displays its Save As dialog box.

6. **In the Save as type drop-down, select Microsoft Excel add-in (*.xla).**

7. **Click Save.**

A new add-in file is created, and the original XLS version remains open.

Opening the add-in

To avoid confusion, close the XLS workbook before opening the add-in created from that workbook. If you don't close the XLS workbook, the Tools menu may have two Change Case of Text menu items (one for the XLS version, and one for the XLA version).

To open the add-in:

1. **Choose the Tools⇨Add-Ins command.**

   Excel displays the Add-Ins dialog box.

2. **Click the Browse button, locate the add-in you just created, and select it.**

   After you find your new add-in, the Add-Ins dialog box displays the add-in in its list. As shown in Figure 22-4, the Add-Ins dialog box also displays the descriptive information you provided in the Properties dialog box.

3. **Click OK to close the dialog box and open the add-in.**

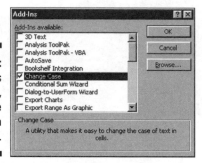

Figure 22-4: The Add-Ins dialog box, with the new add-in selected.

After you open the add-in, the Tools menu displays the new menu item that executes the ChangeCase macro in the add-in.

Distributing the add-in

You can distribute this add-in to other Excel users by simply giving them a copy of the XLA file. (They don't need the XLS version.) When they open the add-in, the new Change Case of Text command appears on the Tools menu. Because you locked the file with a password, your macro code cannot be viewed by others (unless they know the password).

Modifying the add-in

If you want to modify the add-in, you need to unlock it. To unlock it, activate the VBE and double-click the project's name in the Project window. You'll be prompted for the password. Enter your password, make your changes, and then save the file from the VBE (using the File⇨Save command).

If you create an add-in that stores information in a worksheet, you must set the workbook's IsAddIn property to False to view the workbook. You do this in the Property window when the ThisWorkbook objects is selected (see Figure 22-5). After you've made your changes, make sure that you set the IsAddIn property back to True.

You now know how to work with add-ins and why you might want to create your own add-ins. One example in this chapter shows you the steps for creating an add-in that changes the case of text in selected cells. The best way to discover more about add-ins is by creating some.

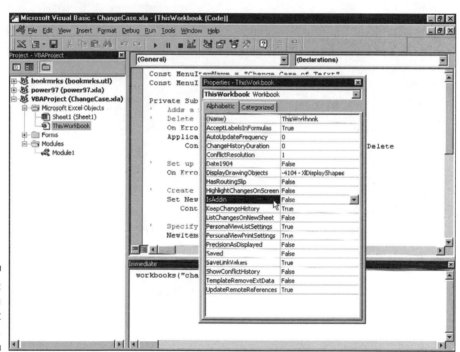

Figure 22-5:
Making an add-in not an add-in.

Chapter 23

Creating Excel Applications for Other Users

In This Chapter

▶ Differences between developing spreadsheets for you and developing spreadsheets for others

▶ Knowing what makes a good spreadsheet application

▶ Guidelines for developing applications that others will use

*E*xcel programmers develop two basic types of spreadsheets: (1) spreadsheets that only they will use, and (2) spreadsheets that other people will use. This distinction often determines how much effort you need to put into creating a spreadsheet. Developing spreadsheets for your use is much easier than developing spreadsheets that others will use.

In this chapter, I provide general guidelines for developing spreadsheets that others will use. But even if you're the only person who uses your spreadsheet creations, you might discover some helpful hints.

What Is a Spreadsheet Application?

Excel programming is essentially the process of building applications that use a spreadsheet rather than a traditional programming language such as C, Pascal, or BASIC. In many cases, people other than the application developer use these applications.

The definition

Without further ado, here's my working definition of a *spreadsheet application:*

> A spreadsheet file (or a group of related files) designed so that someone other than the developer can perform useful work without extensive training.

Based on this definition, most of the spreadsheet files you've developed probably don't qualify as spreadsheet applications. You may have hundreds of spreadsheet files on your hard disk, but you probably didn't design most of them so that others can use them.

Throughout this chapter, I use the terms *developer* and *end users.* The developer is the person who creates and maintains the application (that's you!), and the end users are the folks who benefit from your efforts (this group also could include you).

What makes a good application?

Like witches, there are good spreadsheet applications and bad spreadsheet applications. How can you tell them apart? A good spreadsheet application

- ✔ Enables end users to perform a task they probably couldn't otherwise do.

- ✔ Provides an appropriate solution to a problem. The optimal approach for solving a problem doesn't always involve designing an application that works in a spreadsheet environment.

- ✔ Does what it's supposed to do. This might be an obvious prerequisite, but many applications fail to meet this test.

- ✔ Produces accurate results and is free of bugs.

- ✔ Performs its job using appropriate, efficient methods and techniques.

- ✔ Traps errors and helps the user correct them.

- ✔ Does not allow the user to accidentally (or intentionally) delete or modify important components.

- ✔ Offers a clear, consistent user interface, so the user always knows how to proceed.

- ✔ Contains formulas, macros, and user interface elements that are well documented.

✔ Provides a design that enables developers to make simple modifications without making major structural changes.

✔ Presents an easily accessible help system that offers useful information on at least the major procedures.

✔ Is based on a *portable* design — that is, the application runs on any system that has the proper software (in this case, a copy of Excel 97).

You can create spreadsheet applications at many different levels, ranging from simple fill-in-the-blanks templates to extremely complex applications that use custom menus and dialog boxes — and may not even look like spreadsheets.

Application Development, Step By Step

No simple recipe exists for developing a spreadsheet application — besides, this isn't a cookbook. Fact is, everyone develops his or her own style for creating spreadsheet applications.

With that said, I'm ready to provide you with some *general* guidelines that I find useful. At the very least, the information in this chapter can help you improve your own development style.

Here's a list of activities that spreadsheet developers typically perform. You won't necessarily perform all these steps for every application, and the order in which you perform them may vary from project to project:

✔ Determine the needs of the user.

✔ Plan an application that meets those needs.

✔ Determine the most appropriate user interface.

✔ Create the spreadsheet, the formulas, the macros, and the user interface.

✔ Test and debug the application.

✔ Make the application bulletproof.

✔ Make the application aesthetically appealing and intuitive.

✔ Document the development effort.

✔ Develop user documentation and online help.

✔ Distribute the application to the user.

✔ Update the application when necessary.

I describe these activities in the following sections.

Determining user needs

The first step in developing an application usually involves identifying exactly what the end users require. Skipping this step (or guessing what the users' *might* need) often results in additional work later in the development process because you have to adjust the application so that it does what it was supposed to do in the first place.

In some cases, you know the end users very well — you may be one yourself. In other cases (for example, a consultant developing projects for a client), you know little or nothing about the users or their situation.

Here are a few tips for making this phase easier:

- ✔ Don't assume that you know what the users need. Second-guessing at this stage almost always causes problems later in the development process.

- ✔ If possible, talk directly to the end users of the application, not just to their supervisor or manager.

- ✔ Learn what, if anything, the users currently do to solve the problem. You may be able to save some work by adapting an existing application.

- ✔ Identify the resources available at the users' site. For example, try to determine whether you must work around any hardware or software limitations.

- ✔ If possible, find out which systems will be used for running your application. You need to consider whether your application must run on slower systems.

- ✔ Understand the skill levels of the end users. This information helps you design the application appropriately.

- ✔ Determine how long the application will be used. This often influences the amount of effort you put into the project.

One final note: Don't be surprised if the project specifications change before you complete the application. This often happens, and you're better off *expecting* changes rather than being surprised by them.

Planning an application that meets user needs

After you determine the end users' needs, you might be tempted to jump right in and start fiddling around in Excel. Take it from someone who suffers from this problem: Try to restrain yourself. Builders don't construct a house without a set of blueprints, and you shouldn't develop a spreadsheet application without a plan.

How formal you make your plan depends on the scope of the project and your general style of working. You should, however, spend at least *some* time thinking about what you need to do and come up with a plan of action.

Take some time to consider the various ways you can approach the problem. A thorough knowledge of Excel pays off here by helping you avoid blind alleys before you get to them.

More specifically, you need to consider some general options at this stage, including the following:

- **File structure:** Should you use one workbook with multiple sheets, several single-sheet workbooks, or a template file?

- **Data structure:** Should the application use external database files or store everything in worksheets?

- **Formulas or VBA:** Should you use formulas to perform calculations or write VBA procedures? Both have advantages and disadvantages.

- **Add-in or XLS file:** In most cases, you probably want your final product to be an XLA add-in. But an XLS file is sometimes preferable.

- **Version of Excel:** Does your application need to work with Excel 95 and Excel 5? If so, you'll want to use one of these products for your development work. (And you can't use any features that are new in Excel 97.) If the application must work also with Excel for the Macintosh, you'll need to test it using both products.

- **Error handling:** Anticipate possible errors and determine how your application will detect and deal with error conditions.

- **Use of special features:** Don't reinvent the wheel. For example, if your application needs to summarize lots of data, consider using Excel's built-in pivot table feature.

- **Performance issues:** The approach you take ultimately determines the overall performance of your application. Start thinking about the speed and efficiency of your application now — don't wait until the application is complete and users are complaining about it.

- **Level of security:** Excel provides several protection options for restricting access to particular elements of a workbook. You can make your job easier by determining up front exactly what you need to protect — and what level of protection you want.

You have to deal with many other project-dependent considerations in this phase. The important point is that you should consider all options and avoid settling on the first solution that comes to mind.

I've learned from experience that you shouldn't let the end user completely guide your approach to solving the problem. For example, suppose you meet with a manager who tells you the department needs an application that writes text files, which will be imported into another application. Don't confuse the user's perceived need with the solution. In this example, the real need is to share data — using an intermediate text file is just one possible solution. In other words, don't let the users define their problem by stating it in terms of a solution approach. Finding the right approach is *your* job.

Determining the most appropriate user interface

When you develop spreadsheets that others will use, you need to pay special attention to the user interface. By *user interface,* I mean the method by which the user interacts with the application — clicking buttons, using menus, pressing keys, accessing toolbars, and so on.

Excel provides several features that relate to user interface design:

- Dialog box controls placed directly on a worksheet
- Custom dialog boxes
- Custom menus
- Custom toolbars
- Custom shortcut keys

Consider all your options, as well as the skill level and motivation of the end users. Then decide on the interface elements that make the most sense.

Developing the application

Okay, you've identified user needs, determined the approach you'll take, and decided on the user interface. Now you can get down to the nitty-gritty and start creating the application — the step that comprises most of the time you spend on a project.

The approach you take for developing the application depends on your personal style and the nature of the application. Except for simple template-type applications, your application will probably use VBA macros.

I can't be more specific here, because each application is different. In general, try to keep your VBA procedures short and modular.

Testing the application

Every computer user encounters software bugs. In most cases, such problems result from insufficient testing that fails to catch all the bugs.

After you create your application, you need to test it. This is a crucial step, and you might spend as much time testing and debugging an application as you do creating the application in the first place. Actually, you should test extensively during the development phase. After all, while you write a VBA routine or create formulas in a worksheet, you want to make sure that the application works as it should.

It's often a good idea to recruit one or more users to help with the testing. I've found that using a few good beta testers is an excellent way to uncover problems that I have overlooked.

Although you can't test for all possibilities, your macros should handle common types of errors. For example, what if the user enters a text string instead of a value? What if the user cancels a dialog box without making any selections? What happens if the user presses Ctrl+F6 and jumps to the next window?

As you gain experience, issues like these become second nature, and you account for them with little effort.

Making an application bulletproof

A user can easily destroy a worksheet. Erasing one critical formula or value often causes errors throughout the entire worksheet — and perhaps in other dependent worksheets. Even worse, if the user saves the damaged workbook, the corrupt version replaces the good copy on disk. Unless the person using your application has a backup procedure in place, the user could be in trouble — and *you'll* probably be blamed!

If other users — especially novices — will be using your worksheets, you need to add some protection. Excel provides several techniques for protecting worksheets and parts of worksheets:

- ✔ Locking specific cells (using the Protection tab in the Format Cells dialog box) so that they can't be changed. This takes effect only when you protect the document with the Tools⇨Protection⇨Protect Sheet command.

- ✔ Protecting an entire workbook — the structure of the workbook, the window position and size, or both. This takes effect when you use the Tools⇨Protection⇨Protect Workbook command.

✔ Hiding the formulas in specific cells (using the Protection tab in the Format Cells dialog box) so that other users can't see them. Again, this takes effect only when you protect the document with the Tools➪Protection➪Protect Sheet command.

✔ Locking objects on the worksheet (using the Protection tab in the Format Object dialog box). This takes effect only when you protect the document with the Tools➪Protection➪Protect Sheet command.

✔ Hiding rows (Format➪Row➪Hide), columns (Format➪Column➪Hide), sheets (Format➪Sheet➪Hide), and documents (Window➪Hide). This helps prevent the worksheet from looking cluttered and provides some protection against prying eyes.

✔ Designating Excel workbooks as read-only to ensure that they cannot be overwritten with any changes. You access this option by choosing the Options button in the Save As dialog box.

✔ Assigning a password to prevent unauthorized users from opening your file (using the Options button in the Save As dialog box).

✔ Using an add-in, which doesn't allow the user to change *anything* on the add-in's worksheets.

The appropriate level of protection, and how you implement it, depends on the application and who will be using it.

Making it look good

You've undoubtedly seen examples of poorly designed user interfaces, difficult-to-use programs, and just plain ugly screens. If you develop spreadsheets for other people, you should pay particular attention to how the application looks.

The way a computer program looks can make all the difference in the world to users. And so it goes with the applications you develop with Excel. End users appreciate a good looking user interface, and you can give your applications a much more polished and professional look if you devote some additional time to design and aesthetic considerations.

Evaluating aesthetic qualities is very subjective. When in doubt, keep your worksheets simple and generic looking. Here are a few tips:

✔ **Strive for consistency.** This includes fonts, text sizes, and formatting. When designing dialog boxes, for example, try to emulate the look and feel of the Excel dialog boxes as much as possible.

✔ **Avoid the gaudy.** Just because Excel lets you work with 56 colors, you don't have to use them all. In general, use only a few colors and no more than two fonts.

✔ **Keep it simple.** Developers often make the mistake of trying to cram too much information into a single screen or dialog box. A good rule of thumb is to present only one or two chunks of information at a time.

✔ **Consider the hardware.** If your application will be used on laptops, make sure that you use color combinations that look good (and are legible) in monochrome, too.

✔ **Think modular.** Make it easy for the user to figure out what's what. For example, you can separate different parts of a worksheet by using background colors or borders.

Documenting your efforts

Assembling a spreadsheet application is one thing — making it understandable to other people is another. It's important that you thoroughly document your work. This helps *you* if you need to modify the application (and you will), and it helps anyone else who needs to work on the application (after you get that big promotion).

How do you document a workbook application? You can either store the information in a worksheet or use another file. You can even use a paper document if you prefer. Perhaps the easiest way is to create a separate worksheet in which you store comments and key information about the project.

Use comments liberally throughout your VBA code. An elegant piece of VBA code may seem perfectly understandable to you today — but come back to it in a few months, and you may be scratching your head.

Developing user documentation and online help

In addition to your programming documentation, you need to develop user documentation. You have two basic choices: paper-based documentation or electronic (online) documentation.

Online help is standard fare in Windows applications. Fortunately, your Excel applications can provide online help — even context-sensitive help. You can develop help files and display a particular help topic on demand. Although developing online help requires quite a bit of additional effort, this may be worthwhile for a large project. To simplify the process, I suggest that you acquire any of several software products designed for creating Windows help files.

Distributing the application to the user

You've completed your project, and you're ready to release it to the end users. How do you do this?

It depends. You could simply hand over a disk, scribble a few instructions, and be on your way. Or you may install the application yourself. Another option is to develop an official setup program that automatically installs your application. You can write such a program in a traditional programming language, purchase a generic setup program, or write your own setup program in VBA.

You also need to consider the issue of providing support for your application. In other words, who gets the phone call if the user encounters a problem? If you aren't prepared to handle routine questions, you need to identify someone who is. In some cases, you may specify that the developer handles only highly technical problems or bug-related issues.

Updating the application when necessary

After you distribute your application, you're finished with it, right? You can sit back, enjoy yourself, and try to forget about the problems you encountered (and solved) during the development of your application. In rare cases, yes, you may be finished. More often, however, the users of your application will not be completely satisfied.

Sure, your application adheres to all *original* specifications, but things change. After seeing an application work, users often think of other things the application could be doing. That's right, I'm talking about *updates*.

When you need to update or revise your application, you'll appreciate the fact that you designed it well in the first place and that you fully documented your efforts. If not, well . . . you learn from your experiences.

Part VII
The Part of Tens

The 5th Wave — By Rich Tennant

"C'MON BRICKMAN, YOU KNOW AS WELL AS I DO THAT 'NOSE-SCANNING' IS OUR BEST DEFENSE AGAINST UNAUTHORIZED ACCESS TO PERSONAL FILES."

In this part . . .

For reasons that are historical — as well as useful — all the books in the *...For Dummies* series have chapters with lists in them. This book is no exception. The next three chapters contain my own Top Ten lists, which deal with tricks, frequently asked questions, and other Excel resources.

Chapter 24

Top Ten VBA Tips and Tricks

● ●

*T*his chapter contains a list of ten clever tricks I've developed (or acquired from other users) over the years.

Getting VBA Help, Fast

When working in a VBA module, you can get instant help regarding a VBA object, property, or method. Just move the cursor to the word that interests you and press F1.

Speeding Up Your Macros

If you write a VBA macro that produces lots of on-screen action, you can speed things up significantly by turning off screen updating. To do so, execute the statement: `Application.ScreenUpdating = False`.

If your macro uses a custom dialog box, make sure that you turn screen updating back on before you display the dialog box. Otherwise, moving the dialog box on the screen leaves an ugly trail.

Avoiding Excel's Questions

Some VBA methods cause Excel to display a confirmation message — which requires the user to click a button. For example, the statement `ActiveSheet.Delete` always displays a dialog box that asks for confirmation.

To eliminate such confirmation messages, execute the statement: `Application.DisplayAlerts = False` before the statement that causes the confirmation messages.

To reinstate the confirmation messages, use the statement: `Application.DisplayAlerts = True`.

Displaying One Procedure at a Time

Normally, a Code window in the Visual Basic Editor (VBE) shows all the procedures in the module, one after another. If you find this distracting, you can set things up so that only one procedure is visible. Activate the VBE and choose Tools⇨Options. Click the Editor tab in the Options dialog box and remove the check mark from the Default to Full Module View check box. Then you can use the drop-down lists at the top of the module window to select the procedure to view or edit.

Using With-End With

If you need to set a number of properties for an object, your code will run faster if you use the With-End With construct. The following code doesn't use With-End With:

```
Selection.HorizontalAlignment = xlCenter
Selection.VerticalAlignment = xlCenter
Selection.WrapText = True
Selection.Orientation = 0
Selection.ShrinkToFit = False
Selection.MergeCells = False
```

The next code performs the same action but is rewritten to use With-End With:

```
With Selection
    .HorizontalAlignment = xlCenter
    .VerticalAlignment = xlCenter
    .WrapText = True
    .Orientation = 0
    .ShrinkToFit = False
    .MergeCells = False
End With
```

Reducing the Size of a Workbook

In many cases, you can significantly reduce the size of a workbook — especially a workbook with modules you've heavily edited — because Excel does not do a good job of cleaning up its symbol table. To clean up the mess Excel leaves behind:

1. **Save your workbook.**

2. **Select a module or a UserForm in the Project Window.**

3. **Right-click and choose Remove from the shortcut menu.**

4. **When asked whether you want to export the module, click Yes.**

5. **Repeat Steps 3 and 4 for each module and UserForm — but keep track of the modules and forms that you remove.**

6. **Choose File⇨Import File to import all the modules and forms you deleted.**

7. **Save your workbook again.**

You'll usually find that the new workbook is much smaller than it was.

Avoiding a Workbook_Open Subroutine

If your workbook has a Workbook_Open subroutine (a procedure that Excel executes automatically when the workbook is opened), you can prevent Excel from running this macro by pressing Shift while you open the workbook.

Using Your Personal Macro Workbook

If you've developed some general-purpose macros, consider storing them in your Personal Macro Workbook — which is opened automatically whenever Excel starts. When you record a macro, you have the option of recording it to your Personal Macro Workbook. The file, PERSONAL.XLS, is stored in your XLSTART directory. The Personal Macro Workbook will be created the first time you record a macro to it.

Displaying Messages in the Status Bar

If you develop a lengthy macro, use the Excel status bar to display the progress of the macro. To do so, write some code that periodically executes a subroutine, such as the following:

```
Sub UpdateStatusBar(PctDone)
    Application.StatusBar = _
      "Percent Completed: " & Format(PctDone, "0%")
End Sub
```

This subroutine uses one argument — a value that ranges from 0 to 1.0. The subroutine simply displays a message that indicates the percent completed. To return the status bar back to normal, execute the following statement: `Application.StatusBar = False`

Forcing Yourself to Declare All Variables

Declaring every variable that you use in your code is an excellent practice. For example, if you use an integer variable named Count, you declare it as `Dim Count as Integer`.

Declaring your variables as a particular data type makes your code run faster, and also helps avoid typographical errors. To force yourself to declare all variables, insert the following statement at the top of your module `Option Explicit`.

If you would like this statement to be added to each new module automatically, activate the Visual Basic Editor and choose Tools⇨Options. In the Options dialog box, click the Editor tab and place a check mark next to Require Variable Declaration.

Finding the Excel 97 Secret Window

Try this:

1. **Open a new workbook and press F5.**

2. **Type X97:L97 and press Enter and then Tab.**

3. **Press Ctrl+Shift and click the Chart Wizard button on the Standard toolbar.**

You'll be greeted with a full-screen animated image. Use the mouse to move around.

Chapter 25

Top Ten VBA Questions (And Answers)

● ●

*I*n this chapter, I answer the most frequently asked questions about VBA. These questions appear time after time on the online services I monitor.

1. **When I execute my macro, everything that happens flashes on the screen. Can I execute the macro without showing what's happening?**

   Yes. Insert the following statement to turn off screen updating:

   ```
   Application.ScreenUpdating = False
   ```

   For best results, insert this statement just before the point in your macro where the screen updating normally occurs. Using this statement has a nice side effect: Your macro usually executes much faster.

   To turn screen updating back on, execute this statement:

   ```
   Application.ScreenUpdating = True
   ```

2. **Is there a utility I can use to translate my XLM macros into VBA?**

   No existing utility does this, and it is very unlikely that anyone will ever write a utility for this purpose. Such conversions must be performed manually. Because Excel 97 can execute XLM macros, however, you don't really need to convert them.

3. **Is there a utility that will convert my 1-2-3 macros to VBA?**

   No. My advice is determine exactly what the 1-2-3 macro does and then write a new VBA macro to perform the same task. In most cases, you will not be able to do a line-by-line translation, so it's usually more efficient to start from scratch.

4. **Is there a utility that will convert my Excel 5/95 dialog sheets to Excel 97 UserForms?**

   Yes! You can get a free copy of my Dialog-to-UserForm Wizard from my Web site:

   ```
   http://www.j-walk.com/ss/dlgwiz.htm
   ```

This utility does not convert your VBA code. You'll need to adapt your old code to work with the converted UserForm.

5. Can I stop Excel from showing messages while my macro runs? For example, I'd like to eliminate the warning message that appears when my macro deletes a worksheet.

The following statement turns off most Excel warning messages:

```
Application.DisplayAlerts = False
```

6. Is there a VBA command to select a range from the active cell to the last entry in a column or a row? (In other words, how can a macro accomplish the same thing as Ctrl+Shift+down arrow or Ctrl+Shift+right arrow?)

The VBA equivalent for Ctrl+Shift+down arrow is

```
Range(ActiveCell, ActiveCell.End(xlDown)).Select
```

For the other directions, use the constants: XLToLeft, XLToRight, and XLUp.

7. How can I make my VBA code run as fast as possible?

Here are a few tips:

- Make sure that you declare all your variables. (Use Option Explicit at the beginning of each module to force yourself to declare all variables.)

- If you reference an object (such as a range) more than once, create an object variable using the Set keyword.

- Use the With-End With construct whenever possible.

- If your macro writes data to a worksheet and you have lots of complex formulas, you may want to set the calculation mode to manual while the macro is running.

- If your macro writes information to a worksheet, turn off screen updating by using `Application.ScreenUpdating = False`.

8. I upgraded to Excel 97, and now I can't find the Menu Editor. Where did it go?

It went to the big bit bucket in the sky. In Excel 97, you modify the menus by using the View➪Toolbars➪Customize command. There is, however, a major caveat: Modifications that you make to the Worksheet menu bar are permanent. Therefore, if you want your menu changes to be in effect only for a particular workbook, the best approach is to use VBA to make your menu modifications (see Chapter 20 for details).

9. My application will be used by people running Excel 5 and Excel 95. Which version should I use to develop my macros?

For best results, use Excel 5 for your development. And make sure that you test it thoroughly using Excel 95 and Excel 97. Unfortunately, later versions of Excel are not always 100 percent compatible with earlier versions.

10. **I need to create a simple macro for someone who is stuck in a time warp and still uses Excel 4. How do I record a macro in the old XLM macro language?**

No can do. Although Excel 97 can execute XLM macros, the capability to record such macros is not supported.

Chapter 26
Top Ten Excel Resources

● ●

*T*his book is only an introduction to Excel programming. If you hunger for more information, you can feed on the list of additional resources I've compiled here. You can discover new techniques, communicate with other Excel users, download useful files, ask questions, access the extensive Microsoft Knowledge Base, and lots more. Several of these resources are online services or Internet resources, which tend to change frequently. The descriptions are accurate at the time I'm writing this, but I can't guarantee that this information will remain current.

The VBA Online Help System

I hope you've already discovered VBA's online help system. In Excel 97, it's better than ever — and amazingly thorough. It's there, it's free, and (for the most part) it's accurate. So use it.

Microsoft Product Support

Microsoft offers a wide variety of technical support options (some for free, others for a fee). For complete information on how to contact Microsoft for technical support, choose Help⇨About Microsoft Excel. Then, in the dialog box Excel displays, click the Tech Support button. You'll find details on various ways to get help directly from Bill Gates (well, probably one of his employees).

Internet Newsgroups

One of my favorite Internet hangouts is the Usenet newsgroup, `comp.apps.spreadsheets`. Although this newsgroup deals with all spreadsheets, most of the traffic focuses on Excel.

Microsoft also has its own news server, with hundreds of newsgroups devoted to Microsoft products — including a dozen or so newsgroups for Excel. These newsgroups are *not* part of Usenet, so you'll need to set your newsreader software to access the (NNTP) server at msnews.microsoft.com. Following is a list of the Excel-related newsgroups at msnews.microsoft.com.

microsoft.public.excel.123quattro

microsoft.public.excel.charting

microsoft.public.excel.crashesGPFs

microsoft.public.excel.datamap

microsoft.public.excel.interopoledde

microsoft.public.excel.links

microsoft.public.excel.macintosh

microsoft.public.excel.misc

microsoft.public.excel.printing

microsoft.public.excel.programming

microsoft.public.excel.queryDAO

microsoft.public.excel.sdk

microsoft.public.excel.setup

microsoft.public.excel.templates

microsoft.public.excel.worksheetfunctions

If you would like to search old newsgroup messages by keyword, point your Web browser to http://www.dejanews.com.

Internet Web Sites

Several World Wide Web sites contain Excel-related material. A good place to start your Web surfing is my very own site, which is named **The Spreadsheet Page**. Once you get there, you can check out my material and then click some links to visit other Excel-related sites. The URL is http://www.j-walk.com/ss/.

And don't forget about Microsoft's Excel Web site. To get the latest on Excel, go to http://www.microsoft.com/excel/.

For lots of other useful Excel stuff, try this site: `http://www.microsoft.com/MSExcelSupport/`.

To search Microsoft's Knowledge Base to find the answer to a specific question, go to `http://www.microsoft.com/kb/`.

Internet Mailing Lists

Two Internet mailing lists deal with Excel:

- **EXCEL-G:** Excel General Q & A List
- **EXCEL-L:** Excel Developers List

To subscribe to one of these lists, send e-mail to `LISTSERV@PEACH.EASE.LSOFT.COM`.

The subject line of the message doesn't matter. In the body of your message, include `SUB listname Your Name`.

For example, if your name is Bill Gates and you want to subscribe to the Excel Developers List, send e-mail with `SUB EXCEL-L Bill Gates` in the message body.

You'll receive return mail that describes the list and provides complete instructions.

Online Services

If you subscribe to Compuserve, you should definitely check out the Excel Forum (**Go Excel**). You'll find several hefty libraries of files to download, plus a lively (and very informative) question-and-answer forum.

If you're an America Online subscriber, the Applications forum has many Excel files you can download.

The Microsoft Network is Microsoft's foray into the world of online services. If you're a subscriber, check out the available Excel information. After logging on, do a global search for *Excel*, and you'll get a list of pointers to various areas.

Local User Groups

Many larger communities and universities have an Excel user group that meets periodically. If there's such a user group in your area, check it out. These groups are often an excellent source for contacts and sharing ideas.

My Book

Sorry, but I couldn't resist the opportunity for a blatant plug. I've received tons of positive feedback on *Excel 5 For Windows Power Programming Techniques* and *Excel 95 For Windows Power Programming with VBA* (both published by IDG Books Worldwide, Inc.). The Excel 97 edition should be available in the summer of 1997.

The book covers all aspects of Excel application development in detail, with lots of useful examples on the companion CD-ROM.

My Power Utility Pak

Okay, this is the last plug. I promise. Use the coupon in the back of this book to get your very own (free!) copy of my Power Utility Pak — a dynamite collection of quality Excel utilities and custom worksheet functions. And for a nominal fee, you'll be able to access the complete VBA source code so that you can see exactly how it works. You'll find dozens of useful techniques that you can adapt to your own needs.

My E-Mail Address

I'm always happy to try to answer questions that readers submit (time permitting). All I ask is that you be very specific and avoid broad questions such as, "I need a macro to track my company's sales. What should I do?"

To contact me directly, use my e-mail address `john@j-walk.com`.

Index

• Symbols •

& (ampersand)
  concatenation operator, 108
  type-declaration character, 101
' (apostrophe), comment character, 93–94
* (asterisk), multiplication operator, 108
@ (at sign), type-declaration character, 101
\ (backslash), integer division operator, 108
^ (carat), exponentiation operator, 108
$ (dollar sign), type-declaration character, 101
= (equal sign), assignment statements, 107
! (exclamation point), type-declaration character, 101
- (minus sign), subtraction operator, 108
% (percent sign), type-declaration character, 101
+ (plus sign), addition operator, 108
# (pound sign), type-declaration character, 101
/ (slash), division operator, 108
_ (underscore), continuation character, 40

• A •

absolute recording mode, 81
accelerator keys, assigning. *See also* hot keys
  check boxes, 254
  option buttons, 259
Accelerator property
  CheckBox control, 254
  OptionButton control, 259
Add Watch dialog box, 196–197
add-ins. *See* Excel add-ins
AddItem property, 273
Address property, 119
alert messages, disabling, 214
Alt+F8, hot key, 24
Alt+F11, hot key, 33
ampersand (&)
  concatenation operator, 108
  type-declaration character, 101
And operator, 108
apostrophe (') comment character, 93–94
arguments
  in custom functions, descriptions of, 339–340
  in custom functions, overview, 329–330
  definition, 60–61, 67
  in methods, 60–61

arrays
  declaring, 109
  dynamic, 110
  multidimensional, 109–110
  redimensioning, 110
Assign Macro dialog box, 72
assignment statements
  = (equal sign), 107
  definition, 106
  examples, 107
asterisk (*), multiplication operator, 108
at sign (@), type-declaration character, 101
author's Internet address, 7
Auto Data Tips option, 46
Auto Indent setting, 47
Auto List Members option, 45–46, 135
Auto Quick Info option, 46
Auto Syntax Check option, 45
automatic calculations, disabling, 213
AutoSize property, 261

• B •

backslash (\), integer division operator, 108
BeforeClose event, 163–164
BeforeDoubleClick event, 167–168
BeforeRightClick event, 168
BeforeSave event, 164–165
BeginGroup property
  menus, 314
  toolbars, 300
BoundColumn property
  ComboBox control, 255
  ListBox control, 257
Break mode, hot key for exiting, 193
breakpoints, 193
bugs
  definition, 189
  identifying, 190
  types of, 189–190
  vs. syntax errors, 190
BuiltIn property
  menus, 314
  toolbars, 301

• C •

Caption property
  menus, 314
  toolbars, 300

• E •

• R •

• X •